Compassion and Calculation

Transnational Institute Series

The Transnational Institute is an independent fellowship of researchers and activists living in different parts of the world, who develop innovative analyses of world affairs.

It serves no government, political party or interest group.

Other titles available in the TNI series:

Short Changed:
Africa and World Trade
Michael Barratt Brown and Pauline Tiffen

People and Power in the Pacific:
The Struggle for the Post-Cold War Order
Walden Bello

Dark Victory:
The United States, Structural Adjustment
and Global Poverty
Walden Bello et al.

Beyond Bretton Woods:
Alternatives to the Global Economic Order
*Edited by John Cavanagh, Daphne Wysham
and Marcos Arruda*

Blue Geopolitics:
United Nations Reform and the Future of the Blue Helmets
Vicenç Fisas

The Debt Boomerang:
How Third World Debt Harms Us All
Susan George

The Democratisation of Disempowerment:
The Problem of Democracy in the Third World
Edited by Jochen Hippler

The Next Threat:
Western Perceptions of Islam
Edited by Jochen Hippler and Andrea Lueg

Pax Americana?
Hegemony or Decline
Jochen Hippler

Central Asia After the Empire:
Yuriy Kulchik, Andrey Fadin and Victor Sergeev

Bonn & the Bomb:
German Politics and the Nuclear Option
Matthias Küntzel

Palestine in Crisis:
The Struggle for Peace and Political Independence After Oslo
Graham Usher

For information about forthcoming titles in this series contact
Pluto Press

Compassion and Calculation

The Business of Private Foreign Aid

Edited by
David Sogge
with Kees Biekart *and* John Saxby

Pluto Press
LONDON • CHICAGO, IL.

with

Transnational Institute (TNI)

First published 1996 by Pluto Press
345 Archway Road, London N6 5AA
and 1436 West Randolph, Chicago
Illinois 60607, USA
in association with
the Transnational Institute (TNI),
Paulus Potterstraat 20, 1071 DA, Amsterdam

British Library Cataloguing in Publication Data
A catalogue record for this book is available from the British Library

ISBN 0 7453 0975 5 hbk

Library of Congress Cataloging-in-Publication Data are available

Impression 02 01 00 99 98 97 96 5 4 3 2 1

Designed and produced for Pluto Press by
Chase Production Services, Chipping Norton, OX7 5QR
Typeset from disk by Stanford DTP Services, Milton Keynes
Printed in the EC by J.W. Arrowsmith, Bristol

Contents

Lists of Illustrations

Figures

Boxes

Acknowledgements

This book is a product of help. Undertaken by a private organization addressing some of the same issues facing private aid agencies, the Transnational Institute, it was the recipient of insight, information, time and material support generously given. As a privileged beneficiary in this helper–helped relationship, the editor would like first to acknowledge a debt for lessons learned over the years from those he knows in different private aid agencies, and from those in the South whose special views of the agencies, through their telescopes and microscopes of experience, are so illuminating. Unfortunately, space and discretion allow mention of only a few directly of help in this project, mainly in the North:

Staff of the Transnational Institute, especially Jochen Hippler, Basker Vashee, Laurian Zwart, and Mariël Otten; and TNI fellows and associates, including John Cavanagh, Susan George, Andrey Fadin, Myriam Vander Stichele, and Peter Wahl.

Persons with knowledge of the aid agencies from first-hand experience, including: Jacques Bastin, Pierre Beaudet, Sally Burrows, Ian Cherett, Constantino Casasbuenas, Hugo Couderé, Rui Gonçalves, Silvia Ricchieri, Paul Robson, Corrie Roeper, Theo Ruyter, Simon Stocker, Eileen Sudworth. David Harding deserves special mention for trenchant comments on early sketches of several chapters. Finally my partner Florrie de Pater, for many years an agency insider, supplied discernment and distractions.

Persons in institutions of research and higher education, including Mark Duffield, Paul Hoebink, Liisa Laakso, Alison van Rooy, Pantalis Sklias, Mariano Valderrama, Frits Wils.

Persons who gathered information on assignment to this project, and provided useful insights besides: Robert David, Edgar Pieterse, William Sweet.

Niala Maharaj merits special mention for her editorial advice and sub-editing of drafts of most chapters.

For its financial support to this project, particular thanks are due to an organisation of the official aid system, the Finnish International Development Agency (FINNIDA) of the Ministry of Foreign Affairs of Finland.

Finally, the colleagueship and energy of the other authors of texts appearing here must be gratefully acknowledged. Debate and preparation of a number of texts took place in continual and close collaboration with John Saxby in Ottawa, who furnished feedback to the editor and initiated discussion among associates in Canada, creating a virtual sub-project there; and with Kees Biekart in Amsterdam, who provided stimulating comment and important nuances throughout. Of course no one among the above mentioned should be held responsible for any of the book's failings in editorship.

Note: A number of contributors to this book, including the editor, have been employed by private aid agencies under contracts which stipulate that information about the agencies acquired during one's employment shall be held strictly secret, and that disclosure of such confidential information to the media is explicitly forbidden. Every effort has been made here to respect these contractual requirements. Thus, for example, documentation only in open circulation has been cited. Any lapses in respect to these obligations are wholly unintended.

David Sogge
Amsterdam
January 1996

Notes on Contributors

Kees Biekart is a Fellow at the Transnational Institute, Amsterdam, where he coordinates its programme on Democratisation. He is author of several reports and articles on European agencies and NGOs involved in Latin America.

Alan Fowler is a consultant, analyst and writer specialising in non-governmental development organisations, with which he has worked since 1978, mostly in sub-Saharan Africa. A former programme officer with the Ford Foundation, he co-founded in 1991 the International NGO Training and Research Centre (INTRAC) in Oxford.

Issiaka-Prosper Lalaye is a social scientist. He teaches philosophy, anthropology and sociology at the Université de Saint-Louis, Senegal. He is a member of the South–North Network Cultures and Development.

John Saxby has worked with private aid agencies in Southern Africa and Canada for more than twenty years. He has a Ph.D. in political economy. He lives in Ottawa, Canada, in a house full of canoe paddles, hockey sticks and outmoded paradigms.

John Schlanger, a Brazilian-born social scientist, works with IBASE (Brazilian Institute of Social and Economic Analysis), a leading NGO based in Rio de Janeiro. For more than twelve years he worked in Novib, a major private aid agency in The Netherlands, where he came to head the Latin America programme desk.

Edith Sizoo is a founder and coordinator of the European regional base, in Brussels, of the South–North Network Cultures and Development. A former General Secretary of PSO, an association of private aid agencies in The Netherlands, she has written and lectured widely on culture-conscious approaches to development cooperation.

Ian Smillie is a writer and consultant on development issues based in Ottawa, Canada. A founder of a private aid agency, Inter Pares, and former Executive Director of CUSO, he is author of, among other works, *The Alms Bazaar: Altruism Under Fire – Non-profit Organisations and International Development.*

David Sogge works as an independent consultant based in Amsterdam. Since 1970 he has come to know private aid agencies as a staff member in field and home office positions, and as an advisor to them and their local grantees, chiefly in southern Africa.

Yash Tandon is a Ugandan political economist, currently an independent development consultant based in Harare, Zimbabwe. He has served on the faculties of a number of universities in eastern Africa, Britain and the United States, and was formerly a TNI Fellow. He has published and lectured widely on North–South issues, including the phenomenon of private aid.

Simon Zadek is Research Coordinator of the New Economics Foundation in London, where he heads NEF's social audit work with enterprises and non-governmental organisations. He has carried out a number of evaluations of NGO programmes financed by official and private aid agencies.

Preface

Private aid agencies have turned generosity into charity with few questions asked. Lionised by the contented classes and reformers alike, they have been largely exempt from serious scrutiny, sheltered by an endearing public image and the patronage of the far larger official aid system. Yet whiffs of scandal around front offices, and whispers about fiascos in field projects, have put some agencies – and by extension, the industry of which they are a part – under clouds of public doubt and misgiving.

While not ignoring the plumes of smoke rising above occasional fires of scandal and fiasco, this book does not aim for sensational scoops. Rather, it poses a few straightforward questions about crises besetting agencies at deeper levels:

- A crisis of legitimacy and accountability: Who owns the agencies?
- A crisis of purpose and motivation: Should laws of the market rule?
- A crisis of performance in the South: Do agencies make any difference?
- A crisis of significance in the North: Do agencies bear witness in full measure as they shape meanings and emotions about the South?

Each of these is addressed in the book's main chapters. Accompanying them are shorter pieces on salient themes, particularly those with a Southern perspective. Taking a sceptical but not cynical stance, it probes what they actually do, what drives them, and what they could become.

An overview of the organisations and their contexts appears in Chapter 1.

This book arose from concerns and experiences among associates of the Transnational Institute (TNI), an independent and decentralised fellowship of scholars, researchers and writers from the South, the United States and Europe committed to critical and innovative analyses of North–South issues. The fact that TNI itself has enjoyed the support and collaboration of several private aid agencies only strengthened its interest and curiosity in the subject. From Jochen Hippler, TNI's Director from 1993 to 1995, came the original suggestion to create this book. Its contents emerged in discussions among TNI fellows and associates, including a seminar jointly organised with the Instituto de Estudios Transnacionales, Cordoba, Spain, in November 1994. The project corresponds with broader TNI interests in issues of conflict, democratisation, and new social movements – and in particular the role of Northern and international institutions affecting the prospects for the South.

List of Acronyms

ACN	Action Canada Network
AFREDA	African Relief and Consultancy Association
AFSC	American Friends Service Committee
BRAC	Bangladesh Rural Advancement Committee
CARE	Cooperative for Assistance and Relief Everywhere
CCFD	Comité Catholique contre la Faim et pour le Développement (Catholic Committee against Hunger and for Development)
CIDA	Canadian International Development Agency
CIIR	Catholic Institute for International Relations
CSPA	Center for the Study of Policy Attitudes
CUSO	formerly Canadian University Service Overseas, now legally known as CUSO
DAC	Development Assistance Committee of the OECD
DPI	Disabled People's International
GATT	General Agreement on Tariffs and Trade
GIF	Group of Institutes and Foundations
IAF	Inter-American Foundation
IBASE	Brazilian Institute of Social and Economical Analysis
ICCO	Interchurch Organisation for Development Cooperation
ICRC	International Committee of the Red Cross
ICVA	International Council of Voluntary Agencies
INTRAC	International NGO Training and Research Centre
IRENE	International Restructuring Education Network Europe
ISCA	International Save the Children Alliance
MSF	Médecins Sans Frontières
NAFTA	North American Free Trade Agreement
NCO	National Commission for Development Education
NCRP	National Committee for Responsive Philanthropy
NEF	New Economic Foundation
NGDO	non-governmental development organisation
NGO	non-governmental organisation
OECD	Organization for Economic Development and Assistance
ORAP	Organisation of Rural Associations for Progress

RAFI	Rural Advancement Foundation International
RMALC	Mexican Action Network on Free Trade
RONGEAD	Network of European NGDOs on Agri-Foodstuff and Development
SCF	Save the Children Fund
SIDA	Swedish International Development Agency
Six-S	Se Servir de la Saison Sèche in Savane et au Sahel (Using the Dry Season in the Savannah and the Sahel)
SNV	Stichting Nederlands Vrijwilligers (Dutch Volunteers Foundation)
SOLAGRAL	Soladarités Agro-alimentaires
TNI	Transnational Institute
UNHCR	United Nations High Commission for Refugees
UUSC	Unitarian Universalist Service Committee
VSO	Voluntary Service Overseas
WUSC	World University Service of Canada
ZOPP	Zielorientierte Projekt Planung (Objectives-oriented project planning)

1

Settings and Choices

David Sogge

After decades of quiet and respectable middle-class existences, private aid agencies have come up in the world. Their representatives sit with diplomats and commanders of expeditionary forces; their spokespersons interpret crises for millions of television viewers. Chequebooks open to them, funds have flowed easily. Aid agencies have therefore multiplied and grown, a few achieving the size and status of transnationals.

Yet even as they get bigger, their small-scale approach remains at the heart of their appeal. Their work is popularly equated with development at the grass-roots and person-to-person relief of suffering. As high-profile members of an expanding 'third sector' on which many hopes ride, they have become emblematic of practical altruism. A Canadian parliamentarian's recent speech nicely captures the prevailing view:

> Government ... is tapping into the collective wisdom, talents, and strengths that are 'out there' in the realm of civil society and the private sector. ... NGOs have always served as our collective conscience, and as a vehicle for direct citizen participation in nearly all the areas that affect our lives ... These groups are closest to the people. They know what is needed. And they have a credibility that government often lacks. Not being bound by the political agenda of the day, they can act quickly and creatively. They can experiment and try new approaches.[1]

But is this fame and popularity to last? For decades, images of charitable good works, like the *National Geographic*'s charming photographs of poor but worthy people in exotic lands, have transmitted a reassuring message: Life in non-western places isn't easy, but with some help things will work out all right.

The trouble is, things are not working out all right. Poverty is not being cured as promised. On the contrary, misery and menace in many poor regions appear only to grow worse, threatening upheavals and migratory waves to richer regions. Worried publics, who believe that

1

foreign aid is much bigger and more important than it really is, begin to wonder if it is being well-spent. So too do many doubters with inside views of the aid industry. And at the receiving end, in poorer regions, opinions about private aid are decidedly mixed.

By the mid-1990s, following a giddy period of rising public status and revenues, many agencies have found themselves under mounting stress from within and without. They face paradoxes and painful questions:

> Do the agencies' good deeds really make a difference? Or are aid workers just 'useful idiots' whose projects collapse once they go home or they stop sending money? Is their effect rather to mask root causes, provide reassurance to better-off but troubled Westerners, and divert attention from ugly realities of powerlessness and desperation? Are they driven only by voluntary and high moral purpose, or have they become mere businesses, where value-driven pursuits are crowded out? Indeed whose values are driving them? For whom do they speak? Who really owns and controls the private aid agencies?

Mainly out of public earshot, close to and within the private agencies, these questions are provoking self-doubt and debate. This book draws on those not-so-public debates. It aims to make them accessible and useful to a broader public, including readers in the South, many of whom feel left in the dark about the agencies. The issues are not trivial, since they concern well-known institutions said to be driven by the most exemplary of motives, compassion, and the most admirable of utopian ideals, emancipation from the servitude of poverty and exclusion.

Fearing to Tread on Angels?

Raising these questions is not without risks. The emancipatory ideals of some private aid agencies – expressed, for example, in their support to new social movements – are not universally welcomed. Indeed many organisations pursuing such ideals, including a few private aid agencies, face a battery of hostile interests with powers to cripple or destroy them by slashing their subsidies, imposing gag rules, or pillorying them in public.

Some may seize on portions of this book to pour more scorn on foreign aid where it fails to adhere to neoliberal orthodoxies. Red-baiting may be out, but some other spectres – the barbarian cultures

Box 1.1: What Kinds of Organisations are at Issue?

This book concerns chiefly *non-profit organisations based in Northern countries*[2] *purporting to relieve suffering and promote development in poor areas, especially Southern countries.* These comprise endowed foundations with international programmes, religiously-based bodies, emergency relief agencies, technical assistance and volunteer-sending organisations – in short, organisations whose chief vocation is the transfer of material or financial resources.

Private aid agencies form a subset of a larger and much more diverse category, namely that of *non-governmental organisations, or NGOs.* Here are also found, North and South, community and membership associations, non-profit advice-giving bodies, activist groups, and so on. This book's main focus is *not* on this wider community. In contrast to other writings, this book avoids using the term NGO when referring to private aid agencies, as just defined. To conflate Northern and Southern bodies, those that transfer resources, those that receive them, and those that do neither is to invite confusion.

What distinguishes private aid agencies from other NGOs is their greater command over tangible resources. Some agencies may be puny, but relative to most types of NGOs, they are powerful. The power dimension allows closer pursuit of the political sociology of these organisations: who owns them and what relations they bear to the state and social movements. Chapter 2 explores these matters in greater depth; it depicts them graphically on pages 42–3.

However, contributors to this book make frequent mention of an NGO that is not an agency: the *knowledge-based NGO.* Sometimes allied with private aid agencies, these organisations do not make grants, send used clothing or place volunteers abroad. Their stock-in-trade is analysis and information, concentrating on action-research or media for public education and advocacy. Examples include the Institute for Agriculture and Trade Policy, the New Economics Foundation, and the Rural Advancement Foundation International.

Agencies and other NGOs in turn are nested in a much broader category, the *non-profits.* These range from churches and trade unions to universities and private hospitals to professional sport leagues and art museums. Another label attached to this category is 'third sector', sometimes referring to almost everything outside the for-profit business and governmental sectors.

Putting precise boundaries around each category is difficult. Many ties of affiliation and parentage blur distinctions among aid agencies, NGOs and non-profits. For example, some advocacy NGOs are spin-offs of aid agencies, and vice-versa; or some universities, trade unions and professional groupings operate foreign-focused programmes which can resemble small-scale aid agencies. The field is getting crowded and overlapping.

Although chapters in this book make allusions to the broader non-profit world and draws parallels between private aid agencies and domestic social service non-profits in the North, this book does *not* deal with this far greater universe but focuses on one small branch of it.

of the South and the counter-cultures of an left-elitist 'New Class' in the North – will continue to be conjured up. Playing on fears and resentments regarding poor people or their allies is an old stratagem; today it has new impetus through well-oiled opinion-making machinery. Thus there are reasons for caution in raising questions about the agencies where emancipatory efforts could be damaged.

The contributors to this book have no wish to see such outcomes. But they also refuse to see agencies as angels above criticism. A muffled, impoverished debate out of public earshot cannot serve emancipatory agendas, including those the private aid agencies say they wish to pursue. The writers share a conviction that agencies' potentials to realise their professed ideals is of course what makes their activities worthwhile, indeed precious to us all. In this sense, the attitude underpinning this book is one of optimism.

The Humanitarian Branch, and its Roots

Behind well-polished official appearances, it can be hard to detect the original spirit and purpose inspiring people to set up an agency in the first place. Yet that inspiration can still tug at an agency from its past, influencing choices today. The reader will find extensive overviews of agency history in other works;[3] a brief review here must suffice.

Many agencies grew as initiatives of middle-class citizens concerned about victims of war and other catastrophes, as with the International Committee of the Red Cross and Oxfam UK, or to the plight of children, as with the various national Save the Children bodies and the Foster Parents Plan (also known as PLAN). Similar responses also arose from churches and mission groupings, as with the Christian Children's Fund.

Inspiring a more recent, post-war generation have been notions of 'relief and development' through material and technical aid, often through direct operations and volunteers (Voluntary Service Overseas – VSO, the Canadian University Service Overseas, now formally known as CUSO, Water Aid), or, most commonly, by supplying funds for projects. Some work from a base in organised religion (Caritas, American Jewish World Service) or from a secular base (German Agro-Action, Novib). Most depend on government or private donations, but a small but important number rely on their own, endowed funds (Rockefeller Foundation, the Rowntree and Cadbury trusts).

Viewed broadly, agencies can trace their origins and inspiration to four social and institutional streams:

- religious institutions and their norms;
- secular expressions of compassion and solidarity, some linked with ethical and social movements and professional associations, among Northern middle classes;
- private philanthropies of monied families and corporations, and
- government authorities in the realm of foreign policy.

While some agencies remain anchored firmly in these streams, many have drifted to points where streams flow together. Domestic interest group politics have brought about alliances, compromises and hybrid organisations. In some European countries, for example, church and secular initiatives have gained virtual statutory status as recipients of church taxes or government subsidies. US government interests have dictated the vocations of numerous private agencies in meeting US foreign policy objectives, for example in helping penetrate overseas markets for US foodstuffs, coping with populations displaced by wars in Asia, or in promoting 'birth control'.

Agencies have grown alongside domestic social welfare systems, drawing on the same political and moral sources of inspiration. Organised pressure from below, fear of upheaval above, and prevailing notions of Christian solidarity helped to curb a liberal ideology of individual responsibility for risk, misfortune and 'backward' zones. Such pressures and fears helped collectivise that responsibility through social insurance, measures to protect the least advantaged, and revenue redistribution programmes to uplift poor regions. Rhetorically at least, private and public *foreign* aid bear the stamp of *domestic* public welfare principles, even if the principle of universality, hence any notion of entitlement, immediately falls away. Some of the differences among western European, Scandinavian, and US private aid agencies may be traced to the norms informing their respective social welfare systems: the broad, corporatist, but non-redistributing approach of Germany, France and Canada; the egalitarian, redistributive systems of Scandinavia; and the means-tested minimalism of the United States.

The variety of private aid agencies is also traceable to the kinds of organisational models people had to work by, and social strata underpinning them. Early private aid had only a few basic models: the private family foundation, the Christian mission society, the Red Cross and the solidarity group of the kind seen in the Spanish Civil War.

Government steering of altruism was often present, but the initiative and most of the material backing was private and voluntary.

The endowed foundations were trend-setters. They took the long view. Unlike most private aid agencies, foundations have never chosen the strategy of the small charity project and emergency aid. John D. Rockefeller had abandoned this 'retail' philanthropy even before setting up his foundation in 1909–13. The strategic approach of his 'scientific' philanthropy resembled some progressives' notion of social planning and policymaking – except of course that it was wholly in the hands of the super-rich.

Henry Ford, whose accumulated wealth later served to build the foundation bearing his name, at first had a wholly different outlook. He wanted nothing to do with philanthropy. Rather, he tried using surpluses to set up a profit-sharing plan for his employees. Asked for his views at Congressional hearings in 1915 about the private foundations, Ford responded:

> They may and probably do do some good. Of course they are not adequate. But my idea is justice, not charity. I have little use for charities or philanthropies as such. My idea is to aid men to help themselves ...[4]

In the event, Ford's employee-shareholder idea got sidelined. For ruling elites, philanthropy was the safer bet. The large philanthropic trusts moved ahead strategically, exercising crucial influences over domestic policies – especially those concerning social services and welfare. And, as noted in Chapter 5, they also shaped the discourses guiding foreign aid programmes for close to fifty years.

The post-war era of US dominance, the Cold War and competition for clients among newly decolonised lands began rapidly changing, and to some degree eclipsing, pre-war patterns of altruism centered on citizen and church initiative. The emergence of the official aid system began spawning and driving 'private' aid agencies like CARE (Cooperative for Assistance and Relief Everywhere), whose tasks, often defined by government contracts, were shaped by foreign policy aims. For the older generation of agencies, driven almost entirely by citizen initiative, government subsidies created new possibilities for wider scope and impact, but also new dilemmas about compromising autonomy and sacrificing the voluntary spirit.

The new United Nations system of aid, relief, policy formulation and assertion of universal rights initially posed the possibility that recipients could influence the terms under which the rich provided aid to the poor. But other outcomes in most of the UN system – technocratic and bureaucratic elite strata on a world scale – have largely nullified those prospects. Nevertheless the hope of ending charity, of making the helpers answerable to the helped, and of establishing something like mutuality, remains an ideal. Whether private aid agencies can risk vocational suicide and put mutuality in the place of 'cold charity' is an open question.

Unaccountable Power in the Saddle

Agencies have become numerous, and salient, at a moment when the world political economy is changing at unprecedented speed. The conjuncture has seen a particularly violent collision of two organising principles and forces long in tension with each other: that of economic liberalism and its accumulating classes, and that of social protection and the classes hurt by unconstrained workings of the market.[5]

Neoliberalism is clearly now in the ascendant. The forces of social protection are suffering such setbacks that even observers in the middle of the political spectrum grow fearful. The editor of the Sunday edition of the British newspaper the *Independent*, no tribune of the Left, tells it this way:

> The ever-restless ideology of commerce now rides over and through us, it sometimes seems to me, like those images of Death in the plague years – cutting down some populations, allowing others to survive and prosper, with a finality and randomness that allow no argument. The idea that it is the best, and indeed the only, mechanism to secure human happiness has infected us with a medieval fatalism; there goes the market riding by with his scythe on his charger, nothing can be done. It also poses a threat to politics, if politics are taken as the demonstration of how we wish to live. For what is the point of them if that question has already been answered?[6]

Poverty and exclusion, the things justifying the aid agencies' existence, loom larger than ever, both in the North and in the South. Labour-saving technologies, demographic growth, and razor-wire barriers to immigration combine to deny growing numbers of people any hope of gaining decent livelihoods.[7] This raises the spectre of permanent castes of 'insiders' and 'outsiders', winners and losers – in a word, global apartheid. Combined with rising fears about the environment, these chilling trends have begun eroding the broad consensus favouring conventional growth, though not yet to the point of decisive measures to curb it.

A sober reckoning suggests that to brake these trends would require material, political and conceptual resources far surpassing those of the world-wide aid industry, let alone the lively but relatively lilliputian agencies of private aid. Action by public authorities is going to be indispensable. Voluntary action and civic initiative may be vital, but they lack means and broad legitimacy. Yet other trends pose the question: When problems accumulate to the point where they can be tackled only via public authorities, will those authorities still have means to do so?

There are worrying signs that they will not. Their means are slipping away at an accelerating rate. Transnational firms now straddle the world as colossi. 'Contented', better-off minorities, identified so acutely by John Kenneth Galbraith, are successfully mounting pressures to shrink the collective sector, delegitimise state powers of intervention on behalf of the poor, and pass social responsibilities to unaccountable private agents. Big firms and financial markets are steadily freeing themselves from public obligations, including taxation. Public revenues are proportionately shrinking. There is downward pressure on government expenditure, especially that meant to benefit people least able to defend their interests. All this puts in question the legitimacy of public welfare systems at home and official foreign aid efforts abroad.

Driven by dogmas that gained ground in the Thatcher-Reagan era, and by the explosive growth of money-power of banks and bond traders since the early 1980s, these economic measures have been accompanied by efforts to transform the political stakes permanently. The aim is to shift decision making about fundamentals of economic life away from public purview and debate.

Many state services, and with them significant powers over public policy, are placed in the hands of unelected authorities such as quangos – the quasi-NGOs notorious in Britain as well-paying sinecures for Tory party hangers-on, and in The Netherlands as bloated institutions with poor accountability to the public.[8] Those capturing the streams of benefits here constitute new private interest groups. The careers of some private aid agencies are rising on the same wave of privatisation. Indeed some of them are effectively quangos.

Paradoxes abound. Trends thrusting agencies into prominence also erode their legitimacy and the material basis for their existence. Agencies founded on principles of peace and justice find themselves caught up in relief efforts that effectively feed conflicts and hinder the achievement of justice. While their environments are proving less predictable and tractable, the question of where they are to anchor themselves grows more urgent, both in the South and in the North.

Non-profits and Welfare Provision in the North

Even social democratic politicians are capitulating to interests who say that declining Northern well-being stems from excessive collective sector outlays on social services, particularly for the poor. In the United States, politicians compete to slash welfare programmes and drive the poor out of their areas. In the European Union, where the Maastricht articles of confederation require caps on state borrowing and national budget deficits, the trimming of collective sector services has also begun. Dismantling welfare may lighten fiscal burdens, but it has come at a cost to democratic practice. The Reagan and Thatcher administrations, according to one study, owe their success in cutting welfare to sneaky, non-democratic methods, mainly obfuscation: 'Never tackle problems head-on. Conceal what you are doing. Shift the blame on to others. Always cover your tracks'.[9]

Have non-profit social service agencies been used in this cynical assault on the poor, and on democracy? The shedding of state responsibilities has meant in any case new tasks and dilemmas. Devolution of welfare services to them – contracting-out – has spawned hundreds of 'non-profits for hire'. They care for the elderly and infants, provide counselling and job placement services to the young and housing and neighbourhood improvements for entire communities. In some cases this may yield responsive and adequate services, especially where the contracting public authority follows a transparent, enforceable mandate to see that services are delivered and human needs satisfied. But such circumstances are hardly universal, at least in the United States. Non-profits on contracts may lose (or never gain) value-driven identities. Their orientation shifts away from constituents and toward funding authorities. Some begin to resemble their paymasters, turning rigid and bureaucratised.[10]

In their response to market forces, non-profits are proving no more immune than for-profit businesses from self-dealing, political cronyism, shoddy services, misleading advertising and evasion of public oversight. In the United States, some non-profits have been exposed as 'warehouses of wealth', recalling earlier public outcries over abuse of charitable status to cover massive tax avoidance, price-rigging of health services and political manipulation.[11] In 1993, in a scathing article on the non-profits, *Time* magazine enjoined its readers to 'Remember the Greedy'.[12]

Such bad publicity may help explain why the crisis in confidence in *state-run* welfare measures may not be as serious as the neoliberal critics claim it is. A recent poll suggests that 80 per cent of the US public believes that 'government has a responsibility to try to do away with poverty'; in 1964, 70 per cent held such a view.[13]

Despite a dented image, the non-profit sector continues to grow. One study suggests that more than half of all non-profits were created since 1960, and that, when the enormous health care and university sectors are included, 'third-sector' operations account for 5 per cent of rich countries' gross domestic products.[14] An all-party panel of the British Parliament has urged that non-profits in Europe 'be given full "social partner" status in the European Union, on a par with industry and trades unions'.[15]

In a word, mainstream non-profits are gaining stature. The public gets an impression that 'something is being done'. In some cases quite effective work *is* being done. But there are real risks that what is being conjured up is a smokescreen, a cheap and expedient way for public authorities to sidestep basic obligations.[16]

If deep undertows are eroding the political consensus in Northern countries about obligations to the poor and excluded on home ground, conventional foreign aid is being swept from its moorings by a powerful riptide.

Conventional Foreign Aid: 'A Problem Posing as a Solution'

Having grown rapidly in the 1960s and 1970s under Cold War and mercantilist pressures to boost Northern exports, the official aid industry began losing momentum in the 1990s. With overall DAC (OECD Development Assistance Committee) aid volume 6 per cent lower in real terms than the two previous years' totals, 1993 may have been the turning-point. As Northern economies' gross domestic products expand, smaller proportions of them go toward foreign aid.[17]

Northern publics continue professing adherence to principles of altruism. They still see foreign aid as a moral obligation, but they have grown sceptical about it in practice. Voters and their representatives have little stomach for more stories about 'clientalism, shady deals, corruption and public aid for private benefit',[18] or about the high-flying lifestyles of its elite managers, the 'lords of poverty'. Reinforcing perceptions of waste and malfeasance are exaggerated notions of the claims aid budgets make on taxpayers; Americans for example harbour inflated fantasies about foreign aid, estimating that its share of the national budget is 15 to 33 times greater than it actually is, namely about 1 per cent.[19]

Is foreign aid as badly spent as most people think? With all forms of aid lumped together in this way, the question cannot be answered with a single, resounding Yes or No. It all depends. There is evidence that official aid has been quite important, even decisive, in helping certain countries and communities get through times of extreme stress, such as when rebuilding after war or depression. Taiwan and the two Koreas are foremost examples from the 1950s and 1960s. In a number of African countries today, aid is simply indispensable to the functioning of government, basic public services and vital investments for the future.

But in other instances there is evidence of the futility and even perversity of outcomes of official aid. Neoliberal critics scorn it for its statist, Keynesian starting-points. Their opponents on the Left call attention to the ways it imposes the growth model, distorts economies and governments in the South, 'internationalising' them and breaking down their reciprocity with citizens, for example. They doubt the claims made about aid's positive contribution to social equity. After reviewing, and debunking, the exaggerated claims made for conventional (in this case, large-scale, World Bank-orchestrated) aid, David Korten concludes:

> It all comes down to what has become a widely recognized, though freely ignored, truth. International assistance is only useful in supplementing domestic resources within the context of a disciplined national policy environment that encourages the efficient and equitable use of all available resources, both foreign and domestic. In the presence of such conditions the need for external assistance is greatly reduced. In their absence, aid is of little help – and is usually counterproductive ... Where discipline is lacking, assistance is more likely only to produce profits for suppliers and contractors, finance profligate lifestyles for the rich, relieve pressures for domestic tax collection, subsidize the exploitative extraction of natural resources, mask economic mismanagement, release other funds for military expenditures, reduce pressures for essential social reforms, aid capital flight, add to debt burdens, and make recipient governments beholden to foreign interests.[20]

At best only 5 to 15 per cent of official aid is spent in anti-poverty categories, despite assertions that from 30 to 44 per cent goes to 'basic needs'.[21] Rather, advancing Northern commercial and political interests, including the selling of loans and transmitting economic and political doctrine, are foremost on many aid agendas.[22] A recent 'aid-for-arms' scandal in Britain led one tribune of the environmental movement to denounce mainstream aid as 'little more than a slush fund fuelling a corrupt and corrupting system of patronage politics', adding that 'the familiar rhetoric of "conquering poverty" is a cynical deception'.[23] Can such charges be so easily dismissed?

Overlooked amid the claims and counter-claims about official aid and Northern intervention is how relatively insignificant aid can be – especially for poor people. Aid agencies, both private and official, draw a lot of attention to their work in support of war victims and refugees; yet in post-war Mozambique, an aid-dependent country *par excellence*, aid agencies furnished direct help to only a small fraction of all Mozambican refugees and displaced persons, most of whom restarted their lives unaided.

Poor people, like everyone, prefer to rely, where they can, on means they can control. That usually comes down to relying on their own devices. They survive chiefly through shrewd use of local circuits of goods, services and migrant labour. Here and there, a flow of benefits from a foreign aid programme may fit into a survival strategy for a while. But Africans, Asians and Latin Americans organise their own richer-to-poorer flows with great efficiency. Earnings sent home to poor areas by family members working in richer areas often account for far greater transfers of resources, with far less leakage and overhead costs, than foreign aid. Such private flows are sometimes organised to sustain not just families, but community investments, as with village associations in West Africa supported by emigrants working in Europe.[24] Much of the aid industry carries on in complete ignorance of such huge but unregistered systems of self-help.

Yet pumping up the legitimacy of official aid depends on its maintaining an acceptable public profile and broader constituency. Private aid agencies have been exemplary as the 'soft, cuddly face of official aid'. Other non-profit contract-holders in universities and city councils now also form modest lobbies for official aid. To legitimate and protect itself, the official aid system is today taking on other aims and allies. New goals are put forward, such as stemming the flow of immigrants and refugees to the North or caring for asylum-seekers on home ground; and broader tasks, such as relief interventions that somehow keep a lid on complex political emergencies;[25] and new institutional colleagues, such as police, military and even espionage agencies.[26]

Thus as evidence of the failings of conventional aid mounts,[27] and scepticism grows among aid workers and journalists (who can reel off many anecdotes of absurdity and waste in the aid business),[28] many in the agencies would like to see a radical overhaul of the official aid system, beginning with the institutions that run it. Yet beleaguered and compromised, private aid agency top managers find themselves obliged to defend it, increasingly with strange bedfellows.

Box 1.2: On Hobbyism and Learning Disabilities

Insiders to private aid agencies will recognise at once the truth of the following remarks, made by a seasoned observer of the aid industry, mainly about an agency of the official aid system – but not only official aid, as the reference to the Ford Foundation suggests:

> There's an interesting project cycle that goes with [the agency's] system, and it has three phases: First there's a new group with a terrific idea, and they go through the 'fantasy generation' stage where everybody's all excited ...
>
> But because of staff turnover and rotation, implementation is often done by a very different group than the one that designed the project. The new staff find themselves in what one might call the 'damage control' phase – because the project never works out the way the designers fantasised it. Then they go through *another* cycle of turnover in staff, and this new group comes into the mission, reviews the old portfolio, and says, 'My God! What a mess! How could they have done this?!' They go through the final 'slum clearance' phase, where they wipe it all away and start with a new fantasy.
>
> These bureaucracies have got to transform. The question is, how do you make that happen on a sufficient scale? Even the Ford Foundation, a relatively small organization, has no internal learning mechanism.[29]

Forward to Oblivion?

From Right to Left, and especially in the political mid-field, private aid agencies have gained glowing plaudits. For the contented Right, hostile to government, they fit neatly into game plans to shed collective responsibilities. For the discontented Left, they embody the principle of social protection and solidarity against the impoverishing effects of *laissez-faire* economic dogma. For most people, however, private aid's chief virtues hinge not on politics but on the altruistic gesture. All together, the convergence of different interests helps explain why the agencies and their Southern NGO counterparts have been lionised, and why publications on private aid and its outcomes bear such optimistic titles as *Democratizing Development*, *Making a Difference* and *Hope at Last*.

But now the bloom is off the rose. Criticism – some of it wholly dismissive of private aid – has begun to surface. The gap between claims and actual performance, and the marketing techniques used to camouflage it, are slowly being exposed. These have brought other observers to publish quite different conclusions about the agencies, with pessimistic or sceptical titles like *The Orchestra of the Titanic, The NGOs: Mercenaries of the Global Village or Guardians of the Ghettos*, and *Naked Emperors or Full-Fledged Partners?*[30]

The persistence of poverty and social exclusion, especially in regions where private aid agencies have been most assiduously and visibly at work – Sub-Saharan Africa, South Asia and Central America – suggests an easy conclusion: private aid, like official aid, is clearly not up to the job. But that is to pit them against absurdly large tasks, like those that faced heroes of myth and legend down through the ages.

That publics continue showing no objection to agencies being cast in roles of mythological proportions suggests a willing suspension of disbelief, and careful stage-management. Most agencies have long been sheltered under a 'cloak of love', both of their own making and of those who need or use them. Gross simplifications of the problems they claim to tackle merely add to the mystique. One important sim-plification is that the victims have only themselves to blame, and that the problem is far away in the poverty zones and the killing fields. Whole chapters of history fall from view. Poverty and power in the North disappear. Together with a general lack of accountability to the public, these dense covers have allowed agency failings to go unnoticed and unaddressed.

Who owns the agencies, and what makes them run?

This book seeks to hold private aid agencies up against the light of several issues under-illuminated in debates up to now. The first cluster of issues concerns control, ownership, identity and legitimacy. Who really owns and controls the private aid agencies? What drives them? To whom are they ultimately accountable?

Private aid agencies have grown in number and size on rising streams of revenue, especially from the official aid system. And those official funds look likely to increase: at the March 1995 Social Summit, US Vice-President Gore announced that within a few years more than 50 per cent of all US non-military foreign aid would be channeled through non-governmental organisations (in 1993 it was 17 per cent). Northern private aid agencies stand to get most of this. But Southern NGOs, hitherto seen by Northern agencies as their 'natural partners', are increasingly eligible and attractive channels for official aid. Direct funding of Southern NGOs is expected to grow from currently modest levels (an estimated 10 per cent of all funds reaching Southern NGOs come directly from Northern governments in the early 1990s) to considerably more. This will complicate relations among official aid bodies, Southern governments, and local NGOs, and exacerbate tensions between all three and the private aid agencies.[31]

Privatisation of official aid looks like a bonanza. But it will force agencies lacking real constituents or an independent source of income, and bound to a strategy of tangible resource transfer, into a corner. They must join the scramble for contracts or perish. Meanwhile, their former 'partners' among Southern NGOs will begin competing with them for funds.

Competition for funds from donating publics and the accompanying struggle for positive attention in the media continue to concentrate the minds of agency managers. The effective deregulation of this market, and massive entry of newcomers, are profoundly affecting agency choices, including how they structure and manage themselves. Rule by the backroom boys for marketing and public relations is a charge no longer so easy to dismiss. Do the agencies risk becoming mere businesses, where value-driven pursuits are crowded out?

For agencies concerned to remain non-governmental and thus able to pursue emancipatory agendas, the future looks troubled. *There is, in short, a mounting crisis of control and ownership.* This can manifest itself in revenue problems, as when a government slashes its life-giving subsidies. But a chain of consequences follows for their basic strategies, even identities. For they risk being wedded to an endless succession of short-term projects based on a dubious model of modernisation, or to stints in soup kitchens under tents set up by military task-forces. Willy-nilly, they come to legitimate things they say they oppose, just as social service 'non-profits for hire' in the North appear to legitimate truncated systems of public welfare and the rule of social Darwinism. Do private aid agencies risk becoming one more problem posing as a solution?

For the contributors to this book, the promise of the agencies to deliver on their ideals depends at minimum on their control over their own agendas, and thus their ability to keep a critical (if often necessarily negotiated) distance from the far larger institutions of the official aid system and interested parties in the charity market and media. At issue is the legitimacy of agencies as *agents* of voluntary, civic initiative. In some cases the debate extends all the way to basic *identity*: 'Is our agency an international aid organization that happens to be headquartered in country X, or are we an organization *rooted in the society of country X* that addresses issues of poverty and exclusion internationally?'

The most important of those choices go to fundamental purposes and identities: Whether to anchor their work in emancipatory agendas, and to root or ally themselves with others pursuing those agendas North and South, including social movements, other non-profits and responsive public authorities; or to follow agendas set by institutions with other vocations, which may at best be indifferent to emancipation.

Other choices facing the agencies – about professionalisation, scaling-up, and other instrumental measures to improve performance – are also important, but ultimately secondary to the choices of identity, ownership and direction.

What difference do they make?

The second cluster of issues concerns *impact*, in the North as well as in the South, intentional and unintentional. What *do* the agencies actually accomplish?

Giving priority to the poor, alleviating poverty and relieving victims of crisis, empowering community groupings and women, and casting spotlights on chronic wrongs and conflicts: these are among the main purposes private aid agencies set for themselves.

Many assume they are making good these claims. Funds have been kept flowing on that promise. No agency seems to quit the field, and more agencies professing such purposes enter it every year. Yet this may reflect not the strength of performance, but one of gravest weaknesses: funding is only poorly linked with actual outcomes – if it is linked at all. Agencies are rewarded chiefly for spending and being active; they are almost never punished when that spending and those activities come to nothing, or entail unwelcome side-effects. Why should results not carry more weight?

One reason is that agencies can just keep moving. Staff can often 'escape into the future' through a succession of short-gestation, photogenic projects and 'partners'. Sustainability becomes somebody else's problem. It is easy to disclaim responsibilities of paternity of their projects, left in the care of local people – like unwed mothers with 'love child' babies.[32]

Moreover, aid fashions change, new staff arrive, a new crisis spot grips world attention, and it is time to assemble a new portfolio – appropriate technology is out, small-scale credit is in; public administration is out, natural resource management is in; Somalia is out, Rwanda is in, and so on. This 'continuity of discontinuity' afflicts not only private aid agencies of course, but it seems especially marked among them.

That funding is not anchored in performance runs parallel to agencies not being accountable to those whose life-chances depend on outcomes. In a word, neglect of impact implies a rootlessness, and thus aimlessness.

But what is actually known about outcomes? How closely do the claims match actual practice, and in what measure do the practices achieve the aims? Until quite recently, there has been little evidence one way or another. Few agencies, like other public and non-profit organisations,[33] have had their work assessed *independently*, systematically and in depth, and fewer still have published the results. Private aid agencies are notoriously persistent in demanding information from project holders in the South. A few hammer the World Bank and IMF for *their* lack of transparency. Yet most agencies themselves show great parsimony, and nervousness, when it comes to revealing information about the full range of their successes and failures.[34]

This culture of secrecy has raised suspicions, placing state-subsidised agencies in the firing line of public debate, and forcing them to undergo special investigations. Chapter 4 considers the findings of a number of these semi-independent studies. Chapter 5 assembles findings from an even less well-studied matter: agency impact at home in the North.

Back to the Future

In a charged and rapidly shifting sphere of clashing interests, private aid agencies find themselves in positions similar to that of a donor-driven development project in Africa that

> was not simply acting on a system in place, but was itself acted on; grabbed and pulled and twisted every which way by forces it did not understand or have the means to deal with ... it quickly found itself in the position not of a craftsman approaching his raw materials, but more like that of a bread crumb thrown into an ants' nest.[35]

Shallow-rooted and accountable to few at home, grabbed by the marketing boys, pulled by the media and twisted by official funding authorities who must move their money before the fiscal year lapses, agencies are vulnerable to a host of forces with seductive but ambiguous powers. A rising number of interested parties are concerned – with good reason, as Chapter 4 suggests – about the impact and ultimate meaning of their activities in the South. These vulnerabilities grow with every passing year.

At the same time, a few agencies are awakening to their comparative advantages in seeing and exposing important realities of poverty and exclusion in the South, sometimes with a shock of recognition: some of those realities are little different in the North. In their public standing, finances and guiding paradigms, agencies, are in a word, challenged.

As suggested throughout this book, they will face further public probing and attacks. This public exposure may never reach the depths of demagoguery prevailing today around domestic social welfare programmes. Rather, it may replay the pressures endowed foundations have faced periodically in the United States. The effect of those public conflicts was largely conservative, leading most foundations to play it safe and support only the tamest charitable causes. But a few have withstood right-wing attacks and cautiously moved toward 'responsive philanthropy' which emancipatory social movements have pressed them to do for decades.[36] A further upshot has been the appearance of watchdogs, and their practice of keeping an eye on the foundations.

Hence figures likely to arise on the agencies' terrains are monitors – groups or persons with *watching briefs* about the private aid agencies. People who donate, the agencies' consumers, are getting choosier and seek better information about the product they are buying. The second and fourth chapters of this book pose such possibilities, and present forcefully the need for improved public transparency and accountability.

Challenged by watchdogs North and South, agencies face pressures to reform. Those with clear vocations as contractees will seek, and perhaps find, shelter under the wings of their patrons in the official aid system. As effective quangos, some may evade full public scrutiny. Therefore it is that rather larger category of agencies supported both by public and private funding which must change itself unaided. As argued in Chapter 2, that challenge is a radical one: to 'reinvent' themselves.

Notes

1. Hon. Jean Augustine, MP, speaking to the Annual General Meeting of Partnership Africa-Canada, 29 September 1994, Hull, Quebec. Thanks are due to John Saxby for this quotation.

2. While charities and other organised expressions of compassion are woven into the fabric of life in some non-Western societies, and while a few aid agencies modelled on Western lines have sprung up in Southern countries in recent years, the organisations considered here originate in the North Atlantic countries and Japan.

3. In B. Smith, 1990, *More Than Altruism: The Politics of Private Foreign Aid*, Princeton University Press, Princeton NJ, and P. Burnell, 1991, *Charity, Politics and the Third World*, Harvester Wheatsheaf, Hemel Hempstead, for example. For a country-by-country review of the private aid agency sector, see I. Smillie and H. Helmich (eds), 1993, *Nongovernmental Organisations and Governments: Stakeholders for Development*, OECD, Paris.

4. Quoted from US Senate documents in B. Howe, 1980, 'The Emergence of Scientific Philanthropy, 1900–1920: Origins, Issues, and Outcomes' in R. Arnove (ed.), *Philanthropy and Cultural Imperialism: The Foundations at Home and Abroad*, G.K. Hall & Co., Boston, p. 44.

5. Karl Polanyi places this 'double movement' at the centre of his famous 1944 treatment of capitalism, *The Great Transformation*, Beacon Press, Boston, Chapter 11.

6. Ian Jack, 'How to Survive the 21st Century. Part Three: Society', the *Independent on Sunday*, 9 April 1995.

7. A sobering synthesis of these trends appears in P. Kennedy, 1993, *Preparing for the Twenty-First Century*, HarperCollins, London.

8. In Britain, where quangos manage £50 billion ($75 billion) a year, malfeasance has become so rampant that local government leaders have proposed that 'quango board members be made personally responsible for costs if they act in unlawful ways'. (*Financial Times*, 29 September 1994.) In The Netherlands, where quangos manage about $100 billion in public monies every year, the President of the government's General Chamber of Audit, after issuing a stinging report, said that Dutch quangos were in an 'unbelievable mess' and called for a parliamentary investigation. (*The Netherlander*, 8 April 1995.)

9. *The Economist*, 15 July 1995, in a review of Paul Pierson, *Dismantling the Welfare State?*, Cambridge University Press, Cambridge.

10. See S.R. Smith and M. Lipsky, 1993, *Non-profits for Hire: The Welfare State in the Age of Contracting*, Harvard University Press, Cambridge.

11. For an overview of scandals in the early 1990s and citizen efforts to call non-profits to account in the United States see: National Committee for Responsive Philanthropy, 1994, *The New Age of Non-profit Accountability*, Washington DC. In 1993 the Attorney General of the State of Massachusetts issued a report on charitable fundraising. Following a broad survey, it revealed that of 158 fundraising campaigns, the average charity itself received about 29 cents of every dollar raised; only 12 per cent of the charities received more than half of gross revenues raised in their names. Pocketing the lion's share were the professional fundraisers, advertisers, and other go-betweens. See F.C. Genovese, 1995, 'A Report on Charitable Giving', *American Journal of Economics and Sociology*, January, pp. 105–6.

12. Adam Zagorin, 'Remember the Greedy', *Time*, 16 August 1993. The article's sub-head: 'Exploiting their tax-exempt status, a growing minority of nonprofits put themselves before the poor'.

13. From a report by the Center for the Study of Policy Attitudes, Washington DC, as reported in *Left Business Observer*, No. 67, December 1994, p. 7.

14. L.M. Salamon and H.K. Anheier, 1994, *The Emerging Sector in Comparative Perspective: An Overview*, Institute for Policy Studies, Johns Hopkins University, Baltimore.

15. Sandra Greaves, 'MPs call for single European market for voluntary sector', *Third Sector*, 28 July 1994.

16. See T. Funiciello, 1993, *Tyranny of Kindness, Dismantling the Welfare System to End Poverty in America*, Atlantic Monthly Press, New York; and M. Miller, 1992, 'Citizen Groups: Whom Do They Represent?' *Social Policy*, Spring, pp. 54–6.

17. See T. German and J. Randel, 1995, *The Reality of Aid 95*, Earthscan, London. This excellent 'alternative DAC' report was also published for the years 1993 and 1994 by ActionAid, EuroStep and ICVA.

18. The 'four concrete pillars' of French relations with countries in the South, according to Claude Julien, 'Politiques hallucinées', *Le Monde Diplomatique*, August 1993, p. 11.

19. S. Kull, 1995, *Americans and Foreign Aid. A Study of American Public Attitudes. Summary of Findings*, Program on International Policy Attitudes, Center for the Study of Policy Attitudes and the Center for International and Security Studies at Maryland, University of Maryland, p. 1.

20. D. Korten, 1991, *International Assistance: A Problem Posing as a Solution*, The People-Centered Development Forum, Manila, mimeo, 8 April 1991.

21. The gaps between anti-poverty rhetoric and actual allocations have been quite wide, it appears, with the 'progressive' donors, as illustrated in a study of Dutch official aid up to the mid-1980s: P. Hoebink, 1988, *Geven is Nemen. De Nederlandse Ontwikkelings- hulp aan Tanzania en Sri Lanka*, Stichting Derde Werld Publikaties, Nijmegen.

22. Among important statements of this view is R.E. Wood, 1986, *From Marshall Plan to Debt Crisis: Foreign Aid and Development Choices in the World Economy*, University of California Press, Berkeley. Pantelis Sklias, in doctoral research currently underway at the Institute of Development Studies, Sussex, is using a similar framework to study European private aid agencies' relationships with European Union authorities. (P. Sklias, personal communication, 1995.)

23. *The Ecologist*, 'Lies Dam Lies and Ballistics', Vol. 24, No. 2, March/April 1994, p. 44.

24. In Cape Verde, remittances are equivalent to two to three times all foreign aid provided to that country; the disproportion is even greater when it is recalled that much registered official aid is (in salaries and overheads for example) never spent for goods and services in Cape Verde. In labour-exporting zones from Central America to northeast Africa to the Philippines the story is much the same. See Charles Condamines, 'Ces Immigrés, atouts du développement', *Le Monde Diplomatique*, Decembre 1993, p. 25, and Panos Institute, 1993, *Quand les Immigrés du Sahel construi- isent leur pays*, L'Harmattan, Paris.

25. A chilling scenario of apartheid on a world scale, in which relief agencies, accompanied by military forces, 'manage' sanguinary crises in the Southern periphery, and thus facilitate Northern (arms-length) coexistence with an imploding South, is elaborated in M. Duffield, 1995, 'Protracted Political Crisis and the Demise of Developmentalism. From Convergence to Coexistence', draft discussion paper, University of Birmingham.

26. In 1994, controversy erupted in Washington DC when the CIA issued a report pressing for more US foreign aid on grounds of national security. The CIA thus thrust itself on to the turf of the State Department, 'which is principally responsible for overseeing U.S. work with various U.N. agencies and *independent groups that conduct humanitarian relief*' (emphasis added). See R.J. Smith, 'Foreign Aid Needs to Increase', *Guardian Weekly*, 25 December 1994 (based on a *Washington Post* report).

27. Among popular critiques are: F.M. Lappé, 1980, *Aid as Obstacle: Twenty Questions about our Foreign Aid and the Hungry*, Institute

for Food and Development Policy, San Francisco; B. Erler, 1985, *Tödliche Hilfe: Bericht von meiner letzten Diensreise im Sachen Entwicklungshilfe*, Dreisam Verlag, Freiburg; and S. Brunel, 1991, *Le gaspillage de l'aide publique*, Hachette, Paris.

There are valid doubts, such as those expressed by the Dutch academic expert in aid, Paul Hoebink, about the usefulness of broad, generalizing studies such as R. Cassen *et al.*, 1986, *Does Aid work? Report to an Intergovernmental Taskforce*, Clarendon Press, Oxford, and P. Mosley, 1987, *Overseas Aid: Its Defence and Reform*, Wheatsheaf, Brighton. See P. Hoebink, 1995, 'Herijking Achterstevoren: De Jacht op Fantomen in het Nederlandse Ontwikkelingsbeleid', *Derde Wereld*, 13:4, pp. 21–35.

Studies concentrating on one zone or type of institution tend to yield sounder bases for judgement. Many of these suggest conclusions that are at best equivocal about the outcomes of official aid. Its poorest record – indeed its most egregious detrimental outcomes – are in Africa; see N. van de Walle, 1996, 'The Politics of Aid Effectiveness' in S. Ellis (ed.), *Africa Now*, Netherlands Ministry of Foreign Affairs (DGIS), Heineman and James Currey, The Hague, Portsmouth NH, and London, pp. 232–50. See also M. Lipton and J. Toye, 1991, *Does Aid work in India? A Country Study of Official Development Assistance*, Routledge, London; P. Mosely, J. Harrigan and J. Toye, 1991, *Aid and Power: the World Bank and Policy-based Lending*, Routledge, London; and J. Morton, 1994, *The Poverty of Nations: The Aid Dilemma at the Heart of Africa*, British Academic Press, London.

28.   Examples include: the swingeing attack on mainstream (mainly World Bank and United Nations) aid by G. Hancock, 1989, *Lords of Poverty*, Macmillan, London; and a personal memoir from Yemen of the farcical side of private agency aid work, T. Morris, 1991, *The Despairing Developer*, I.B. Taurus, London.

29.   David Korten, in an interview appearing in *In Context*, No. 28, reproduced in *Quid Pro Quo, Journal of the South–North Network Cultures and Development* (Brussels), No. 17/18, June 1994, p. 34.

30.   J. Clark, 1991, *Democratizing Development. The Role of Voluntary Organizations*, Earthscan, London; M. Edwards and D. Hulme. (eds), 1992, *Making a Difference. NGOs and Development in a Changing World*, Earthscan Publications, London; M. Sinclair, 1990, *Hope at Last: A Guide to Grantmaking in South Africa*, Henry J. Kaiser Family Foundation, Washington DC; H. Achterhuis *et al.*, 1993, *Het Orkest van de Titanic. Werken aan andere Noord-Zuid Verhoudingen*, VUB Press, Brussels; B. Hours, 1992, 'Les ONG. Mercenaires du village planétaire ou gardiennes des ghettos', *L'Homme*

et la Société, No. 105–106, juillet–décembre, pp. 35–50; De Ekster-molen Groep, 1994, *Naakte Keizers of Volwaardige Partners? Rol en Plaats van de NGO-Beweging in de Internationale Samenwerking*, NCOS, Brussels.

31. This paragraph draws on D. Fowler, 1992, 'Distant Obligations: Speculations on NGO Funding and the Global Market', *Review of African Political Economy*, No. 55, pp. 9–29.

32. A metaphor used by Edith Sizoo; see Chapter 6 of this volume.

33. See A. Wildavsky, 1987, *Speaking Truth to Power*, Transaction Books, New Brunswick, NJ.

34. See Y. Tandon, 1991, 'Foreign NGOs, Uses and Abuses: An African Perspective', *IFDA Dossier*, 81, April–June, pp. 68–78. Even after seven years of on-and-off public debate in The Netherlands about official and private aid, there is still widespread doubt about transparency. See for example Frans van der Steen, 'Ontwikke-lingswerkers blokkeren hulpdebat', *De Volkskrant*, Amsterdam, 18 February 1995. For experience with private aid agencies see, for example, P. Smit, 1991, *Nederlandse Landbouwprojekten in Afrika*, doctoral thesis, University of Amsterdam, especially pp. 44–9.

    Non-transparency over aid is certainly not confined to private aid agencies. A damning 1992 report by Price, Waterhouse over European Union aid in the Africa-Caribbean-Pacific countries was deliberately withheld from the public, further confirming widespread suspicions that the aid industry has a lot to hide.

35. J. Ferguson, 1990, *The Anti-Politics Machine: 'Development', depoliti-cization and bureaucratic state power in Lesotho*, Cambridge University Press, Cape Town, p. 225.

36. In the US, the National Committee for Responsive Philanthropy has been active since the time of major congressional investi-gations in the mid-1970s. Other watchdogs, such as the National Charities Information Bureau and the American Institute of Philanthropy, have also sprung up.

Interlude: Looking Back from 2010[1]

Simon Zadek

Once Upon a Golden Age ...

It all came to a head in the second half of the 1990s, although the underlying roots have a far earlier origin. The 1980s had been a golden era for what was then known as the 'non-governmentals'. From relative obscurity, NGOs became a centre of attention. They offered a vision of an active and responsible civil society underpinned by flexible, effective and accountable institutions. They offered, in short, themselves.

And they were accepted. They symbolised what the by-now emas-culated state sectors could no longer provide – a moral representation of the excluded. They were the guardians of faith of a people's democracy, latter-day Davids exposing the grubby, ineffectual and at times destructive deeds of marauding Goliaths. By the end of the 1980s, the NGOs – private aid agencies foremost among them – were a force that could not be ignored. Well financed and publicly acclaimed, they took on roles from providers of state-funded services, to legal challengers of corporate and state activities. Then the 1990s dawned ...

Globalisation and Its Malcontents

As you will recall, this was intended to be the period when the glob-alisation of trade and community would be realised via the General Agreement on Tariffs and Trade (GATT) agreement, CNN and the global shopping arcade on the Internet. It's quite strange to think about that dream in retrospect, given what actually happened.

The severe recession created by the globalisation adventure had the same effect on NGOs as it did on their main sparring partner, the corporate sector. They were, after all, both products of the same underlying processes. It was therefore logical that they should share the same patterns of development. During the early 1980s, many private aid agencies had over-expanded. In the leaner times of the

1990s, most agencies saw financial shortfalls as the heart of the problem. Agency staff's livelihoods began to compete for importance with the livelihood strategies being promoted for the world's poor, many of whom had meanwhile become clients, customers, users and, of course, 'partners'.

Agency leaders began to echo the corporate solution: retrenchment for survival. The extremities of the movement's early proponents were replaced by the managerial style of the period, 'corporate neo-liberalism'. Downsizing and de-layering was the order of the day, albeit smothered in the NGO language of decentralisation and empowerment. The same management consultants who had helped to construct the Babylonian aid edifices of the 1980s returned to advise solemnly on how to take them down again. This time, however, they had added redundancy counselling services to their colourful brochures, and talked intently about inter-agency competition, the returns from cold-call invasive marketing, and the need for a couple of more serious crises in the South to make up the funding shortfall.

Charity money, however, proved addictive. When they had it – money, that is – there seemed to be more and more strings attached. When they didn't have it, their enormous bureaucracies (and their many dependent sub-contractors) grew hungry, angry and frightened. Substance abuse, and real dependencies, had set in during the 1980s. More and more of the stuff was needed, even although it was clear that the more they had, the more were the values and other strengths of the agencies compromised in its use.

Transnationals Face South

Particularly dire was the situation of the Northern transnational agencies – or what were known as 'development non-governmentals' or 'private foreign aid agencies'. They had built up enormous organisations and associated financial commitments during the early neoliberal period. They had extended their scope through development programmes, lobbying and campaigning, and, in particular, disaster relief work. The official aid system of governments and international agencies, and the public, had willingly funded these moral crusades through promises of increased efficiency, effectiveness and an approach to participation that evaded the problematic role of the state, especially those democratically elected.

This helped propel the meteoric growth in the number of Southern NGOs who implemented the projects and kept pushing the cause of decentralisation and delegation so as to get more of the power over the funds. These Southern bodies had by the early 1990s outgrown their subordinate status. They were demanding a more than equal share of the cake. The agencies found themselves limited to an ever-diminishing set of activities. Funding from governments and international agencies flowed directly to the growing cadre of Southern NGOs, who in turn took the international stage by storm. They insisted on direct representation rather than the earlier indirect routes to power through their Northern colleagues. Some Southerners launched their own fundraising organisations in Europe and North America, particularly following the success of the newly elected African National Congress in attracting money directly. No part of the agencies' operations were safe at that time from the deadly pincer movement of invasive funding pressures and the rising of the South.

Matters of Measurement

Meanwhile the agencies fell prey to a serious case of measurement neurosis. New and expensive forms of accounting were introduced just at the time the agencies were cutting and downsizing. Measuring impact became a sort of institutional pass-the-parcel exercise. Funding agencies weaved an increasingly crazed, bureaucratic nightmare around their 'clients' in response to their own internal pressures. Agencies spent more and more time and money to fulfill these reporting requirements, and thus had to reduce the time and energy available for getting the job done. Agencies passed the buck to their Southern partners, instilling the same fear around reporting requirements that had been imposed on them. The facts of poverty became buried under a wealth of conceptual transformations. Impact assessment became an industry unto itself. Talk of indicators, targets and evaluation processes became the newspeak of the age, often substituting for the facts of power relations, exploitation and poverty.

The Emperor's Ragged Clothes – Legitimacy in Question

The changes resulting from the crisis in the 1990s unfortunately came about largely despite the stands taken by many agencies. A few medium-sized agencies moved towards new forms of accountability. But these relatively minor cases had no real ripple effect because of the obstinacy of the largest agencies, most marked in the so-called 'Seven Brothers'.

Drawing their nickname from the term 'Seven Sisters' applied by Anthony Samson to the seven largest oil companies, the Seven Brothers were a group of private transnational aid agencies that directly or indirectly controlled about 60 per cent of the funds passing from North to South via non-governmental hands. They dominated much of the lobbying space created during the 1980s, so they set the agenda in the media campaigns for hearts, minds and money. The fortunes of the NGO community lay in the image that these few organisations created for the public, the state, and, to a lesser degree, the corporate sector.

The resistance to change shown by the Seven Brothers and other agencies meant that the first real changes came about involuntarily, not via internal reflection and change of heart. The underlying structural issues became a crisis for the agency community when some of the more embarrassing aspects became public. It almost seemed a corollary of the increasing legitimacy of agencies in the eyes of the official aid establishment. From there, it was mostly downhill. A number of spirited journalistic investigations were undertaken – particularly one from the Trans Oceanic Institute, a renowned, European tabloid-style research institute based in The Netherlands. The book produced by this institute included a series of disclosures about malpractice, shoddy performance and outright cynical behaviour in high profile agencies.[2] These disclosures were, as many of those in the know have since argued, unrepresentative. However, the damage was done, and the floodgates opened.

The immediate effect was the outbreak of a fierce public debate in Europe and North America, with numerous allegations and counter-allegations flying through the media. Kinder critics portrayed the agencies as bloated bureaucracies in which well-meaning ethical and political initiatives had been buried in a paperchase and a sweaty morass of circular consultation. Enemies derided them as a self-serving elite unwilling to submit themselves to the very forms of accountability that they insisted upon for others. Amidst this invective and confusing debate, officials working for government and inter-national bodies quietly secured themselves. Programme approvals were mysteriously delayed and existing programmes were placed on hold pending the completion of some obscure technicality. This bureau-cratic retreat did not remain secret for long, and when publicised, it precipitated a steep decline in publicly-raised funds.

A major joint review of agency funding was ordered by the World Environment Organisation; its sister company, the World Bank; the anti-corruption agency based in Berlin, Transparency Incorporated, and a consortium of corporate sponsors. The European Commission and the United Nations eagerly scrambled to join this consortium, albeit as junior partners, because they saw it as a way of distracting public attention at a time that they themselves were under intense scrutiny by the international community. The contents of this joint review report, *Development Challenges for the 21st Century: The Role of the Non-Governmentals*, were pretty ghastly, with accusations of ineptitude combined with crass naïveté verging on corruptness-by-error.[3] The outcome of this review was all too predictable. Funding declined dramatically, and in a number of cases the accreditation rights – the lifeblood of these organisations by then – to major national and international policy fora was withdrawn.

There was, it must be said, some malicious exaggeration in the response of governmental and international bodies. For over a decade, bureaucrats and technicians from these organisations had been repeatedly held to moral account by small, badly organised agencies that had little expertise and absolutely no direct accountability. Here was finally their chance to take revenge for earlier humiliations such as the Wapenhans critique of the World Bank, and the legal ruling against the British government over the tying of funds for the Pergau Dam in Malaysia to their purchase of arms. Here finally was the opportunity to beat the agencies with their own moralising stick.

It is ironic that moralism was the one weapon that the private aid agencies had not reckoned could be used against them. They should have been warned by the media campaigns waged against a number of so-called 'ethical businesses' over this period. Even more ironic, perhaps, was that the bureaucrats who took their revenge in this way were drawn from among the same people who, only a decade or so earlier, had built their own careers by supporting the emerging non-governmental giants. These international bureaucrats had become a roving expert group on how to work with any type of agency. They ran newly emerged, assertive departments within organisations that were otherwise more or less moribund. Many of these bureaucrats in fact came originally from the agencies themselves, the very organisations which had become their clients and contractors. This made it all the more sad to see how quickly they turned away from the agencies, playing a central part in naming the very deficiencies that they had been so central in creating.

The agencies were in a shambles, as a domino effect tore through their ranks. Already demoralised by retrenchments that had alienated many of their Southern partners, the Seven Brothers met together in closed sessions to find a common approach to this problem. The central issues, they agreed, were legitimacy and accountability. The essential challenge was, broadly, 'What gives an organisation the

right to take funds with the stated aim of doing good for others?'
What could guarantee in the 'eyes of the beholder' that the organisation really intended to do what it said? How could one ensure that
this was what the intended recipients of this wealth of goodness
really wanted? Success was of course, important. However, public
opinion polls taken at the time showed that most people in the
North did not really believe that the facts of poverty in the South
would significantly change, certainly not at any large-scale level.
Similarly, an in-depth survey commissioned by Shell and carried
out by the World Environmental Organisation highlighted the fact
that 'success' was understood as a demonstration of trying the best
one could in difficult circumstances, not demonstrating significant
positive outcomes.

Southernising

A radical 'Southernisation' process began as a way of rebuilding
legitimacy. Southern NGOs had not suffered the same sort of
undressing in the media as had the agencies (another interesting story
which seems to be coming to the surface at the moment). It was
therefore possible for the agencies to regain at least some of their lost
legitimacy in the eyes of the North – and so their funding – by
demonstrating the increased control over decision making by NGOs.

A series of mergers between key Northern agencies and Southern
NGOs started taking place. Those agencies who failed to merge, or
who failed to merge quickly enough, found themselves subjected to
predatory 'asset stripping' of people, programmes and funding sources
by other NGOs from the North and the South. Most of those with
the 'ride it out' philosophy eventually had to change tack. A number
of them left it too late and had to close their doors for good.

Biting the Hand that Once Fed

The old adage, 'It never rains, it pours' proved to be devastatingly
applicable in this period. The 'controlled' mergers were, in most
cases, sufficient to move the new organisations onto a new plateau
of stability, but the South was still restless. The experiences in the
mid-1990s of mass demonstrations against GATT in India, and the
uprising in Chiapas following the signing of North American Free
Trade Agreement (NAFTA), offered a taste of one form of resistance
to what was seen as the high-handed approaches taken by agencies
in the South. The embarrassment caused by these demonstrations,

and the small but well-publicised loss of lives of agency officials and demonstrators (particularly in one awful case where agency officials turned out to be armed, and fired on a peaceful demonstration in a fit of fear), pushed agencies that had been slow on their feet to appreciate the need for change.

But then, a number of community organisations in the South suddenly began bringing cases against agencies to the international courts. Most accused the agencies of expropriating personal and community-based information for fundraising, and then using the money for unrelated purposes. Others charged them with making 'false promises'. (An interesting study of this period suggests that this strategy was the brainchild of a consortium of Southern companies interested in acquiring aid-funded contracts then in hands of the Northern agencies. These companies, it appears, were being fed with information and legal advice by a large Northern advertising agency, Media Development Inc., that was building a reputation in public fundraising for Southern development-oriented organisations.) Legal history was made where peasant and urban communities shrewdly used intellectual property rights legislation and privacy laws. Some high-profile agencies found that their opponents were the very organisations with whom they had campaigned against GATT regulations on intellectual property rights. The merger strategy took on a more urgent note, so as to co-opt community organisations which posed the greatest legal danger. This led to the establishment of offshore legal registration in several NGO havens, notably Norway and Switzerland.

The End of the Non-Profits

The idea of non-governmentalism, it will be recalled, was to enable a balance of autonomy from the state; an orientation towards non-financial gains, and a governance structure that sought to secure accountability in relation to stated aims. Exactly how this was achieved varied from place to place, but broadly built on the idea of 'trusteeship' associated with do-good organisations. That is, the trustees who effectively had the only legal right to direct the organisation were chosen by a group that usually acquired this right through historical precedent, and were representative only in the sense of having a legitimised concern for the same issues as the organsation.

The trustee model, in its various forms, was legitimate only until it was really tested. It could not withstand the pressures of a complex matrix of activities involving large volumes of resources, and major conflicts of interest regarding the use of these resources. Most of all, it became subject to challenge the moment the overall legitimacy of the agencies became open to doubt.

It became widely accepted that the traditional model of agency ownership – which was basically no formal ownership at all, leaving effective ownership in the hands of unelected officials – was inadequate. In 1999, drawing partly from a government-sponsored in-depth analysis of the non-governmental sector in the UK, produced in 1994,[4] a law was passed through the English Parliament marking the end of non-ownership status for all but a few (rather archaic) cases. The agencies, of course, resisted. They took the English government to the European Courts in an effort to overturn this shift in legal status. But times had changed since the Europeans could be counted on to temper English excesses. The European Court not only confirmed the original judgement, but made strong recommendations that the approach be pursued at a European level. The counter-move had backfired. By the turn of the century, the whole notion of 'non-governmental' as a form of (non)ownership was effectively over.

New Forms of Accountability

It would be gratifying to be able to say that a new form of ownership arose phoenix-like from the ashes to support appropriate forms of accountability for non-governmental organisations. This did not happen, although there was a period of intense and often creative innovation in new forms of accountability and ownership. Rather, a range of existing models of accountability was taken up by different agency-like organisations.

Institutional Federalism
This was probably the most common form adopted. It was quite similar to the 'Europe of the Regions' model that had been rejected by the European Union in the mid-1990s. Each part of newly-merged organisations acquired a vote according to various possible measures of size; the more conservative organisations tended to weight votes according to monies provided, whereas the more radical ones gave weight to how many people each part represented. The heads of the parts, many of which were in the South, made up the Board of Directors. This approach seemed to work particularly well for those organisations that were in practice controlled by their staffs, since it tended to consolidate decision making within the organisation's (extended) boundaries, rather than extending decision making to outside insti-

tutions, groups and individuals. This model was therefore often preferred by agencies oriented towards service delivery rather than advocacy and campaigning.

Block-Vote Model
Some agencies went for a variation of the block-voting formulas adopted by numerous political parties and trade union movements in the 'socio-corporate' era of the 1960s and 1970s. World Services International (WSI), for example, created a voting structure that gave funder stakeholders an aggregate block vote of 25 per cent, community organisations (the intended beneficiaries) 55 per cent, and staff the remaining 20 per cent. At the time, this approach seemed particularly attractive to agencies wishing to secure long-term funding relationships with a small number of institutional sources, and to focus activities on a small and stable number of communities. It was also an approach of relevance to agencies faced with legal action from the South, as was the case for WSI.

The WSI experience was particularly interesting in how subsequent power battles shifted the effective locus on control back towards the staff. The model they adopted should have given the community organisations effective control. However, the staff and funders managed from the outset to operate a divide-and-rule approach which gave them effective power. When this no longer functioned, the staff themselves organised a workers' buy-out (with support from the funders), leaving WSI in its current well-known form as the only agency workers' cooperative, in many ways resembling the institutional-federal model. WSI now provides a range of services, in practice doing a lot of cheap sub-contract work for other agencies.

One-Person-One-Vote Model
Of the large agencies, TransFam adopted the most radical approach of all, a one-person-one-vote system across their one million members. This was not, it must sadly be said, because they were the most radical organisation prior to the period of change. It was TransFam, some may recall, that became the focal point of mass demonstrations in the late 1990s, and had to cope with the largest number of litigations. Eventually, faced with imminent bankruptcy, TransFam signed the famous Delhi Accord in 2001. The over 3,000 closely-typed pages of the Accord spelt out a deal whereby TransFam would become owned by all those people who had received grants directly through them over a specific period. In return, the various litigations were dropped, and the relatively widespread intimidation of TransFam's officials ceased. It was quite a depressing affair at the time; today it

is seen as a low point in the collapse of the dinosaurs. It is somewhat ironic therefore that the TransFam model is now seen as the most radical to emerge from that period.

Enter the NICs

In that period there were, however, a set of organisations that voluntarily embraced radical transformations in accountability and ownership. These are the so-called 'new internationalist conglomerates' (NICs). These did not form a coherent community of organisations, but were a motley category that had acquired the name 'NICs' along the way, largely because of the ways in which they coped with the crisis of the late 1990s.

The NICs did, however, have a few fairly common characteristics. Firstly, although most of them were originally Northern NGOs, they were different from aid agencies of the traditional resource-transfer school. They grew out of operational, educational and lobbying work within and usually about their own communities and countries. Thus, although they did have an international profile, they brought with them a distinctly and unashamedly Northern internationalist perspective. This Northern root also meant that the NICs had a different sense of accountability. The intended beneficiaries of the private aid agencies had only limited access to the Northern media. But the beneficiaries and collaborators of the NICs could make their views heard in exactly those institutional spaces where the NICs could most easily be confronted and, if necessary, held to account. Thirdly, the NICs were generally smaller and younger than the mainly middle-aged aid agencies. They thus suffered much less from institutional inertia, bureaucratisation and internal vested interests.

But the really critical difference was that the NICs were of the information rather than the development age. Hence their other nickname, the 'New Information Consolidators'. They generated and shared knowledge, not funds. They moved information, not freight. They fostered development education, research, lobbying and campaigning, rather than funding physical projects.

These features gave the NICs an altogether different organisational form. In them, authority was far less hierarchically organised, since generating and sharing knowledge was much more about reciprocal relationships and respect. Their relationships with each other and with beneficiaries tended to be far more open-ended, involving less dependencies, fewer reporting structures, and, in general, a far higher level of voluntarism. The NICs did not therefore face the same sorts of difficulties encountered by other types of agency, particularly those that emerged before early neo-liberalism, during the 'development' period.

Conclusions and Lessons

The last twenty years have been quite remarkable. Looking back, it seems quite obvious that the changes should have been expected. However, at the same time it was all pretty unexpected. Even those most committed to change had got stuck in a visionless vision, one that was able to see what was wrong, but just couldn't discern what to do. Everyone seemed to be looking for the 'Big Story' and missed the massive events that were unravelling on their own doorstep. That is, until these events stood up and slapped them in the face.

This should not really be a surprise. It is difficult to see problems clearly when you are right on the middle of it all. This is not merely due to ignorance or malice. We prefer often to hang on to redundant utopias. Our certainties of what is wrong are not matched by a clarity of what would be an achievable 'right'. This state of 'perplexity', as Manfred Max-Neef describes it, is the 'outcome of a situation for which we cannot recognise a precedent, which has kept us in a dead-end alley and barred the road to imaginative, novel and bold solutions'.[5] The only route forward, André Gorz confirms, is to 'find a new utopia, for as long as we are the prisoners of the utopia collapsing around us, we will remain incapable of perceiving the potential for liberation'.[6]

This story is a lesson for us all. We may be pleased at the changes that have taken place; the new forms of private aid agencies, and the NICs. But history challenges us all not to repeat the incredibly myopic behaviour of the late twentieth century. After all, it might have turned out very differently, and may still do so in the future.

Notes

1. The author draws upon an earlier version of this scenario in S. Zadek and M. Gatward, 1995, 'Transforming the Transnational NGOs: Social Auditing or Bust', in M. Edwards and D. Hulme, *Non-governmental Organisations: Performance and Accountability*, Earthscan, London, pp. 193–205.
2. TransOceanic Institute, 1996, *The Private Agencies: Rulers or Ruled?*, TransOceanic Institute, Amsterdam.

3. World Environment Organisation/World Bank, 1998, *Voluntary Action in the 21st Century: A Reassessment*, WEO, Tehran.

4. HMSO, 1999, *Private Service Operators Act, White Paper*, London; B. Knight, 1994, *The Voluntary Sector in the UK*, Centris, London.

5. M. Max-Neef *et al.*, 1991, *Human-Scale Development: Conception, Application and Further Reflection*, Apex Press, New York.

6. A. Gorz, 1989, *Critique of Economic Reason*, Verso, London.

2

Who Owns the Private Aid Agencies?

John Saxby

Mythology, Image and Some Awkward Questions

The private aid agencies have enjoyed a flattering mythology as public-spirited bodies rooted in 'civil society'. By self-portrait and others' descriptions they are voluntary associations of altruistic citizens, distinct from the state and the corporate sector, responsive to their beneficiaries, accountable to their constituencies, and advocates of the poor and dispossessed of the Third World.[1]

Clearly the private aid agencies are now part of the mainstream, the public sphere, the political arena. In short, they have been politicised. Whether consciously, enthusiastically, or otherwise, the agencies are now part of a web of relations of power and privilege, of negotiation, alliance and dispute with state, parastatal, and other non-government bodies. This puts them under scrutiny – a novel, often unsettling, but undoubtedly healthy situation. Practitioners, academics, politicians and bureaucrats are beginning to look beneath the myths. UN officials acknowledge important questions about funding, voluntarism and participation.[2] A professor of public administration asserts that agencies' and other NGOs' participation in public policy dialogues raises searching questions about their representativeness and legitimacy.[3] More pungent are comments from 'insiders': 'So who are you accountable to? Not to any membership. You're accountable to Consumer and Corporate Affairs, that's who you're accountable to.'[4]

Aid budgets are now under attack. After the quantum increase of the last decade, they are being cut back. In 1995, Canadian federal aid was reduced by 15 per cent and the portion assigned to agencies slashed by nearly 20 per cent. Many agencies received no grants at all.

Further cuts are planned. In its official explanations, the Canadian government put commercial considerations at the heart of foreign policy, reducing resources for both domestic social programmes and for foreign aid.[5] Right-wing politicians have asked for even more cuts, challenging the usefulness of grants and tax expenditures in support of charities.[6] And, within the media, historically sympathetic to the sector, questions are being raised about the fundraising ethics of private aid agencies, their corporate style and their mythology of frugal efficiency. Journalists sympathetic to the agencies speak of a 'crisis of confidence' that mirrors doubts about the efficacy of the general aid 'project'.[7]

Boards and managers of private aid agencies have generally responded to the funding crisis by trying to maintain revenue and expenditure levels. Yet there is a deeper issue here, one rarely acknowledged by the agencies themselves, which should force a redefinition of 'the problem' they face. More than a crisis of confidence, a crisis of *identity* is at the heart of the issue.[8] What kind of organisations are private aid agencies, after all? Are they really 'civic' or non-governmental organisations? Who owns them? To whom are they accountable? What legitimacy do they command in the public arena?

As the opening chapter of this book makes clear, most agencies are profoundly vulnerable in political and financial terms, and are facing powerful challenges to their programming role. They may not be able to summon the independence, political clout and legitimacy that their precarious circumstances demand. So these questions, obscured by the prevailing mythology, must now be faced.

At issue are the legitimacy, credibility and autonomy of the 'community' of private aid agencies as progressive citizens' organisations, and as organs of civil society. The weaknesses of the sector will eventually force a reconsideration of the agencies' basic character, and a shaking-down and sorting-out seems inevitable. This kind of 'rationalisation of the market' has transformed countless other institutions, communities and lives in the last decade. But aid agencies face a dual dilemma. Questions of accountability and legitimacy pose a moral problem. Any shortcomings on this front will also leave them poorly positioned and ill-equipped to handle a serious practical problem, the political, financial and programmatic challenges enveloping them.

What Sort of Organisations are the Private Aid Agencies?

Autonomous agents or 'hired guns'?

The agencies unquestionably have allowed (or have they sought?) a growing level of financial dependence on government in the last decade – now well over 50 per cent in some countries. The Organization for Economic Cooperation and Development (OECD) estimates official funding to be now 'crucial' for at least half of the largest private aid agencies. There is a symbiosis at work here as well, of course: governments have come to depend on agencies as 'delivery vehicles'. As much as 25 per cent of official aid in Northern countries is channelled through NGOs. In some sectors, such as emergency relief, the figure is much higher, often approaching, and occasionally exceeding, 50 per cent.[9]

Such an intimacy compromises any role for the private aid agencies as forthright critics of official policy. The disparity in money and political power between themselves and their governmental bedfellows is so great that any symbiosis is decidedly asymmetrical. Can we reasonably speak any longer of 'independent' agencies collaborating with the state? The vulnerability of the agencies is obvious, but one must ask whether governments value an independent voluntary sector, or whether the NGOs see themselves as anything more than 'hired guns'?[10]

Internal democracy and membership sovereignty? Or the 'iron law of oligarchy'?[11]

Politically, the agencies have shallow roots in civic soil, with vestigial membership sovereignty, and limited accountability to their membership, constituencies, and those they serve. Rarely do they meet the standards of 'transparency' they ask of others.

It is not at all uncommon for an agency to be governed by a Board of Governors or Trustees which perpetuates itself. It may thus conform to national legal requirements but not be accountable to a membership base, let alone to those the agency serves. It is therefore in no political or constitutional sense a citizens' association.

Staff have particular privileges of power, however modest their salaries. Typically, they choose the agencies' Southern 'partners' and make recommendations and decisions about resource allocations among these partners. Programme plans, proposals and budgets are generated by staff, as might be expected; rarely, however, are Southern voices and faces around the tables of boards and programme committees where the choices are made. Staff constitute the primary, even exclusive, channels for information flowing among 'partners' in the South, institutional funders, private donors, volunteers and members in the North.

Some would say there's good reason for this. Norman Uphoff argues that 'service organisations ... are entitled to function as oligarchies'.[12] To allow beneficiaries to decide resource allocations would verge on conflict of interest, and would breach the fiduciary obligations of board and management. Whether such behaviour is 'justified' or not, one can reasonably ask whether oligarchies deserve the image of 'participatory' organisations, or are well suited to the task of 'democratizing development'.

So What's at Stake for the Aid Agencies?

So long as these patterns of ownership and accountability persist, the agencies' legitimacy is open to challenge, their effectiveness doubtful. Such fundamental weaknesses in character must provoke scepticism about their capacity to respond to the crisis noted in Chapter 1. Can they summon the skills, resources and clout to intervene on issues of global social justice, on North–South relations in the political arenas of the North or in multilateral forums like those of the United Nations? Do they have the imagination to change their historic programming roles and political positions – to build more equitable and solidary relations with 'partners' in the South, in support of social movements there; and to make common cause with movements for social justice in the North?

They will have to recognise that they are in a political milieu, and begin to act politically, in a conscious way, as some are already doing. They will have to meet criticisms; mobilise supporters, advocates and beneficiaries to argue their worth, and show to friends and critics their financial strength and viability. They can choose now to rebuild themselves as citizens' organisations, agents of a community of interest in the North, firmly rooted within those societies; to work for social justice, for sustainable economies and societies in the countries of the North as well as the South; to make common cause with and learn from citizens' movements in the North, while bringing in the accumulated knowledge of international work, and to build links of solidarity with Southern peoples and their organisations.[13]

If they do not do this, the process already in motion in countries like Canada and Britain will probably continue apace. The 'rationalisation of the market', driven by cuts to official aid budgets and faltering private donations, has already led to the closure of agencies, mergers, involuntary 'downsizing' and the attendant disruptions in programming. Willy-nilly, there will be realignments of political position, with some agencies openly embracing conditionality and the role of 'public service contractor',[14] and others asserting an independent stance. Still others might become transnational fundraising enterprises.

There are no guarantees, of course. The changes advocated here are probably not in themselves sufficient to ensure survival for the agencies, at least as relevant actors. Certainly they cannot replace wisdom, creativity, agility, or good luck. Nor is a solid membership by itself any guarantee of a commitment to social justice – witness the strength and effectiveness of the National Rifle Association in the United States.

Remaking the agencies in this fashion requires scrutiny of their political and financial ownership, and of the link between that ownership and the broad social role the agencies play. We can borrow some of the central concepts – 'accountability', 'ownership' and 'legitimacy' – from the agencies themselves. They and other NGOs have campaigned, and rightly so, for greater openness and accountability from international financial institutions like the World Bank and the International Monetary Fund. Their advocacy has helped put these principles onto the public agenda, and so to make them vital to any remaking of the agencies as independent organs of civil society.

Yet there is surprisingly little to draw on. The 'discourse' is rudimentary, the issue critical but largely unexamined. Notions like 'ownership', 'accountability' and 'representation' are often brandished but rarely unpacked in debates within and about the agencies, and receive little scrutiny in the literature on the agencies.[15]

A few working definitions, then. 'Accountability is the obligation to answer for ... responsibilities.'[16] Within a private aid agency, the board (of directors, governors, or trustees) is the ultimate locus of responsibility and accountability. A contract lies at the heart of accountability: an agreement on shared values or purposes, results and (usually) sanctions. 'Accountable to whom?' thus also carries the question 'for what?'. There is a core notion of reciprocity and mutual obligation between people or organisations. Also implied is some equity or comparability in power.

'Ownership' may well have acquired buzzword status within the liturgy of organisational development. For all that, there is a critical question here: who does the organisation belong to? Ownership of many types of organisations resides in its members, exercising their rights through a general meeting, annually or as required by law. They are comparable to shareholders who own equity in a corporation, or members of a cooperative.

This is all straightforward enough. 'Accountability' and 'ownership' are matters of organisational roles and responsibilities (though performance may be another matter entirely.) 'Legitimacy' is a more diffuse notion, though no less important for that.[17] It signifies rightful authority, bestowed upon an organisation by a recognised source. (The legitimacy of a democratic government, for example, derives from the continuing and active consent of those governed.) For an organisation like a private aid agency, 'legitimacy' can be ascribed or earned, and probably never guaranteed. And within the definition offered here, there remains the question of who confers and recognises legitimacy. Two critical components are:

- duly constituted (internal) authority – a board of governors elected by and accountable to the owners (members). A sovereign membership delegates authority to the board to govern the organisation,[18] and
- some real measure of accountability to those the agency serves. Brian Murphy puts it well: 'Above all the NGOs need to become more accountable to those in whose names they have justified their very existence as "humanitarian" organisations.'[19]

In some measure, too, legitimacy is surely about performance – the need for consistency between professed mission and actual behaviour; for demonstrable competence in managing organisational affairs; perhaps for expertise. Here, though, the notion of legitimacy becomes elusive, even unsatisfactory, not least because those judging performance and competence in an agency are rarely those it claims to serve. Nevertheless, the link between legitimacy and action has to be addressed.

The role or broad social and political position chosen by an agency is surely part of any agency's claim to legitimacy. This is a composite of its identity, its working relationships, its public stance on issues of global development. Evidently a subjective matter for both an agency and its observers, this consideration none the less has to be included in any assessment. Any judgment here will reflect the choice the agency makes between the options described in the opening chapter: alignment with official policies, or opting for a more civic existence and building a popularly-based public agenda.

A Typology of the Private Aid Agencies

The agencies' patterns of political and financial ownership and accountability give us a rough-and-ready political sociology. The accompanying Figure 2.1 shows five basic variants across a spectrum.

At one end are agencies which are essentially public service contractors, accountable to an official aid body via the contracts which

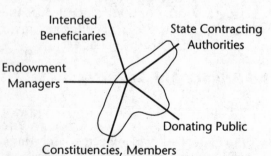

Figure 2.1 A Typology of Private Aid Agencies

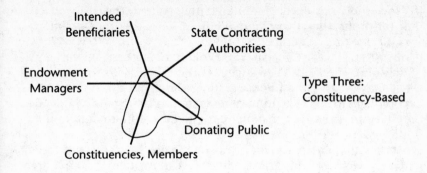

Type Three:
Constituency-Based

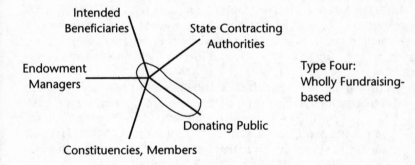

Type Four:
Wholly Fundraising-
based

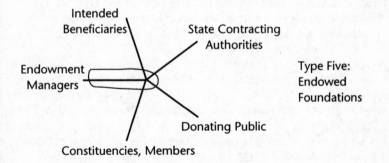

Type Five:
Endowed
Foundations

finance their existence. Nominally independent, they are, indeed, not-for-profit non-governmental enterprises rather than voluntary or citizens' organisations. Examples include CARE, WUSC (World University Service of Canada), VSO (Voluntary Services Overseas), SNV (Stichting Nederlands Vrijwilligers – Dutch Volunteers Foundation). They may be involved in private fundraising, but this is essentially a complement to their primary revenue source. Typically, they do not have an extensive constituency or membership structure, nor an independent institutional base.

At the other end of the spectrum are the privately endowed foundations, such as Ford, Rockefeller, Mott, Rowntree and Cadbury. Here, accountability is limited, private and direct: the endowment managers report to the trustees.[20]

In between are a diverse group of agencies with different configurations of funding, social and institutional bases. Among the agencies 'proper' – those established with the express purpose of aiding poor people in the South – one can identify several variants:

- European agencies like the Friedrich Ebert Stiftung or ICCO (the Interchurch Organisation for Development Cooperation). These have an established institutional base (the German Social Democratic party, and the Dutch Protestant churches and related trade unions respectively) and significant state funding, but few funds raised from donors within the public at large.
- Organisations whose budgets show a mix of funding from state agencies and private donors, but which have a limited base or infrastructure in the form of institutional affiliation or constituency committees. An example is the international relief agency, Médecins Sans Frontières (MSF).
- Agencies which include state and private funding, and a defined constituency or institutional base. Examples here would include several Oxfams, the Canadian agency CUSO, and church-related bodies such as Caritas or Development and Peace.

There is another grouping of organisations whose primary vocations are not in overseas aid. They are primarily membership-based. Examples include cooperatives and coop associations active in international development, unions with funds for international solidarity or humanitarian assistance, and municipalities. The grouping could be expanded to include professional bodies such as bar associations or medical associations. They finance their work from members' donations, public giving, and, unevenly, but increasingly from state funding. Such organisations are not agencies 'proper' –

their international development work is an outgrowth from their original raison d'etre, and their role as aid agencies is surely ancillary. Nevertheless, they and others see their international work as an organic development, a reflection of the globalisation of issues in every sector. To some, they are the future: their combination of sectoral expertise and a secure membership/funding base threatens to make the 'traditional' agency passé.[21]

The figure also includes a fourth type of private aid agency, one of recent origin. Organisations like BandAid or Comic Relief are purely fundraising-based, the project of pop stars like Bob Geldof. Necessarily, they are almost personalistic in their provenance and existence, relying on the box-office drawing power of their founders or fronting artists.

The Accountability Thing

It was 'the vision thing' that finally sank George Bush. The agencies may not be in quite so dire straits, yet the trinity of accountability, ownership and legitimacy poses some searching questions for them. These can be grouped under several sub-heads:

- Who are the 'publics' of an aid agency? To whom is it accountable?
- For what is an agency accountable, and how?
- How do we describe and account for an agency's positioning and role?
- Who or what confers legitimacy?

The publics: to whom is an agency accountable?
Through its Board, an agency is accountable to diverse publics:[22]

- donors, who donate money to finance the work of the agency;[23]
- its owners or members;
- the state as legal and public regulator, grantor and/or customer;
- 'partners' – those people or organisations the agency works with to design and deliver its programmes;
- the people or organisations the agency serves with information, services, money, human resources, etc.; a common term is 'the beneficiaries', sometimes 'customers' or 'clients; sometimes the usage extends to 'partners'.
- 'interested parties', which might include the following:

  - other agencies (The list here is long and may include individual agencies or councils and associations in the same sector, staff

unions, affiliated organisations, and members of a coalition or consortium);
- inquisitive folk like journalists and academics;
- moral supporters;
- concerned citizens.

Staff – those who administer the agency's affairs – are in a peculiar position. They bear operational responsibility, through the chief executive officer (CEO), or equivalent, for programmes, budgets, public relations, personnel and so on. Their work is governed by internal relations of accountability to the board and management, but they are not accountable for the agency as a whole.[24]

Volunteers – people who donate their time and services to the organisation – often find themselves in an anomalous or marginal position. Agencies are frequently lodged within the voluntary sector, and count voluntarism among their strengths.[25] Many large aid agencies can trace real voluntary beginnings to groups of independent citizens, often young people, working on shoestring budgets in church basements and community halls. Vestiges of that era may remain, in the form of local committees for fundraising and educational work. Yet, as agencies have become 'professionalised', control over resources and operations have increasingly become the preserve of staff. Most agencies' *voluntary* character now is often limited to their unpaid boards. There may be nothing wrong with this – it simply belies the myth of agencies as voluntary, citizens' organisations.

Accountability: Objects and Mechanisms

Two related issues arise: for what is the agency accountable? and how is this accountability established and honoured? The answers differ for the various publics.

Donors

The donor relationship is a contract built upon an exchange of values. The agency is responsible to ensure its work embodies the values of the contract and for sound management of its affairs. Typically, reporting, mutual education and information exchange are all key components of the contract. There is a sanction which is regularly checked: the donor renews or withdraws her gift of money. But how informed is the contract? How fully and candidly do agencies describe their budgets and activities as they solicit and report on donations? How do agencies respond to donors' ideas and perceptions, and how do they try to shape them?[26]

Owners

In a membership organisation, members are sovereign, and delegate their authority to the Board via an annual assembly. The Board then becomes responsible for the active governing of the agency. This relationship is the 'centre of moral authority' for the Board, hence of the agency as a whole, which underpins its general mandate or mission. The 'contract' is the mandate and power given to the Board, including goals, methods of work and reporting requirements; the sanction is the members' potential revocation of that power, or indeed their quitting the agency. There are variations, of course. The Board itself may be an agency's membership, renewing its own mandate and recruiting new members.

The State

The public authority performs a regulatory function via an agency such as a Charities Commission or a Department of Consumer and Corporate Affairs. Agencies must show their compliance via bylaws, a duly constituted Board, a satisfactory annual financial audit and annual report, or be defrocked or disbarred. This relationship provides an arms-length check to ensure 'peace, order and good government' within an agency. However, it is a 'passive' or *ex post facto* check. It is sometimes ineffective in preventing misappropriation of funds, as recently occurred in Oxfam Québec. There are other instances of bad business judgment, even leading agencies to the brink of insolvency, as in 1990 with War on Want in Britain and in 1991 with WUSC in Canada. In these cases, however, the problem would seem to lie with inadequate internal accountability, between management and the Board.[27]

But the state has come to play a critical role in the life and work of many agencies, as primary funder.[28] In this role, the state shapes programmes, perspectives and operating systems, often displacing any original voluntary character of the agencies, aligning agencies to the requirements of the official agenda of the day. Hence, the state has moved far beyond original role of 'supporter', 'funder' or 'customer' to a status closer to that of principal owner. In such circumstances, an agency's most comprehensive and elaborate statements of accountability are its contracts with the official development aid agency. Sanctions in such a situation are less a matter of cutting off official support entirely, than of shaping its use through increasing conditionality.[29]

Partners

This is one of the sacred terms of the development lexicon. But it is also what in Papuan pidgin is called a 'something nothing' word. It covers the waterfront, from Lester Pearson's *Partners in Development* to an official 'Partnership Branch' to individual agencies to the relations between agencies and organisations they work with in the South. Considerable reverence attaches to 'partnership', yet it has been described by one commentator as an effort by those in the North to address the imbalance of power inherent in the donor-recipient relationship.[30] A recent paper by Brian Murphy begins to demythologise the notion effectively. Examining the roots of the word, he makes it clear that 'partnership' implies separation when solidarity, collaboration and conspiracy are needed to promote an agenda of social justice.[31]

Nevertheless, the word and all its attendant baggage exist (much like the acronym 'NGO', perhaps) and its persistence requires acknowledgement and attention. In its most common usage, it refers to cooperation between Northern and Southern agencies to develop and deliver programmes and projects.

A recent study of partnership, done for the Canadian coalition Partnership Africa Canada, reveals some of the issues that lie embedded in the notion of 'partners' and 'partnership'. Prominent within the basic principles of the relationship is a Southern demand for mutual accountability and transparency. At the same time, very little practical detail is offered to elaborate or realise this principle. There are suggestions for mechanisms to promote a more equitable relationship: information exchange, advisory forums, proposals for joint planning and programming, protocols of understanding. All worthwhile and effective in the right hands, but no real examination of relationships of accountability, their substance or modalities.[32]

This apparently paradoxical silence may be revealing. Despite the changing roles of NGOs North and South, there remains a significant imbalance of power and resources. This is especially so when one speaks of the private aid agencies, the largest of the Northern NGOs. It is still the prerogative of Northern agencies to make the choice of partners.[33] They are the ones who fund programmes, initiate evaluations. Precarious as agencies' revenues are from both state and private sources, they still exceed in quantity and security the revenues available to most Southern NGOs or community-based organisations.

At the same time, however, as long as Northern agencies are aid agencies, they need Southern 'partners' to spend money and legitimise the Northern agency and its work, to provide evidence of its relevance. A symbiosis, albeit unequal, underpins the relationship. It bears an uncanny resemblance to the agencies' relationship with Northern official donors.[34] Not surprisingly, official use of 'partnership' often rankles with the agencies (and NGOs more generally). Not surprisingly either, basic relationships of accountability are poorly served by partnership-cum-dependency: on the whole, there is little definition of accountability beyond the narrow financial sense. Any notions of sanctions and reciprocity – essential to our earlier definition at least – are seriously compromised by an unequal donor/recipient relationship. There is a reality check for the agencies, a question simply posed but less easily answered: what would remain of the 'partnership' if one took away the money, that is, took away the aid relationship?

The conventional North–South 'partnership' relationship thus raises some awkward questions when viewed through the lens of 'accountability'. Related questions must be faced as agencies consider new roles, not only as donors but as participants in networks and coalitions, both North–South and within the North. Effective coalition work requires members to be accountable to each other for their performance in pursuit of common objectives and for their use of shared resources. But there are often significant differences in the resources on offer. Just as in a donor/recipient 'partnership', this difference in resources can compromise the nominally equal membership required for building a coalition. There may also be key differences in internal patterns of accountability, especially if agencies are collaborating with representative, membership-based organisations. The question 'Whom do you represent?' must be answered when it comes from allies, perhaps even more so than when it comes from critics. How many agencies could answer it well?

Beneficiaries

Webster's defines 'beneficiary' as 'anyone receiving a benefit', that is, a favour or a charitable act. The word's roots reflect relations of charity; perhaps paternalism. A more cumbersome phrase, 'those the agency serves' seems more appropriate to missions of justice and development. Here, the typical relations of accountability become more complicated, from imprecise to non-existent, and also loaded. Yet it is here that the moral stakes are highest – should an agency not, after all, be in some way accountable to those it is trying to assist, support, or serve? To those who are, after all, the *raison d'être* of the agency? Should not the work of an agency be shaped and assessed by those whose interests they are supposed to promote?[35] Our earlier review of basic principles (see page 41 above) tied the notion of legitimacy to this relationship.

If that assertion holds, then in its relations with those it serves, an agency should be: accountable in some measure for the purpose, implementation and review of its programs; and accountable through

methods that are operational or programmatic, rather than constitutional. These might include joint analysis, strategising and planning;
collaborative implementation, and joint evaluation.

But there are some knotty problems here that challenge the
intuitive view:

- Those served are, typically, far removed in time, space, culture
  and resources from the membership, the formal owners of the
  organisation, and indeed from the Board responsible for the
  agency.[36]

- An agency needs to be advised of the needs of those it serves –
  but the formal incorporation of 'partner organisations' or 'beneficiaries' into a decision-making role verges on conflict of interest.
  What options or mechanisms are available? A defined advisory
  role via councils or fora might work most readily where 'the beneficiaries' are organised and 'organisationally literate' – well versed
  in the politics and procedures of agencies. There are examples of
  such an approach. The Dutch agency Novib, for example, maintains
  a practice of regional consultation with networks of its grantees.
  In a more operational sense, those to be served may help shape
  an agency program as it is developed – though Robert Chambers
  has set out well the biases and blindness at work when staff of a
  Northern agency encounter the realities of power relations within
  the rural populations of Southern societies.[37] An evaluation would
  seem to be a made-to-order opportunity for sympathetic criticism
  and advice from those affected by an agency's programme. Yet
  the private aid sector as a whole is criticised for its continued
  deficiency in using evaluation to learn and to enhance accessibility. Many evaluations indeed are initiated by state funding
  agencies, or undertaken to satisfy their demands for results or
  financial accountability.[38]

- An agency may not even be in direct contact with those its
  programmes are intended to serve – the relationship may be
  mediated by a partner agency such as a Southern NGO which
  administers the programme.

- The sanctions available to 'beneficiaries' may be few and feeble.
  People using a social service agency in the North may be able to
  go to another if they are dissatisfied; or they may complain to a
  local newspaper; or they may seek redress in the courts; or they
  may go to political representatives. Few of these options are
  available to, let us say, a group of women farmers in western Zambia

if they feel a Northern agency has not honoured its commitments. Any leverage they may have is probably indirect at best, and individual rather than collective: they are but one 'project-holder' among many, so their withdrawal of services will have only modest effect. They face the dilemma of people of the South as whole: they are not voters in the North.

Interested Parties

These can provide a substantial measure of informal accountability for the whole range of an agency's activity. Accountability of this type functions primarily via information exchange, typically through the channel of staff (the CEO) or Board. The classic example is media exposure. Agencies have had, on the whole, a remarkably easy ride of it here, though the investigative articles cited at the beginning of this chapter signal a change.

Academic investigation is a potentially important external check on the agencies, as 'development NGO' research becomes a subfield of scholarship in sociology, organisational management and development, public administration and so on. (Though a sceptic might ask whether anointment as an academically respectable field is not also a form of protection.)

Agencies usually belong to inter-agency councils and associations, which create a kind of peer accountability. Agency associations have recently developed codes of conduct and ethics.[39] Their status is voluntary; agencies seem reluctant to appoint peers to police themselves, unlike medical associations that jealously reserve the privilege. A demand from public regulatory authorities might well change the terms of debate; indeed this may be in the wind, as populists of the right challenge the advocacy role of non-profit organisations, and the wisdom of tax expenditures in the form of charitable deductions.

Democratic Legitimacy and the Agency's Social Role

We now have to consider the agencies' legitimacy within public life. The issue turns on the nature of duly constituted authority within an agency and some real account ability to 'beneficiaries', as well as organisational action and the 'fit' between an agency's mission and its social role.

There is a trinity that forms a critical 'core' of the agencies' publics. This grouping underpins the legitimacy of an agency as an independent citizens' organisation:

- its donors – supporters who make a financial commitment to the values they believe the agency represents;
- its members – the constitutional owners of the organisation, who have affiliated themselves to its mission and values;
- those the agency serves – those its programmes are intended to benefit, the object of its mission.

For a Northern service agency whose beneficiaries are in the South, there is an inherent disjuncture among these core publics. This poses a structural challenge to their legitimacy. As Uphoff makes clear, the agencies by definition are not representative bodies – their members and financial supporters are not the people served by the agency. Their claims to legitimacy thus rest all the more on relations of accountability, and, as we have seen, there are some serious questions and shortcomings here. A strategy for the future to enhance the agencies' legitimacy, must attempt to reduce this disjuncture, that is, to reduce the organisational distance among these key publics, and to strengthen the patterns of internal accountability to them.

Equally, though, an agency's role and social positioning must be considered. The claim of legitimacy must rest in part upon behaviour as well as upon democratic ownership and accountability. Here, critics have challenged agencies to redefine their role, their stance on issues of social justice; to stake out their position on the basic choices confronting them, described in the opening chapter of this book. The argument in the broadest sense has been outlined by Brian Murphy. Observing and encouraging agencies which are 'adapting to new realities and taking on more critical roles in the dynamics of social change within a turbulent global economy', he says:

> The role clearly transcends [that] of providers of money and materials for projects and partner NGOs, a role increasingly taken on by Northern governmental and multilateral agencies ... And it certainly transcends the role of project implementation, because increasingly this has become the function of local Southern NGOs, institutions, and community-based organisations ...
>
> A new catalytic role or facilitation role of Northern NGOs largely remains to be defined, in conjunction with Southern NGOs ... The role of Northern NGOs would involve collaborating with Southern

NGO partners as equals ... Central to this vision has been a pre-occupation with communications and the democratization of information flow; collaborative research and analysis; and action networking ... a commitment to a strategy of mutual support [and] collaboration ... on mutually shared goals; ... an emphasis on constructive advocacy in the national and international policy arena.[40]

He goes on to cite Tim Brodhead's call for NGOs to 'find common cause not just North/South but with popular movements and social forces within our own countries'. This means taking positions on issues of injustice, power and privilege. As measured a commentator as John Clark asserts the centrality of the debate about political neutrality – the message that 'development is fundamentally about taking sides', and that 'redistribution [of power and wealth] is highly political and controversial'.[41] This is, of course, the consequence of life in the mainstream, and it means that the longstanding and widely held myth of an 'apolitical' mission and organisational milieu is scarcely tenable – if indeed it ever was.

Recent examples of agencies playing such a role give pointers to 'the future in the present'. One example is the creation and work of the tri-national Mexican-Canadian-US networks focused on continental free trade, particularly the Common Frontiers/Fronteras Communes project, a research-and-analysis effort of the Action Canada Network. Founded in 1987 to fight the US/Canada free-trade agenda, ACN is a multisectoral coalition of labour, student and religious groups, women's organisations, cultural associations, seniors' organisations, anti-poverty groups and a handful of aid agencies. Labour solidarity groups and an ecumenical research and popular-education body took the initiative of a fact-finding trip to the *maquiladoras* of Mexico. In the following year, a counterpart Mexican body, Fronteras Communes, was established as a part of RMALC, the Mexican Action Network on Free Trade. In 1990 the network expanded to the tri-national level, to include labour, churches, and development research and advocacy groups in the US.

The networks have promoted dialogue, research and mutual education among their members, to challenge the official and corporate agendas for continental free trade, and to articulate alternative visions. They have had some impact – most publicly, perhaps, the challenge mounted to US President George Bush's 'fast track' agenda for continental free trade in late 1992.[42]

The history of this work points up some of the opportunities and limits of action by aid agencies:

- Here was an issue that brought 'development' and 'North–South relations' into the political mainstream – economic integration on a continental scale, clearly driven by corporate interests. The issue was joined, moreover, by popular organisations in Mexico, the US and Canada – an obvious example of a 'common agenda' apparently made to order for public education and advocacy by private aid agencies.

- Private aid agencies played only a limited direct role within Common Frontiers. A few Canadian agencies provided some administrative infrastructure and modest grants. More important was the participation of some key individuals. Most of the running was made by labour solidarity groups, religious bodies, and development research/advocacy groups.

- Happily perhaps, money – hence the traditional donor role – was not a key factor. Mexican NGOs received funding from European sources; financial contributions from Canada or the US were limited.

- The coalitions took an explicitly political role, intervening in the major issue of economic justice and development of the day. 'Taking sides' was unavoidable. It may be precisely because of this that most of the larger agencies shied away from the issue. None of the large American agencies joined in, for example. However, the Ford Foundation was alert enough to finance research into an innovative and powerful example of citizens' participation in public life. In a process hemispheric in its import, touching fundamental issues of economic and social organisation, gender, culture, and the environment, engaging popular organisations, banks, corporations and governments, the agencies are curiously distant.

- Perhaps because 'free trade' has been so politically charged, accountability has been a constant theme within the coalitions that have challenged it. The members of the different networks have had to constantly negotiate and redefine their roles and methods of work. This has led to a genuine – not at all easy – dialogue to establish common interests and objectives as a basis for action. Yet the process is obviously dynamic: in July 1994, RMALC, the Mexican coalition, hosted an international conference on 'Integration, Development and Democracy'. This drew activists from several other countries of the hemisphere, working to create a hemispheric social charter to challenge the economistic bottom-line thinking of the official versions of 'integration'.

What to Do? 'Reinvent' the Private Aid Agencies?

Amidst their evident crises, the agencies may also find opportunity. They can choose to reinvent themselves as independent citizens' associations. To do so will require fundamental change. They will have to rebuild and use their political legitimacy. They will have to recast themselves as genuinely civic organisations demonstrably owned by and politically accountable to their members and financially independent and accountable to both individual donors and institutional funders. In their choice of programmatic and political positions, they will have to be open and accessible to those they work with and serve.

A Matter of Choosing ...

The first step is a matter of choosing. An agency will have to make a choice about its basic identity: whether it is at heart an independent, 'civic' organisation; or whether it is in the first instance a public service contractor, a 'delivery vehicle' for the official aid budget and programme.[43]

This is the ethical and political choice outlined in Chapter 1. If an agency does take the 'civic' option, then realising its choice will not be easy or immediate. Nor does the option guarantee wisdom, effective programmes, or financial health. The argument here, however, is that making and realising this choice is a necessary condition if the agencies are to be relevant and viable voluntary organisations rooted in a community of interest. Our focus here is on those agencies that make such a choice. (Not every organisation needs to or will do so. The other option is to become primarily a public service contractor. This takes the organisation closer to a parastatal role, however. It is less a voluntary organisation than a community-based not-for-profit enterprise.)

This choice in turn requires that the agency be clear about the official agenda. This task is simplified by official policy statements such as the recent Canadian budget and foreign policy referred to earlier, and the apparent orthodoxy among the OECD countries that dismisses the option for the poor.

Is There a Prototype of the Civic Private Aid Agency?

To reinvent itself, an agency will have to reduce the present disjuncture among members, donors and those the agency works with and serves. In practice there will be a range of options, techniques and strategies for doing so – 'the project' will vary considerably with the diverse patterns of ownership, accountability, and role, organis- ational culture and national political-legal cultures. Moreover, following Uphoff's argument, so long as the agencies are service organisations there will continue to be a certain structural tension within a Northern agency whose membership is concentrated in, say, The Netherlands or Britain, while those the agency serves are people of the South.

Nevertheless the basic direction cannot be avoided: the central premise of this chapter is that the agencies' credibility and legitimacy in both their Southern and Northern spheres of activity will rest upon their evident definition as independent, accessible and accountable citizens' associations. So, there are critical conditions that must be created, and new directions established, even if the organisational form and substance are still to be designed and built.

Membership sovereignty is surely critical. Without a committed membership base acting through an assembly, an agency risks becoming an example of Michels's oligarchy. Probably a well-inten- tioned oligarchy, perhaps an oligarchy of high competence – but an oligarchy competent and credible as a promoter of 'democratisation'? Hardly. As this chapter argues, many agencies are vulnerable on this count.

Yet there are examples of progressive organisations owned by their members, active on issues closely linked to development. One of the most obvious and notable is Amnesty International. Its membership, exceeding one million world-wide, elects representa- tives to a biennial International Council which elects a Board, determines the agency's mandate, makes policy decisions, and endorses operational and strategic plans for the agency. Less well- known is Disabled Peoples' International (DPI), a world-wide assembly of disabled people and their organisations. DPI is an active and effective advocate for the rights of disabled people. It also runs respected development programmes with disabled people in countries of the South. DPI is governed by a World Council, elected at quad- rennial Congresses. Formed in 1981, it now includes member organisations in 114 countries, representing millions of people of all disabilities. With a modestly-sized central secretariat and budget – no more than 10 permanent staff and an annual budget of less than US$ 1 million – the driving force for its advocacy work and its development programming has been a committed, vocal and articulate membership.

We are not suggesting that this part of the reconstruction project is easy. Amnesty's own experience is evidence enough of that. It recently reorganised its international secretariat, in part to respond to a sense of loss of ownership and control by the membership. It is not obvious what will be the social locus of a 'civic private aid agency'. The impact of global economics is putting communities, regions and national societies under stress, and reshaping them. The middle classes of Western society, a key part of the historic base of support for agencies, are being 'downsized'. Our argument is that an independent future will require a community of people to whom the organisation matters. It may be large or small, geographically concentrated or dispersed, but it will be an active community of interest.

Again, the examples of Amnesty International and DPI are relevant. Both organisations have a strongly voluntary character. Their structures of governance vest sovereignty within a committed membership. Their programmes also rely on substantial contributions by volunteers. There is more at work here than structural change, however: the role chosen by each agency is integral to its success. Both Amnesty International and DPI are obviously engaged in the struggle for social justice and development, and neither is an aid agency. Their métier embraces political advocacy, research and solidarity between individuals and communities. For all their global character, moreover, both have clearly-defined agendas – the human rights of prisoners of conscience and disabled people. And, the continuing relevance and quality of their work are critical to their success in retaining the loyalty and energy of their members.

Basic standards of transparency and ethical behaviour can be readily enough established by 'industry-wide' codes of conduct and rules of disclosure. Good examples abound. The International Council of Voluntary Agencies (ICVA), based in Geneva, has established policy guidelines for relations between Northern and Southern NGOs. These assert the principle of 'multiple accountability' by an NGO, 'to its constituency, its donors, and to the recipients of its assistance'. They ask for 'financial transparency' and a reciprocity between Northern donors and Southern recipients, so that the donor agencies' own financial affairs are open for scrutiny.[44]

Implementation of such codes has been a problem so far – anything beyond voluntary compliance through self-certification has proven elusive. 'Watchdog' agencies for non-profits exist in the United States, but their power is limited to providing information to the public. In this, of course, they are limited by what agencies provide to them.[45] Perhaps the time has come for arms-length 'industry councils' to certify agencies in their respective countries. If the agencies take the lead to establish such bodies, they can only enhance their credibility. The point is, however, that if agencies cannot enforce their own standards, then public regulatory authorities will almost certainly do so, sooner or later. They may do so for less than sympathetic reasons but the issue will be decided by power not sentiment.[46]

A less dour and equally effective approach would celebrate the agencies' work and the achievements of people in the South with awards for excellence. The annual ritual of the Oscar film awards ceremony fairly begs for a countervailing public statement of human decency, good judgement and renunciation of garish excess.

The value of independently established and enforced codes of ethics becomes apparent if we recognise that some agencies will not transform themselves into membership organisations; and that citizens in turn will not all become active members of such organisations. If an agency becomes primarily a public service contractor, for example, it is in effect a not-for-profit enterprise rather than a voluntary organisation. An independent 'seal of approval' is then an important tool for any prospective donor or supporter.

Reciprocity With Those the Agency Works With and Serves

Meeting industry requirements could be seen as necessary 'standard operating procedure'. Part of the reason for them is to open up the agencies, to make their power less formidable, to make the agencies more accessible and manageable to those they work with and for. The strategy here is to encourage reciprocity with those the agency works with and serves – a central theme in the guidelines issued by ICVA, for example. There are some interesting initiatives, techniques, relationships on offer. For example, The New Economics Foundation of London has developed the technique of 'social auditing' to assess the social impact and ethical behaviour of an organisation from the perspective of its stakeholders. For an agency, these would include owners, staff, funders and those served by the agency. The audit is regular, externally validated and publicly available.[47]

There are good examples of consultative programme reviews and planning undertaken jointly between Northern development agencies and Southern counterparts. One which was particularly far-reaching and comprehensive is described in 'North-South Co-operation toward a Society of Citizens of the World'.[48] Between 1988 and 1992, Horizons of Friendship, a small aid agency based in Ontario, Canada, changed its programming from child sponsorship to support for community development aimed at social change and social justice. An extended process of reflection and critical dialogue lay at the heart of this change. Of course there are plenty of examples of agency 'consultation with partners', where Southern opinions are solicited, but where final decisions rest with Northern boards and staff. The

Horizons exercise was different because it became just one of several organisations around the table, its final programming the work of many hands.

Other organisations in effect provide a 'consumer sanction' to those they work with. RAFI, the Rural Advancement Foundation International, is a small, international, knowledge-based NGO. It specialises in research into biodiversity, to support policy advocacy by Southern governments, community and non-governmental organisations, and multilateral bodies. Its métier is information, and those served by its work have a simple measure of ensuring accountability: if RAFI's research is not up to par, its products will not be used, and its credibility will suffer.

These arguments for membership sovereignty, for accountability and transparency, for reciprocity all imply some surrender of the historic power and privilege enjoyed by the agencies, and particularly by their staff and board members. In exchange, however, they gain the prospect (not the certainty) of a new, more 'popular' and democratic lifeblood.

Who Pays the Freight for a Politically Independent Organisation?

Independent financing – a core of informed and supportive donors – is essential to this project. The task of building, rebuilding and maintaining such a financial base will not be easy. Donor funds can come under further pressure from the hesitant 'recovery' of the Western economies: persistently high unemployment levels leads to widespread cuts to social programmes and the appeals of domestic charities. Cutbacks of official aid budgets may well mean fewer public funds for the agencies; hence, private donations, for all their uncertainty, loom even larger in importance. Competition for donations amongst agencies themselves will therefore intensify. With the growth and financial preponderance of the transnational agencies – described in this book by Ian Smillie – it is not uncommon to hear corridor chat about 'oligopolistic competition in the chari-market'.

Can the Agencies Change?

For some, the choice will be made for them – radical cutbacks of state and private funding will mean they disappear, or become very different organisations. Less dramatically and probably more commonly, conditionality may lock agencies into the role of public service contractor, if substantial growth of independent fundraising is not a realistic short-term option.

What will induce the agencies to choose? Assuming that any change of the kind proposed here will not be a once-and-for-all 'event', can they continue to adapt and 'reinvent' themselves? There is plenty of room for doubt. Kelleher and McLaren, writing about organisational change, argue that agencies are in a closed loop.[49] They assert that it is precisely the agencies' lack of popular ownership and accountability which insulates them from the influence of new forces, demands and ideas that might provoke change. Others within the agencies cite generational habits and inertia, and express doubts about the capacity of staff long accustomed to their established roles and prerogatives to imagine and implement the sweeping changes that are required.[50] The question then is how to break the circle. This is no idle question, because it is the people within the 'actually existing organisation' who have to make the initial ethical and political choices, and to map out and carry out the changes in organisational structure and behaviour that follow.

Notes

1. Laura Macdonald, in a resource paper prepared for the Canadian Council for International Co-operation, defines civil society as 'the arena of organised political activity between the private sphere (the household and the firm) and the formal political institutions of government (the parliament, political parties, the army, the judiciary, etc.)' (Laura Macdonald, Undated, 'Non-Governmental Organisations: Agents of a "New Development"?' mimeo, Ottawa.)

   'Flexibility, outreach, responsiveness, participation, independence, innovativeness' are all cited as characteristic strengths of NGOs in a recent United Nations survey. (Francesco Mezzalama and Siegfried Schumm, Joint Inspection Unit, 1993, 'Working with NGOs: Operational Activities for Development of the United Nations System with Non-governmental Organisations and Governments at the Grassroots and National Levels', mimeo, Geneva, p. 4.) In *Bridges of Hope*, 1988 (North–South Institute, Ottawa), Tim Brodhead and Brent Herbert-Copley examine the self-proclaimed principles of altruism, autonomy, participation, efficiency and partnership.

2. Mezzalama and Schumm, 'Working with NGOs', p. 3. A recent survey of NGO/state relationships within the OECD countries cites a growing official scepticism. See I. Smillie, 1993, 'Changing Partners: Northern NGOs, Northern Governments', in *Non-Gov-*

ernmental Organisations and Governments: Stakeholders for Development, I. Smillie and I. Helmich (eds), OECD, Paris, p. 15.

3. Susan Phillips, 'Of Visions and Revisions: the Voluntary Sector Beyond 2000', in *CNVO Bulletin,* 12:3 (Winter 1993), pp. 2–14. Kakabadse and Burns put it this way: 'NGOs ... send representatives to UN sessions, but whom do they represent?' N.T. Kakabadse and S. Burns, 1994, *Movers and Shapers: NGOs in International Affairs,* World Resources Institute, Washington, DC, p. 9.

4. Rita Karakas, 1994, from the author's notes, at a session of CUSO On-Site, Ottawa, Canada, January.

5. Ironically, the anointment of the agencies as part of the political mainstream may prove to be no more than belated public recognition preceding the demise of the sector, or, at the very least, profound upheaval and contraction. A politician's public praise of Partnership Africa Canada, quoted at the opening of the first chapter of this book, was followed a mere six months later by the complete withdrawal of federal funding (to the tune of some C$15 million per year). For an overview, see the Canadian Council for International Co-operation, 1995, 'Budget deals a fatal blow to partnerships', *au courant,* 5,5, Ottawa.

   The trends are widespread throughout the OECD countries. See T. German and J. Randel, 1995, *The Reality of Aid 1995,* Earthscan, London.

6. The National Committee for Responsive Philanthropy, based in Washington DC, in an article entitled 'The war on nonprofits' (NCRP, *Responsive Philanthropy,* Summer 1995), sees the Republican-controlled Congress on a 'revolutionary rampage' against the links between non-profit organisations and the federal government. It sounds an alarm on both budget cuts and legislative proposals to constrain advocacy and public education by non-governmental organisations in the US. These measures found a parallel in Canada, with an MP of the governing Liberal Party challenging the advocacy role of non-governmental organisations (both aid and social-service agencies, as well as advocacy groups) as well as the tax expenditures based on their charitable status. See 'Charity Cases', *Ottawa Citizen,* 22 April 1995. Agencies are not uniformly vulnerable to this sort of attack, however. Smillie notes (in 'Changing Partners', p. 40) that not all OECD countries provide tax deductions or credits for charitable contributions. The scrutiny is not only from the Right, however. In a 1994 report, the NCRP chastises non-profits in the US for inadequate accountability to their constituencies and for the

quality of their programs. ('The New Age of Nonprofit Account-ability', Spring 1994, p. 12.)

7. In May 1995, in a prime-time TV special, the Canadian Broad-casting Corporation alleged that CARE Canada had misspent monies fundraised for food aid to Somalia. CARE responded by suing the CBC, and the publicity has tarnished the image of CARE and other private aid agencies. A sympathetic reporter writes of a 'crisis in confidence' within and surrounding foreign aid and aid agencies (*Ottawa Citizen*, 24 June 1995). In a recent book, an investigative journalist claims environmental NGOs are colluding with corporations and governments: E. Dewar, 1995, *Cloak of Green*, Lorimer, Toronto.

8. This insight, pivotal to the argument in this chapter, is from Ronald Bisson interviews, June and October, 1994.

9. Smillie, 'Changing Partners', 1993, pp. 27–33; German and Randel, 1995, *The Reality of Aid 1995*, p. 115 and passim.

10. Some would argue that agencies, and NGOs generally, do not invest enough in research, are not sufficiently capable of learning from their own experience, to be effective critics and sources of alternative visions. (See, for example, Smillie, 1993, 'Changing Partners', pp. 18–21. D. Kelleher and K. McLaren, with R. Bisson, 1996, *Grabbing the Tiger by the Tail: NGOs Learning for Organizational Change*, Canadian Council for International Co-operation, Ottawa, focuses on the obstacles and possibilities for agencies and voluntary bodies to become learning organisations.)

    This may indeed be so – and such conceptual and behavioural limitations will play their part in determining whether and how agencies can change their historic practice. Nor can one ignore the fact of external legal and political constraint. In 1991, the Charity Commission reprimanded Oxfam UK for its critique of Britain's policy on South African sanctions, for example: Charity Commissioners for England and Wales, 1991, *Oxfam: Report of an Inquiry*, HMSO, London. Our argument here points in a different direction altogether: we are focussing on structural impediments that will constrain even 'the best and the brightest'.

11. Norman Uphoff, quoting Robert Michels's famous *Political Parties*. See Uphoff, N., 1995, 'Why NGOs are not a Third Sector: a Sectoral Analysis with some Thoughts on Accountability, Sustainability and Evaluation', in M. Edwards and D. Hulme, *Non-governmental Organisations. Performance and Accountability*, Earthscan, London.

12. Uphoff, 'Why NGOs are not a Third Sector', p. 20.

13. A role will remain for the state, no doubt, as customer (even a 'high-volume customer', as John Carver would put it) purchasing services or expertise from independent organisations. J. Carver, 1990, *Boards that Make a Difference*, Jossey-Bass, San Francisco, pp. 130–2.

14. Hardly a new phenomenon, of course. Some agencies are open to charges of complicity in official US foreign policy agendas and adventures in Central America and Southeast Asia. See Inter-Hemispheric Education Resource Center, 1988, *Public and Private Humanitarian Aid: Legal and Ethical Issues*, Albuquerque. More generally, Steven Smith and Michael Lipsky describe the growth of the contracting phenomenon: see *Nonprofits for Hire: the Welfare State in the Age of Contracting*, Harvard University Press, Cambridge (1993).

15. Some of the best material is to be found in Carver, *Boards that Make a Difference*, 1990; and in Edwards and Hulme (eds) *Nongovernmental Organisations* 1995, especially the articles by Uphoff and by Zadek and Gatward. See also B. Murphy, 'Canadian NGOs and the Politics of Participation', in J. Swift and B. Tomlinson (eds), *Conflicts of Interest*, Between the Lines, Toronto, pp. 161–212. The problem of accountability and representation is noted, for example, in the WRI paper *Movers and Shapers* by Kakabadse and Burns, and by J. Clark, 1991, *Democratizing Development*, Earthscan, London but concepts are not elaborated or mechanisms examined. The question is why, and the obvious if rather unsatisfactory answer, is that 'accountability' has not mattered enough to warrant investigation.

There is another issue here, which seems to be both symptom and cause of the lack of attention to these key issues. This is the problem of defining the 'NGO sector' itself, and the agencies within that. Faced with the wide variety of agencies that call themselves 'NGOs', and the diversity of their work, observers often rely on the agencies' self-definition for their sample or their characteristics. This results in agencies defined by what they are not – a sometimes serviceable but unsatisfactory approach, as Smillie points out ('Changing Partners', pp. 14–15). More to the point for this chapter, the approach typically yields a description of agencies according to the primary intent of their work, rather than any analysis of their political sociology – their internal constitutional patterns, or their relations with each other, with the state, with popular movements, and so on. (As an example, see the UN document cited earlier, 'Working with NGOs'.) Jenny Pearce, in a 1993 article on NGOs and social change, sets out some of the distinctions among Northern and Southern NGOs by assessing their relationships to popular organisations, and their place in social change. See 'NGOs and Social Change: Agents or Facilitators?' in *Development in Practice* 3:3, 1993, pp. 222–7.

16. H.E. McCandless, 1994, 'The Elected Representative's Role in Public Accountability,' *Canadian Parliamentary Review*, Spring, p. 8; cited by Lawrence S. Cumming in 'Accountability – Rising with the Tide' (mimeo, 1995).

17. Though it is uncommon as well: not to be found, for example, in the indexes of D. Korten, 1990, *Getting to the 21st Century: Voluntary Action and the Global Agenda*, Kumarian, West Hartford; Swift and Tomlinson, *Conflicts of Interest*; Clark, *Democratizing Development*; or G. Scmitz and D. Gillies, 1992, *The Challenge of Democratic Development*, North-South Institute, Ottawa.

18. A Board of Trustees or Governors that renews its mandate annually and selects its own new members may be entirely legitimate in a legal sense, and is indeed a common enough phenomenon. It follows that the base of owners or members is very small in such cases. Norman Uphoff in 'Why NGOs are not a Third Sector', insists that the term 'voluntary sector' properly applies only to those organisations that are representative of and serve a membership. By his reckoning, most charities are not voluntary agencies at all, but are instead within the not-for-profit part of the private sector. By this standard, an agency as a service organisation is indeed 'non-governmental' in a legal sense but hardly qualifies as a 'civic' or popularly based organisation.

19. Murphy, 'Canadian NGOs ...', p. 190. In the same article (p. 168) he clearly describes the cumulative alienation of the broader voluntary sector (in Canada) from those it professes to serve and represent.

20. As noted in Chapter 3, however, asset managers of endowed foundations commonly are the locus of effective authority. In-house 'iron curtains' protect them from outsiders' questions about ethics or about consistency in their programme choices.

21. This is the prescient but anonymous comment of an official of CIDA, 1994.

22. Those with some common interest in the agency and its work. The word 'constituency' could also be used, to denote the supporters of an agency. But, not all publics will be supporters; and in any case, 'support' is always a somewhat hypothetical notion, best known after the fact. The question arises whether there exists a hierarchy of importance among these different publics: who matters most, and why?

23. The donor/agency relationship is described well by US fundraiser, Hank Rosso, as a contract, an exchange of values. The donor gives her money, and in exchange participates in a set of values, those expressed in the mission and programme of the agency. Rosso, The Fundraising School, Indiana University (title of notes and resource information for a course in fundraising).

24. They might be properly called a 'stakeholder'. We've avoided the use of this particular child of modern state/public relations. The word 'stakeholder' regularly appears as part of official 'dialogue' and 'consultations'. It is defined by Webster as 'those holding an interest, usually financial'. But its conventional use reduces different publics and relationships of accountability to a single phrase, and includes no notion of reciprocity. It may also obscure key power relationships – to describe a ministry or department with regulatory and financing power, simply as a 'stakeholder' radically understates the power of those who hold the purse.

25. A recent policy framework drafted by the Canadian International Development Agency, for example, addresses the role of the voluntary sector in development assistance.

26. This is the real issue missed by the CBC in its exposé of CARE Canada's fundraising for Somali refugees (see endnote 7). It is also raised in an article on the fundraising and programme spending practices of Save the Children USA (Michael Maren, 'A Different Kind of Child Abuse', *Penthouse*, December 1995). As noted later in this chapter, codes of conduct for private aid agencies are supposed to curb dissembling with donors, but their effects are open to doubt.

27. See Sandra Greaves, 1992, 'War on Want sues former auditors', *Third Sector*, 5 November, p. 6

28. Cf. Smillie and Helmich, *Non-Governmental Organisations and Governments*; also T. Brodhead and C. Pratt, 1994, 'Paying the Piper: CIDA and Canadian NGOs', in Cranford Pratt (ed.), *Canadian International Development Assistance Policies: an Appraisal*, McGill-Queen's University Press, Montreal, pp. 87–119.

29. Brodhead and Pratt, 'Paying the Piper', pp. 98–102. Clark, *Democratizing Development*, p. 49, cites 'a growing concern' that governments are increasingly telling agencies what projects to submit for funding. Recent Canadian agency experience with CIDA indicates that conformity to government objectives is replacing an historic commitment to 'responsiveness'.

30. Yusuf Kassam, reporting on research into 'partnership', AGM of Partnership Africa Canada, September, 1994.

31. B.K. Murphy, 1993, 'Towards the 21st Century', mimeo, Ottawa, October.

32. Partnership Africa Canada, 1994, 'Report of the Study of Partnership and Institutional Strengthening', mimeo, Ottawa, August.

33. Clark makes the same point (*Democratizing Development*, p. 73), arguing that this makes 'mutual accountability' between Northern and Southern NGOs unrealistic.

34. Completing the circle, as it were, Southern NGOs may see little to distinguish Northern NGO 'partners' from official donor agencies. This unflattering perception stands out clearly in a paper by Muchunguzi, D. and Milne, S., 1995, 'Perspectives from the South: A Study on Partnership', AFREDA, Dar es Salaam, Tanzania, and CIDA, Hull, Canada, mimeo, p. 13.

35. Intuitively, the observer might say 'yes'. Uphoff says 'no', placing more importance on financial accountability to donors: 'There is a fiduciary relationship of NGO staff and trustees to those who provide NGOs with their funds which is greater than their obligation to recipients of NGO benefits. If trust and confidence are not maintained with an NGO's contributors, it will collapse.' Uphoff, 'Why NGOs are not a Third Sector', p. 21.

36. For John Carver, this fact represents one of the central challenges and opportunities for a Board – to discharge its stewardship, it must communicate, engage, learn from those the agency serves. Carver, *Boards that Make a Difference*, pp. 130–47. Carver focused on voluntary agencies in the US; his point holds *a fortiori* for a private aid agency, serving the poor of the South.

37. R. Chambers, 1983, *Putting the Last First*, Longmans, London.

38. Cf. Smillie's comments in 'Changing Partners'. Yusuf Kassam also makes the telling observation that development NGOs seem reluctant to use participatory evaluations, where the parameters are not readily controlled. [Kassam, personal communication, October 1994.]

39. Examples include *InterAction PVO Standards* (1992) in the US, the Canadian Council for International Co-operation's *Draft Code of Ethics* (1993), and the Australian Council for Overseas Aid's *Code of Ethics* (Undated). Oxfam International provides an example of agency-specific codes. See also C. Ball and L. Dunn, 1995, *Non-Governmental Organisations: Guidelines for Good Policy and Practice*, The Commonwealth Foundation, London.

40. In Swift and Tomlinson, *Conflicts of Interest*, pp. 178–9.

41. Clark, *Democratizing Development*, p. 44.

42. A more detailed account may be found in John W. Foster, 1993, 'Redefining governance: the transnationalisation of civic par-

ticipation in North America,' Ottawa, mimeo. See also P. Harvey, 1994, 'North-South organising and hemispheric free trade', in *Canadian Perspectives*, Council of Canadians, Ottawa, Autumn, pp. 22–3. See also C. Thorup, 1991, 'The politics of free trade and the dynamics of cross-border coalitions in US-Mexican relations', *Columbia Journal of World Business*, vol. XXVI, No. 2, Summer, pp. 12–26.

The ACN itself has lost coherence, strength and effectiveness since 1993. The career of such coalitions is an important and fascinating issue in itself; but here, our concern is with the aid agencies' engagement with the coalition and the issues around which it mobilised.

43. The former does not have to mean non-cooperation with state bodies, of course. The political economy of a particular country may make such cooperation possible, even desirable. The key issue here is whether an agency can negotiate that as an independent entity.

44. International Council of Voluntary Agencies, Undated, 'Relations between Southern and Northern NGOs: Policy Guidelines', Geneva, mimeo.

45. NCRP, 1994, 'The New Age of Non-profit Accountability', p. 15.

46. And as the references to legislative action above (endnote 6) make clear, the issue is very much on the political agenda.

47. See S. Zadek and R. Evans, 1993, *Auditing the Market: A Practical Approach to Social Auditing*, Traidcraft/New Economics Foundation, London.

48. Horizons of Friendship, Cobourg, Ontario, 1992.

49. Kelleher, McLaren and Bisson, *Grabbing the Tiger by the Tail*, pp. 4–7.

50. Author's interviews. Some would argue these changes must be accompanied by a major demographic transformation as well – both to make the agencies more open to different roles and structures, and to make them more diversified, more representative of the changing face of civil society in the North.

3

'Laws' of the Market?

David Sogge and Simon Zadek

> We always have to work with the laws of marketing *and* the inspi-
> ration of constituents. But the pressure to follow much more
> intensively the laws of the market is certainly increasing.
>
> Jaap van Soest, Director of Mensen in Nood
> (People in Distress) a Dutch private aid agency[1]

The business of private aid has been booming. But has it been
booming *as a business*?

- In 1994, some 200 private aid agencies, many with no track
  records in emergencies, arrived in eastern Zaire to 'do something'
  about Rwandan refugees then filling the world's television screens.
  Described later as a 'three-ring circus of financial self-interest,
  political abuse and incompetence', agency intervention was a
  bonanza for both old agencies and new, including at least one in
  the business of smuggling out orphaned babies.[2]

- In 1995 journalists in Mozambique revealed that the German
  agency SOS-Kinderhof International, pleading financial constraints, had put two schools in its children's centres – set up for
  war orphans – on a commercial, fee-for-service footing, thus
  catering chiefly for children of the salaried classes.[3]

- In 1994 six Christian organisations in The Netherlands withdrew
  their membership in Novib, a major progressive aid agency,
  because too much board meeting time was spent on 'the chari-
  market and fundraising and too little over content and objectives'.[4]

- In 1995, a journalist citing internal documents of Save the Children
  USA revealed that in 1993, for every $240 provided yearly by a
  child sponsor, 'On average, across the United States, only $35.29
  in funding per child actually reaches the project level.' The rest
  of the money allegedly went to advertisements and bureaucracy:
  'What sponsors are really buying is, as stated in Save's brochures,
  a sense of well-being and "deep satisfaction".'[5]

Commercialisation, competition and opportunism resembling that of the for-profit world, and of public unease about such trends, has been growing apace for private aid agencies. Labelled by economists as lethargic and slow to respond to rising demand, non-profits today are disproving that charge as they grow, multiply and move aggressively into new terrains and vocations.[6]

The spirit of enterprise is advancing boldly. But has the calculating logic of the marketplace begun to crowd out compassion as the organising principle? Has that logic become an imperative so strong that we can speak of agencies being driven by economic laws of motion? Values are supposed to drive the agencies, not acquisitive pulls and pushes. But they have begun behaving otherwise in these times of supreme influence of the acquisitive, contented classes.

Agencies without their own, stable endowments face powerful incentives to pander to the concerns of better-off Northern publics, and to collude with an official aid system, based on claims to effectiveness and relevance that are at best exaggerated. They also face pressures to become more 'businesslike' in structure and culture. This may not be a bad thing. Like many charities, some agencies are poorly structured and staffed. They need retooling and reschooling. But the mainstream remedies forced upon them, often versions of 'market managerialism', may only make things worse. Fixated on cost efficiency, through-put and growth, models borrowed from the for-profit world are going to fit poorly where agency leaders try to be guided by other norms and aims.

Finally, they face an erosion of some essential qualities they are supposed to uphold: the value-based commitment, creativity and energetic engagement of their leaders, co-workers and constituencies. Such tendencies can put in question the continued relevance of private aid agencies, especially now that alternatives are emerging and gaining power in the South and in the North.

The term 'laws of the market' suggests an iron determinism. It implies inescapable forces driving agencies to become mere businesses or contractors, bent on growth, aggressive competition and image improvement. Certainly such trends are invasive, and can influence agency behaviour with such consistency and predictability as to become 'laws of motion'. But they can be challenged where those interested in value-based agencies show some shrewdness and pluck.

Private Agencies as Market Makers

The classic private aid agency, as the introductory chapter notes, was born out of non-market impulses: compassion, voluntary effort, even concern verging on outrage. To depict most of them, especially those created before the Cold War, as firms responding to market signals is as absurd as it is to explain the problems they want to address – poverty and exclusion – by tendentious notions like 'market failure'. Yet today, even those agencies born in innocence show the influence of market thinking. By no means all match the sensational cases and episodes noted at the beginning of this chapter; the extraordinary expenditure patterns of Save the Children USA do not represent the norm. Yet few have not begun playing the game by market rules. Indeed, agencies themselves have helped create the very markets in which they are earnestly competing. Innocence is lost. The bullet, to use a Dutch expression, has gone through the church.

Beyond Brokerage in the 'Market' for Anti-Poverty Remedies

People who are materially poor, by the definitions of conventional economics, generate little 'market' or 'effective' demand. Further, their interests are poorly represented in political life. They lack voice, and exert little real leverage over the supply of goods and services.

In such a situation, *non-market* responses – action and inaction by governments and by actors in civil society – are going to be decisive. Private agencies have carved out a place for themselves in this context. They ask for, and receive, many billions of dollars in direct and indirect official subsidies.

Private agencies are not set up for gain through exchange. Yet they act, not merely as brokers, but as market-makers. They are purveyors of both demand *and* supply. They supply the North with images and information about poverty and crisis in the South, and offer remedies. In the North, this elicits 'effective' or 'market' demand – the spending preferences of donors. In this market the agencies raise funds to supply the South with anti-poverty, anti-crisis remedies. Such market-making has enormous potential power and effect.

For although Northern publics continue to see the tackling of poverty as a prime responsibility of *government, not the private sector,*[7] they are losing confidence that governments are tackling it effectively. The public associates private agencies with selflessness, or at least the lack of any motivation for self-enrichment. It also ascribes to them economic virtues: overhead costs are thought to be low, time is not wasted, bureaucrats get by-passed and agency staff get right to work. Agencies are also thought to have finger-on-the-pulse expertise in matters of acute crisis and the Sisyphean work of fighting poverty. As donors are normally at great physical and cultural distances from those intended to benefit from agency work, they rely on agency information and bona fides. Everything hinges on perception and trust.

Power and Filtered Demand

Examined coldly, 'market' demand for private foreign aid stems not from the poor, but from those with powers over surpluses. These are not only private givers, but increasingly also legislators, bureaucrats and endowment-holders. All can be termed 'funding authorities'. Their perceptions, consciences and political calculations filter the essentially moral demands of the poor.

The situation is fraught with difficulties. Complexity and tension crop up where agencies wish to engage in value-based activities for which demand from funding authorities is weak or non-existent, such as where a certain beneficiary group is poorly known, demonised by major media, or downright unpopular. For example, aid agencies and other NGOs (outside of Sweden and a few regions of Italy) had to work hard in the 1970s and much of the 1980s to drum up public support for groups struggling for democracy in South Africa. That is, agencies sometimes have to create 'market' demand if they are to receive the support they need. They must cultivate good connections with the media to enable rapid structuring of public attention toward emergencies.

The heavyweight funding authorities for most endowed foundations are managers of stock-market portfolios and other assets; they tend to operate behind an 'iron curtain' in which asset management is strictly separated from grant making. Thus, a foundation's project officers may grant funds to an organisation fighting for land and environmental rights while the foundation's funding authorities keep investing in oil companies which ride roughshod over those rights.

The disjunction of 'market' demand and real demands or needs is problematic enough in the case of domestic non-profits hired by governments to provide services to poor citizens (who can potentially reward or punish governments with their votes). In the case of faraway people who have no powers to reward or punish the providers or their donors, things are much more complicated. Power lies with funding authorities, and the aid relationship merely adds to that power. It is instructive here to examine whose needs are being met and what kinds of services and goods are in fact being produced.

What Do Agencies Produce?

To some degree, all agencies are in the business of transferring resources. Some set in motion streams of food, medicine and systems for water supply from the mouths of warehouses to the mouths of children in the South. Or they send money or people to enhance legal aid clinics in poor neighbourhoods. Political or religious messages may be smuggled along, but the basic resource is money or a tangible good or service.

For many, that is all there is to it: resources are transferred and well-being results. An agency supplies field hospitals and people are cured. Another runs a trucking and kitchen operation, and people are fed. Yet another furnishes means to modernise production and, it is supposed, people are pulled out of poverty.

Dealing in Intangibles

For a few, however, there is more to it than resource transfer. Some work to make and transmit *knowledge* and *meaning* – the building-blocks of understanding, received opinion and policy. A few agencies today see this as far more important than providing tangible goods. Indeed, some rule out resource transfers altogether. Rather, they cast their services exclusively as investments in *ideas*. In doing so they generally seek strategic points of leverage, to change the way key institutions such as farm extension units, legal systems, universities, public broadcasters and social movements behave.

The endowed foundations have pioneered such approaches. Some younger organisations have followed. The Ashoka Fellowship promotes the idea of 'social entrepreneurs'; the Intermediate Technology Development Group, among many others, promotes 'appropriate technology'. Such aid agencies have chosen to pay for and even supervise the production, testing and dissemination of new concepts. They represent the research and development branches of development aid.

The 'forming' of Northerners is a significant outcome. This can be explicit, in the case of 'development education' services. Seminars, lectures and video films are chief products. Some agencies' output of publications is now so great that they must publish small catalogues to list them all. Or it can be implicit, as with agencies placing technical workers, teachers and health professionals in Southern countries for a couple of years or less. At the height of the Rwandan refugee crisis in 1994, the German branch of CARE shuttled medical students to refugee camps for stints of just two weeks. Such experiences can have significant impacts – in the North. Today, many thousands of ex-fieldworkers are staffing Northern aid agencies, research and training institutes, and other Northern NGOs. Their formation in the South enhances productivity of institutions in the North, thus illustrating the many-sidedness – and perhaps lop-sidedness – of agency outcomes and who in fact gains from them.[8]

Less common, but frequently claimed, are services aimed at engaging and persuading Northern publics and decision makers on issues of public policy; their impact is discussed in Chapter 5.

Merchandising

First came Oxfam UK's chain of shops on the high streets, then a few agencies began entering markets in normal commodities – tea, handicrafts, clothing – with an eye to gain on exchange. In the 1980s, a number of them took direct, even controlling interest in firms which import goods, produced under humane conditions in poor countries, for sale in Northern markets. Oxfam Trading in the UK and Bridgehead (owned by Oxfam-Canada) are two leading examples. Other agencies have supported the 'fair trade' movement by subsidising the development of 'fair trade brands', research and networking. Sales pitches here can emphasise mutual gain: 'You get good coffee, they get vaccinations.'

Such enterprises as yet raise relatively little revenue; but they have widened agency profiles. Their success has raised the ire of high-street merchants, who charge the charities with unfair competition. However, if they continue riding waves of consumer preferences for ethical and green products, they may grow as enterprises, along with others such as educational tourism.

These, then, are what agencies commonly produce. Putting aside for the moment the issue of impact in the South, these outputs are consistent with both the letter and the spirit of the visionary rationale for their existence outlined above.

The Feel-Good Factor

However, agencies also produce something else altogether. It is rarely acknowledged, but arguably necessary for success in the market for compassion. Intangible, even subliminal, the service is for the giver rather than some receiver far away; it is the service of satisfying a psychological need. Child-sponsorship agencies, for example, satisfy compassionate needs of Northern contributors through elaborate feedback loops supplying letters, photographs and guided tourism to the homes of beneficiaries. Such services are quite central 'products' developed often with a keen eye to what competitor agencies are putting on the market.

Northern demand patterns are shifting with the times. Some people continue giving their money or time to good causes out of a sense of moral duty. In no way are they 'purchasing' anything. Yet in an age when institutional monopolies over moral codes have fragmented,[9] the sense of duty has made way for a desire merely to 'feel good'. One means of release is to exchange money for, among other things, the chance to support good works.

These waters are murky, but are being delved by marketing psychologists and students of contemporary mores alike.[10] The moral imperative for altruism and the weight of obligation are giving way to a broader, less burdened approach. Those who give may still seek relief from a sense of guilt. But it must be relief without the pain, without sacrifice, without solemnity.

In responding to this shifting demand, agencies try to make today's charitable 'product' more attractive, and powerful, as an amalgam of 'feel goods'. Its purchase should be accompanied by some immediate reward, even a momentary pleasure – diversion, a good show, conviviality. Hence the remarkable success of charity concerts, the marathons of comic cabaretiers (for example, Red Nose Day, benefiting Charity Projects, UK) and the popularity of telethons mixing showbiz, sentiment and slices of life from the world of the charity recipients. Such appeals with heavy lashings of entertainment are costly to stage, but audiences pay well for them. They illustrate forcefully the success of a winning formula: painless altruism in exchange for amusement.

All this represents a complex interplay of actions, pressures, negotiations and images. The agencies must constantly manufacture, adjust and deliver them. Failure to deliver appropriate information and images in the North can break the circuit and break the spell.

Funding: Pressures and Displeasures

> If you want to achieve anything in this area then you have to be a businessman and have a feeling for publicity and marketing ... If you don't accept that the law of the market also holds true for the charity industry, you won't get anywhere.
>
> Bernard Kouchner, founder of the French agencies
> Médecins Sans Frontières and Médecins du Monde[11]

Agencies may derive their revenues from four kinds of sources. In rough order of diminishing constraints on their autonomy, these are: agreements for the performance of services financed via the official aid system; gifts either from the gift economy of private contributors or private institutions; endowment yields from stocks, bonds and other assets, and earnings from sales of services or products, including lotteries. Given current trends, the proportion of agency disbursements derived from the official aid system is projected to be about

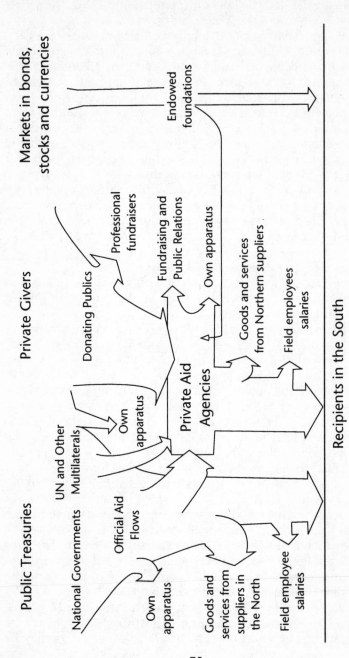

Figure 3.1 Flows of Revenue in Their Northern Setting

50 per cent by the year 2000, as agencies take on more sub-contracting roles.[12] Figure 3.1 depicts flows of revenues within their 'Northern' setting.

Each of these sources tends to impose different imperatives and degrees of freedom in the use of funds. Some require the tying of aid to certain beneficiaries (disaster victims, children, Christians) or to strategic approaches and discourse ('material transfer', 'modernisation', 'solidarity with social movements'), or internal structure (large fundraising apparatus, constituent-maintenance links). Each entails different intensities and types of competition: that among agencies (with new challengers crowding in all the time from the South and from the for-profit world), but also within them, between departments rewarded for different kinds of performance.

Agencies therefore face manifold demands in different markets for compassion. Two are of particular importance: donations from the general public, and taxpayer monies made available through the official aid system. Each is considered in the following pages.

Cultivation of Members or Constituents

Some donors identify strongly enough with a cause or a particular agency to become a 'member' of some kind. They take a broad and consistent interest that can extend to volunteer work. And there are those who give on a more *ad hoc* or impulsive basis. Today, thanks largely to commercialising pressures, the impulsive donation is much in the ascendent, the constituent gift in decline.

Some agencies represent, often literally, the resurrection and continuation of the missionary impulse. Congregations, and broader anonymous memberships of religious movements, are supposed to be the bedrock of finance for religiously-inspired agencies. Those organised along lines of professional interest, or ethnic, residential or employee solidarity may be targeted as potential member-donors. Medical aid agencies target health professionals, for example.

However, constituent loyalty and hence consistency in giving are breaking down. In Germany, for example, increasing numbers of mainstream churchgoers are deregistering as church members to avoid the *Kirchensteuer*, a state-managed tax that in 1993 raised 17 billion Deutschmarks (about US$11 billion) for the churches. This voluntary tax is the foremost economic pillar for German church-based foundations, whose annual budgets make them among the largest private aid agencies in the world.

For agency managers bent on growth, constituency-based fundraising can lack appeal. Capturing the new, 'floating' donor is where the glamour, challenge and potentials for jackpot winnings may be found. Roots and organised constituencies (and their sometimes nettlesome political concerns) are unattractive to the modern enterprise in the charity market. Asked if his agency consciously adopted an apolitical image, a representative of the Dutch branch of Foster Parents Plan (now PLAN International) said, 'Well, perhaps rather an a-religious image, for it's clear that there's no growth there.'[13]

Driven by these market imperatives, agencies risk neglecting natural constituencies and constituency-building. Adam Smith's invisible hand threatens to pull some agencies away from their roots. Especially for those agencies built upon social and religious followings, the dilemma can be acute and distressing. Its echo can be heard in the quotation at the beginning of this chapter, from the Director of the Dutch Catholic aid agency Mensen in Nood – People in Distress.

Public Marketing

The struggle to be better known and valued ('image positioning') and to attract donations away from competitors ('market share'), is concentrating minds of agency managers. It is also putting a squeeze on revenues. Ever-larger proportions of agency budgets now go to public communication efforts. As more agencies enter the market, each has to spend more on advertising to make it stand out from the rest.

And indeed the image-making industries are doing a brisk business. In 1993, Dutch charities, private aid agencies prominent among them, spent 65 million guilders (about US$38 million) on advertising, thereby shooting into the top ten spenders on advertising, just behind beer- and soap-makers.[14] Also doing well are television broadcasters and celebrities' public relations agencies: their fees hike the costs of telethons, sponsorship of 'rent-a-face' disaster tourism under an agency's flag,[15] and sponsorship of concerts and other amusements. Such pricey services are available only to the largest agencies, or joint appeals, such as for African emergencies.

Agencies are caught in marketing games for high stakes – amid rising risks. They stand to lose credibility where donating publics detect disproportions between agency overheads and outputs. More threateningly, publics have begun to get worried when *results* remain so modest. Hence the popularity of flying rescue agencies, which satisfy the craving for instant gratification, even if long-term effects may be nil – or even negative.

Then there are risks of 'poisoning the well'. Selling your product on grounds of apparent helplessness and misery bolsters racial stereotyping and cultural arrogance. In the end it can reinforce donor pessimism and fatigue. 'After years of seeing endless images of starvation and suffering', writes one agency observer, citing two studies of attitudes in Canada, 'Canadians felt an overwhelming sense of despair and cynicism about whether international development assistance does any good at all'.[16] Agencies today make less use of 'famine pornography' than they once did, but the pitiful child, the shriveled brown hand in the palm of the healthy white one, have hardly disappeared. Market competition, and the powerful positions now assumed by the marketing boys, means constant pressure to pay attention to the short run.

Position for Recognition
Gaining and retaining a position in the charity markets tend to put agencies under pressure to gain 'product recognition'. There are several, not always consistent strategies.

Create a single focus, and distinguish it from those of others
For the current frontrunners, the child-sponsorship and medical rescue agencies, the formulas that have worked well are: *Keep the Message Simple and Focused*, and *Make the Giver Identify with the Beneficiary (and Benefactors)*. A single focus to evoke immediate identification – 'only children ... that *one* child ... *our* fresh-faced boys and girls going out there to remedy things'[17] – remains a powerful part of the formula.

For market-oriented managers, abstract themes such as the 'world hunger problem', and 'participatory development processes' provoke big yawns. Even popular issues such as democracy and human rights can prove too abstract for a successful fund appeal. The Dutch humanist aid agency Hivos learned this to its cost in 1994, when it bravely launched a fund drive based on a serious effort to communicate to the donating public concrete examples of participatory development and sustainability. It emphasised mutuality, as it brought poor country observers to monitor Dutch national elections. The message was sound and interesting. But it failed to raise much money.

Claims of special expertise, or techniques in fighting poverty, for example the 'Novib Method' advertised in The Netherlands beginning in 1994, can give a sharp, self-confident, professional profile to a generalist financing agency. Implicit in such a message, however, is a subtle innuendo that other agencies don't have the right formula. Such one-upmanship and 'product differentiation' have upset many in the agency community, whose norms up to now (at least in Europe) discourage aggressive styles of self-promotion. But the growing strength of competition is making pushy, 'American'-style salesmanship the method of choice.

Extend product ranges and assortments

Having long realised that relief and welfare approaches offer no sustainable solutions, a number of agencies had, by the late 1970s, resolved to devote themselves to structural anti-poverty work abroad and policy advocacy at home. Enter market pressures. The sheer financial success of relief aid in the 1980s and 1990s has forced a rethink. Some of the various Oxfams, along with others firmly in the development and institution-building camp, have recently re-emphasised relief aid. Meanwhile, other issues popular with Northern givers are crowding in, from protection of tropical forests to colorful indigenous peoples. Now even the Red Cross, formerly the classic single-focus agency, says 'We do a great many different things. We do everything.'[18]

While it is true that a few agencies have specialised, becoming like boutiques, others have responded to market opportunities and competition by becoming more like all-purpose supermarkets.

Seek public renown via the media

Although not always daunted by rising costs of advertising, agencies make use of media for unpaid advertising in the guise of 'news'. Sometimes an agency can gain a mention on prime-time television merely by issuing a press statement about its offer to help in the aftermath of an earthquake far away. But more often it requires forward planning, investment on the ground and reconnaissance missions – scouting for newsworthy calamities in the making. A shrewd agency manager will see to it that, when the cameras are filming a Northern aid minister's press conference in Rwanda, a relief worker, his agency's logo visible on his plastic helmet, stands prominently within the camera frame. More commonly, an agency official will appear on television news broadcasts as an expert on the background to a crisis. Not uncommonly, when asked to suggest a way out of these complex political crises, agency spokespersons' answers can be breathtakingly simple and self-serving: Help the agencies get on with their mission.

An increasingly tight web of mutual interest binds media managers to private aid agencies. A study mainly focused on Britain ('where the system is operated responsibly') concludes: 'Press advertisements are still of some importance in maintaining an agency's presence, but it is the news that is all-important.'[19]

Timely moves into new countries – provided they are politically popular and favoured by media managers – can be an important growth path. If the zone is not yet newsworthy, agencies can sometimes make them so, and in the bargain make the private aid remedy the leading public answer to a crisis. The siege of Biafra of 1968–9, the Sahelian drought of 1974–5, and the Ethiopian famine of 1984–6 proved financial watersheds for a number of private agencies whose prior involvement in those parts of the world had been minimal or non-existent. Eastern Europe and former Soviet republics have become growth areas of the 1990s – urged on by government, in the case of British aid agencies.[20]

The need for humanitarian intervention, it seems, has never been greater. But is this really the case? Might this perception have something to do with the way public attention is being shaped, thanks in large part to the agency drive to sell itself and its services? One close observer of aid concludes that:

There is no direct correlation between rising relief expenditure and increasing need. The evidence to draw this conclusion does not exist. The situation is more complex. An unknown proportion of rising relief expenditure, for example, is market driven. It stems from the increasing competition of aid agencies and NGOs for relief contracts.[21]

Extend global reach

One of the most successful gambits is to follow the example big business. As explained in Ian Smillie's article (pp. 97–106) enterprising agencies have gone transnational. They raise revenues in the most attractive markets through shrewdly-made advertising campaigns (no broadly-organised local constituency needed) and then channel the money to world headquarters for redeployment. Child sponsorship agencies used just this construction in The Netherlands, where they successfully penetrated the lucrative charity market there.

Diversify the funding base

Aid agencies recommend the same strategy to their grantees: broaden your sources of revenue. To gain autonomy and to grow, it can make good sense. The gambits are many, but some offer better safeguards to the integrity of agency values than others. Corporations have never been significant sources for private aid agencies, although the rise of 'cause-related marketing' has opened that door somewhat. Multinational corporations tend to make their grants directly, bypassing Northern private aid agencies:

Now that most of their profits are made abroad, those companies see philanthropy as the best means of building friendships with government leaders, overcoming regulatory hurdles, capturing the imagination of the emerging middle classes, and opening a dialogue with host communities about how companies can meet their needs. ... Of course there's a danger that companies will misuse the new paradigm to win over citizens with highly publicized social initiatives only to divert their attention from unjust corporate practice, such as underpaying workers or exposing them to unsafe conditions.[22]

More attractive are charitable lotteries, although charities in Britain say they have become net losers to Britain's National Lottery (which has come under fire for effectively redistributing money from poorer people to richer).

Genuinely new, and promising, are joint ventures pivoting on ideas of sustainability and broadening constituencies. Alliances with environmental organisations and municipal governments offer aid agencies both new revenue sources and platforms for advocacy. More radical, in that it shifts the basis of agency work from 'sunk' capital to rotating funds, is the growing association with 'alternative' (community or environmentally active) banks and unit trusts/money market funds. Although not without pitfalls in end uses – the capture of loan funds by entrepreneurial elites, nature conservation funds neglecting poor people's interests – such new funding arrangements open ways away from charity and toward mutuality in the aid relationship.

Help shape the market itself
Western publics have been generous to aid agencies – too generous, some might say, given the ease with which charities are born. With more charities entering the market every year, pressures on agencies mount to sharpen their competitive thrusts and armour themselves against the marketing ploys of others. But open conflict is rarely sought, since it can send everyone tumbling off the high moral ground in an unseemly melée. Gentlemen's agreements, and joint defence of the sector, are preferred.

In the 1970s and 1980s for instance, when new agencies, aided by tax advantages, were entering the market, concern grew about standards of practice and transparency in the charity business. In Canada, Germany, France and the US, associations of established charities, including aid agencies, drew up codes of conduct to persuade charities to come clean with the public. One such code, the French

Charte de Déontologie, wants charities 'saying what they do ... doing what they say ... and rendering a financial account'. While mainly aiming to keep up the reputation of the industry as a whole, these efforts also try to raise barriers to entry, or at least to build the basis for a system of 'quality brand name' agencies. However, the effects of such efforts are in doubt: When AmeriCares, a large and self-professed 'unorthodox' agency with right-wing leanings, pulled out of the US agency trade association InterAction because it found the code of ethics too strict, it did so with complete impunity.[23]

The Market for Funding from the System of Official Aid

> When you have your hands in another man's pocket, you must move when he moves.[24]

Anticipating policy, perhaps helping shape and legitimise it, and then harmonising 'product' assortments to meet official aid system demand has become a major – for some agencies *the* major – strategy for survival and growth. Official frameworks governing funding to private aid agencies differ from country to country. There is no universal model. Political consensus around collective sector responsibilities for welfare tasks and on geopolitical interests can make a big differerence in the degree to which the 'market' of official aid resembles grant making or simple business contracting.

Across most Northern countries, relations between the state and the agencies have become denser and more complex over time. For the United States, where the history of government steering of private agencies goes back decades, one factor has stood out: war. Geopolitical objectives make the 'market' one of contracts for humanitarian action. During the Cold War years, when a US administration wanted private agency involvement, it got it. And where it wanted agencies to stay away, they generally obeyed.[25] Meanwhile, a few courageous agencies, as part of broader citizen movements, challenged those administrations, often with telling success.

In Scandinavia, on the other hand, longstanding consensus politics and corporatist strength of churches, unions and other civil society actors tend to generate harmony, even seamless non-market cooperation between governments and private agencies. Elsewhere, agencies and official aid bodies interact in patterns mixing market and non-market modes. A review of some of these helps fill out the picture.

Manoeuvring in the Market for Official Aid Subventions

For politicians and managers in official aid bodies, who face a host of imperatives to *spend* and defend institutional interests, private aid agencies offer a number of advantages. They can serve useful purposes where official budgets must be spent on time (sometimes at short notice) and renewed without increasing government overheads; where operations are time-bounded, experimental or risky; where beneficiaries may be unpopular at home but important for long-term foreign policy interests; where hands-on knowledge is needed; where a public constituency for aid must be shored up; and where an official aid programme needs a 'human face' for goodwill and political legitimacy.

For private aid agencies lacking generous and consistent contributors and own endowments, the official aid system is virtually the only recourse. Gaining and retaining a position in the 'markets' for official subventions puts agencies on their mettle. They face strong incentives to implement a number of measures discussed below.

Meet eligibility criteria

Government thresholds for conferring formal eligibility range from low, as in Canada and Belgium, to quite high, as in Japan. Professional competence, a track record in the field, capacity to produce auditable financial reports are basic requirements. Much less commonly, governments can insist that an agency be demonstrably rooted in a social constituency. The failure to do so has, it is argued, opened the field to a host of ersatz agencies or parastatals masquerading as voluntary sector bodies.

Adjust country choices, strategies and methods

Governments commonly require (or strongly influence) agency choices over which countries to work in, and which kinds of tasks to fulfill. Global distributions of private aid activity will often match bilateral aid patterns virtually one-to-one. Official aid pressures to accept modernisation approaches, often with high external-input technologies, are commonplace. Agencies also take on board the government planning, budgeting and financial control methods that in turn require sophisticated technologies and specialists to make them work. But the controversy that ensues where agencies' geographical choices do not match official ones, as when a few agencies stubbornly refused to observe the official boycott of Cambodia in the 1980s, is one sign of independence.

With political as well as commercial popularity, official aid spending on emergencies has expanded massively since the mid-1980s. Part of the growth is due to 'market deregulation' as agencies historically assigned special tasks, such as the International Committee of the Red Cross (ICRC), effectively lost their unique standing. Both new and old agencies have adjusted their strategies accordingly, taking up relief, food aid and refugee tasks, or re-emphasised them. Powers to initiate action do not, however, always lie with official aid bodies. A government may only swing into action after a television broadcast from a scene of misery, perhaps decrying the lack of action by aid officials. It was television news, informed by aid agencies, that helped precipitate George Bush's calamitous military intervention in Somalia.

The pursuit of emergency and 'modernization' programming, and the creation of large management apparatuses (for example, big southern NGOs) at the receiving end will usually raise agency turnover without corresponding increases in overheads. Where official aid bodies pay agencies fees to cover their overheads on the basis of a fixed percentage of turnover, agencies are bound to see 'profit' in adopting those programming approaches.

Become a contractee

Governments used to grant most monies on a responsive basis: they *responded* to project proposals private agencies themselves submit and tend to fund between 50 and 80 per cent of all costs. But increasingly they are *taking the initiative* to set the terms of engagement and line up contractors.

Formally, only a modest portion of official funding to private agencies is based on contracts for specific tasks, such as building a hospital, refugee facilities, or rural roads. But in some countries it has become substantial, and UN bodies are becoming explicit in their wish to contract non-profits, including private aid agencies.

In 1991, 37 per cent of all state funds for private agencies in Italy were paid for execution of projects set by government; in Switzerland, the figure was 49 per cent. USAID and the World Bank push a purely market approach, particularly in Latin America. In it, agencies and local NGOs compete with for-profit contractors on the basis of tenders.[26] The World Food Programme and UN High Commission for Refugees (UNHCR contract services from private aid agencies along similar lines. Private contractors are not yet visible in the business of food relief and refugee care, but consulting bureaus have begun to give agencies a run for their money in markets for rural development and training contracts. In Scandinavia and The Netherlands, on the other hand, such overt and direct contracting of private aid agencies for government tasks is relatively rare.[27]

More commonly, official aid patrons create frameworks of incentive and supervision of private aid along less formal lines. Official aid bodies open special funding windows labelled 'Food Aid', 'Country Focus', 'Women and Development', 'Aids and Health' and so on, to which private agencies may apply, and receive 100 per cent funding, often including home office overhead expenses. If such informal means of steering private agencies were taken into account, the 'privateness' of private aid further loses its apparent sharp boundaries.

Press for open-ended subsidisation (join a cartel)
Frustration with the high overhead costs, delays and indifferent quality associated with project-by-project grant making (which is still standard operating procedure in many official systems) has led agencies to lobby governments for longer-term subsidisation, covering 100 per cent of costs. In corporatist northern Europe, where church- and party-based social blocs gained long term claims on state subsidies for foreign aid, and indeed were part of the architecture of foreign aid from its beginnings, such a system has been in use since the 1960s, with seeming success. Introduction of the 'block grant' system by Britain and Belgian official aid agencies, and by the European Union's cooperation ministry, represents an advance for the larger established private agencies.

Admission to the favoured circle is a mark of status as well as financial security. Membership in private consortia with privileged access to special aid 'windows' for particular countries or thematic programmes is likewise a great desideratum, and another mark of insider standing. But are the risks, especially conformity to official aid agendas, worth the price of admission? Perhaps the much-abused, but still democratic form of state subsidy – exemption from taxes for charitable contributions – is the better option after all.

Funding Markets: Loyalty, Exit or Voice?

The public market of charitable giving pushes agencies to conform with donors' wishes to gratify complex bundles of self-centered-cum-altruistic needs. It tends to reward investment in salesmanship, or what is today called a communication strategy. The market run by the official aid system pushes them to conform with institutional imperatives ranging from principled solidarity to the cruellest *realpolitik* including war. It tends to reward investment in loyalty – learning and adhering to official rules and agendas.

Both markets are resource-driven and put great stock by appearances. An agency is what it is seen to be delivering, thus neatly
confirming what Christopher Lasch wrote in his famous critique, *The
Culture of Narcissism*: 'Nothing succeeds like the appearance of
success.' Success is measured by growth – the capacity to absorb and
apply more funds. Up to now at least, few are rewarded because they
yield lasting results, permanent improvements in lives marked by
poverty and exclusion.

The endowed foundations, or those agencies solidly anchored in
a loyal and generous constituency of givers, may be able to ignore
these markets. But most agencies are not so privileged, and have to
stay afloat and navigate on strong and sometimes unpredictable
currents. Some are developing strategies to cope, often by straddling
markets and diversifying funding sources. A few are adopting funding
methods that recast the donor-recipient relationship into one of
greater mutuality and common purpose – such as joint interest in
environmental sanity.

But most remain swept along with the current, and are unable or
unwilling to step back from their predicament, reflect, and exercise
the exit option. One of the reasons for unwillingness stems from the
patterns of behaviour and attitudes that build up within agencies
partially in response to market imperatives. The following section
looks at these internal effects.

The Impact Within

The outward imperatives just described have important implications
for agencies' inner lives. The image of a cosy world of committed voluntarism hardly matches the elaborate organisational machinery
needed to run an agency – especially to run one according to market
rules. In some places, the metamorphosis into enterprise is well
advanced. Salary levels are rising, and in some countries approaching mainstream averages.[28] On a visit to the United States, NGO visitors
from that citadel of managerial accomplishment, Japan, observed that
US private agencies 'seemed like large companies to us. They were
very organised and the staff was very professional.'[29] Is this an echo
of the remark by a visitor to the early Soviet Union: 'I have seen the
future, and it works'?

Granted, inspection of the organisational kitchens of private aid
agencies have rather too often revealed appalling and widespread
mediocrity; many have been plagued by Dickensian, or communard,
management cultures and unsystematic working methods.[30] Recent

research about non-profits, including private aid agencies, is shattering stereotypes. For example, it now looks less tenable to argue that they are more egalitarian and participative than for-profit firms, and staffed by harder-working people motivated by loyalty to the organisation and a common cause.[31] Their capacities to work supportively for their 'partners' can be grossly overstated. A recent report on grantees' perceptions of Northern donor agencies in South Africa notes good points, but also severe shortcomings in private agency performance, often in cumbersome, non-transparent decision making and unpredictability in pay-outs. One or two government donors operating on the same terrain as the private agencies enjoy high reputations with grantees, out-classing the private donors on some points.[32]

Some agencies have therefore thrown themselves into reorganisation processes, hiring pricey mainstream management consultants to set things right. But at the end of these often exhausting, stressful and expensive efforts, management will usually end up emphasising 'delivery', and enhanced capacities to project images to attract resources in the North. Commonly lost in the shuffle, if not dismissed with sneers about granola-eaters and wearers of goat-hair socks, is the energy of commitment.

These accretions of market managerial styles rarely stem from cynical calculation (although these may also intrude), but rather reflect the very pressures described above. Signals from funding authorities in agency markets get amplified *within* the agencies, with significant repercussions. Some illustrations of this process are given below.

Throughput and Growth

Imperatives to 'move the money' are driven by the need to register success in the public eye through volume and breadth of work. These become urgent due to the need for financial security when funding may slump. Thus, agencies and their staffs face both financial and career incentives to raise more funds and achieve a higher throughput of projects, resources, publications, events, etc. A study of Belgian agencies suggests that most value growth over autonomy; they prefer to use their publicly-raised funds not to innovate or improve methods, but rather to gain matching grants from official sources, thereby inflating their turnover.[33] As one agency worker commented, 'without growth over time, how can we measure success?'[34]

The Bottom Line: Margins

The difference between income received and expenditure on a project is a key topic of dispute, negotiation and creative book-keeping.

Margins help cover costs that few funding authorities want to pay for: organisational overheads, advocacy, reserves needed for a rainy day and otherwise unfundable activities.

The drive to gain wide margins resembles rent-seeking, in that revenues gained through margins are *independent* of the quality or effectiveness of the activity. This exposes agencies with weak internal commitments to risks of revenue opportunism. What begin as low-priority projects, such as in relief aid, taken on in order to cross-subsidise high-priority work, can come to dominate, and thus marginalise the work that lay at the heart of the original decision. Where margins are based on percentages (ranging from 3 to 7 per cent in Europe) of a total project budget, agencies face incentives to go for bigger-budget, usually 'modernisation' or large-scale relief projects. This bias collides at once with the credo of the small-scale and critique of large-scale official aid – and frequently collides with positive project results.

As staff costs commonly put major claims on margins, agency managers face incentives to cut those costs. The usual wheeze is the speed-up on the work floor. The aim is to push through a greater volume of revenue-generating projects using existing numbers and qualities of staff. 'It is not uncommon', a recent study notes, 'for a desk officer in a large NGO to be responsible for 50–150 partners. Many overseas department staff are already swamped by an enormous workload ...'[35]

As Ian Smillie[36] and other close students of the issue have pointed out, the portrayal of overhead costs presented to the public and official aid donors – in the range of 5 to 15 per cent – is commonly much lower than actual overhead expenditures, which can easily approach 25 to 30 per cent. This creates a stubborn falsehood, namely, that private aid is cheap. Agencies must build tangled webs of accounting, fitting staff costs into project budgets, for example. Reporting to funding authorities, especially the public, becomes an art of dissembling.

Marketing and Public Fundraising

Pressures on fundraisers to perform, and on senior managers to avoid risks, raise incentives for isolation and self-delusion. Conventional fundraising approaches tend to displace an agency's 'development education' remit. Those with direct knowledge of programmes and issues are marginalised from the process by which agencies construct meaning among their funding authorities, including the donating public at large. Internal factions develop and turn hostile, retreating into their trenches. Fundraisers and senior managers are kept in the dark, play ostrich toward 'bad news' from the field, and avoid con-troversial public issues. They base their public pitch on stories with a happy ending, and on increasingly narrower understandings of what is actually going on.[37]

New approaches to funds and fundraising noted elsewhere in this book are emphasising loans and other forms based on mutual interests. At the same time a few agencies have begun breaking down the firewall between grant-making programme officers and public education/fundraising departments. Common to both is a re-emphasis on the quality and sustainability of interventions on the ground.

Indicator Fetishism

Agencies must feed their official aid system funding authorities with an increasingly narrow diet of information according to indicators easily digested in bureaucracies and in public discourse. Water wells dug and babies jabbed continue to stand for improved child health; proportions of women in training workshops continue to stand for gender balance. Gradually, the production of indicators treating only the very short-run pervades the activities themselves; a longer-run perspective, learning based on real impact, the innovative spark and other 'comparative advantages' of agencies get crowded out.

Evaluation

Evaluation has become a form of accounting to funders, rather than one of accountability to other stakeholders or a basis for self-exami-nation. Funding authorities' evaluation requirements can therefore undermine both internal learning processes and the quality of rela-tionships with Southern grantees and counterparts. Evaluations themselves are not the problem. Rather, it is the uses to which they are put – or not. Inside agencies, and in the specialist literature, it has long been known that agency-managed evaluations are mainly used to grease funding wheels.[38] For grantees, evaluations can be ordeals of high anxiety in a context of unequal power, not of 'part-nership' (a term some agencies use to underscore their legitimacy). Dominant factions in the agencies, on the other hand, have few reasons to pay attention to the content of evaluations, as they are rewarded for keeping the wheels greased and turning along accustomed pathways. They thus collude in dissembling, with corrosive *internal* effects, from 'learning disabilities' to an enfeebled institutional memory.

The foregoing are of course tendencies, not absolutes. They illustrate one side of the equation only: processes arising in the 'natural' response to economic force-fields. They highlight how these pressures distort the work of agencies away from effective efforts with Southern recipients or 'partners', and distort flows of information that are less than complete, often deceptive, or even destructive. The pressures are toward stability, even rigidity; the space for initiative and creativity shrinks. Of critical importance, however, is the impact of the market for compassion within the private aid agencies on the people themselves.

The Human Factor: Nurturing Commitment

The vision for the private aid agencies painted in the first section was about giving 'voice to the voiceless': soliciting a supply response from those that have, and matching it with the needs of those who do not have. It is a vision about fissures and inequities produced by global system, and an institutional response to them.

Missing from this utopian equation, though, is the role of people in this process. It would be possible to paint an alternative scenario that asserted that personal and group commitment lies at the heart of the non-governmental vision. From their early days, the spirit of commitment and energy were writ large in the public perceptions of Northern agencies. And this spirit has certainly flowed in the lifeblood of many that are now household names, such as Oxfam and Christian Aid in Britain, Comité Catholique contre la Faim et pour le Développement (CCFD) in France, and the American Friends Service Committee (AFSC) in the United States.

For reasons outlined in this chapter, however, this spirit has had to submit to enormous pressures the last two decades. The very imperatives that drive the agencies towards being image-makers in competitive Northern markets for compassion, and that create the organisational imperatives and processes described here, erode the personal commitment associated with 'value-based' organisation, management and leadership. The patterns of financial incentives and the career structures meant to motivate agency staff to perform as 'professionals' actively corrode the underlying incentives that energised these agencies in their formative years.

This voluntaristic spirit was, of course, often uninformed and it led to ill-formed decisions and actions. The criticism of 'hobbyism' cannot be ignored. However, there is no obvious evidence that the kind of market-managerial professionalism many agencies now strive for actually furthers fundamental agency values and goals. And there is certainly no evidence proving that this kind of professionalism is more cost-effective, the touchstone of contemporary judgements.

That is not to say that the spirit of professionalism has had no effect: far from it! The forms of professionalism that emerged during the 1980s ensured higher throughput, more resources and a form of managerial efficiency that could be recognised, measured and acknowledged. But instrumental effectiveness of this kind does not necessarily lead to ultimate effectiveness. The instrument of organisation can be forever sharpened while, for the people whose poverty justifies its existence, it doesn't make any difference.

It is this issue that has more recently generated a renewed critique of the tradition of professionalism. Led by the likes of Robert Chambers, there has been an increased call for a *new professionalism* that takes the best of instrumental effectiveness, and the compassionate listening and actions associated with the tradition of voluntarism. Here then has been the recognition that the conventional mode of professionalism that has arisen from the imperatives described above has indeed undermined the essential qualities of effective development workers.

Contesting the Economic Laws of Motion

> You can put lipstick on a pig, give her a purse, and call her Monique, but she's still a pig ... Don't ever get so caught up in running like a business that your revenue needs take priority over your mission.
>
> Laureen Casteel, President, Hunt Alternatives Fund,
> a private endowed agency[39]

This chapter has scanned some of the landscape. Winds blowing across it are buffeting private agencies, forcing many of them to adopt rigid and defensive postures. The scene is one of paradoxes and dilemmas: agencies work ever harder to satisfy Northern needs stimulated by images they make of the South; to raise funds in the name of compassion in a market riven by aggressive competition and cynical *realpolitik*; and to seek efficiencies and business dynamism in ways that fragment the founding spirit of commitment on the alter of managerial professionalism.

These pressures can be thought of as 'economic laws of motion', but they are neither inevitable nor irreversible. Such 'laws' merely promote norms of the game by those directly profiting from such norms. In this sense, these laws are made to be broken. Each section above has given some sense of what it might mean to break these laws.

It is possible to cooperate in markets even if the driving force is towards competition; it is possible to educate people and institutions to respond to complex information about the situation in the South rather than vulgar and often demeaning images; it is possible to manage effectively without distorting information and eroding commitment-based relationships.

The issue is not how an agency can best retreat and quarantine itself from the economy and official aid institutions. No agency can play ostrich and ignore these forces. The issue is rather how to recognise and handle the tensions between those economic currents and the value-based commitments which are supposed to drive the agencies in the first place. To retain those commitments, and reject 'laws of motion' as the pivot of agency work, means paying attention and seeking new paths.

These alternative paths are not easily to find and to follow. It is clearly simpler to 'go with the flow', to respond to the pressures of the market by providing a simple story with a happy ending about how the agencies can do good in the South with other people's money. This approach has worked for many years, and might have some life in it yet. It is only gradually that people in the North are waking up to the fact that all is not as it seems. It might be years before they eventually catch up with the true stories. But they will, of that one can be sure.

Notes

1. Mensen in Nood Director Jaap van Soest, quoted in Jan Landman, 'Tussen Marketing en Inspiratie', *BijEEN*, The Netherlands, October 1994, p. 7.
2. See Chris McGreal, 'Aid Comes with Biblical Strings Attached', *Guardian Weekly*, 25 December 1994. See also John Vidal, 'Mixed blessings of Rwandan aid', *Guardian Weekly*, 9 April 1995.
3. Marcelo Machava, '"SOS" troca pobres por ricos', *Savana* (independent weekly, Maputo), No. 76, 30 June 1995, pp. 1–3.
4. Lidy Nicolasen, 'Het ging te veel om de "chari-markt"', *De Volkskrant*, Amsterdam 7 April 1994.
5. M. Maren, 'A Different Kind of Child Abuse', *Penthouse*, December 1995.
6. See, for example, H. Hansmann, 1988, 'Economic Theories of Non-profit Organization', in W.W. Powell (ed.), *The Nonprofit Sector. A Research Handbook*, Yale University Press, New Haven, pp. 38–9.

7. See Center for the Study of Policy Attitudes (CSPA), 1995, 'Americans and Foreign Aid. A Study of Public Attitudes. Summary of Findings', p. 1; another CSPA 1994 poll showed that 'Despite talk that public support for antipoverty programmes has ebbed since the 1960s, more people now – 80% in fact – believe that "government has a responsibility to try to do away with poverty" than did in 1964, when 70% agreed', *Left Business Observer*, 67, 1994, p. 7. A 1991 poll showed that for the French, the UN, the French Government, and the European Union were the channels of choice for foreign aid, ahead of private aid agencies. CCFD, 'Troisième Barometre CCFD', *Faim Developpment Magazine*, Nr. 85, March 1992.

8. See I. Wilson and M. Nooter (eds), 1995, *Evaluation of Finnish Personnel as Volunteers in Development Cooperation*, Netherlands Economic Institute and Matrix Consultants, Utrecht, mimeo.

9. Attendance at established churches may be dropping in Northern countries, but belief as such is far from dead. The rise of new and sometimes bizarre religious and ideological fellowships, most of them favoured by the same tax laws as private aid agencies, testifies to this. In The Netherlands alone, about one thousand spiritual groupings are said to exist, claiming about 10 million of the country's 15.5 million people.

10. Especially by G. Lipovetsky, 1992, *Le crépuscule du devoir. L'éthique indolore des nouveaux temps démocratiques*, Gallimard, Paris. This paragraph draws on Lipovetsky's findings.

11. *NRC Handelsblad* (Rotterdam), 6 June 1987, cited in G. Rutte, 1989, *NGOs en Financiering (NGOs and Financing)*, doctoral thesis, University of Amsterdam, p. 66. Thanks to Prof. Jan van Heemst of the Institute of Social Studies for drawing the writers' attention to this thesis.

12. Estimations from A. Fowler, 1992, 'Distant Obligations: Speculations on NGO Funding and the Global Market', *Review of African Political Economy*, No. 55, pp. 9–29. Agency income and expenditure are notoriously difficult to pin down with any accuracy. Reporting of agency financial data to the OECD, for example, has been described as 'vitually meaningless', and probably under-reported. See I. Smillie, 1993, 'A Note on NGO Funding Statistics', in I. Smillie and H. Helmich (eds), *Non-governmental Organisations and Governments: Stakeholders for Development*, OECD, Paris, pp. 40–1.

13. Walter van Hulst and Hans van de Veen, 'Wat doen ze met ons geld?' *Onze Wereld* (Amsterdam), July/August 1992, p. 15.

14. *De Volkskrant* (Amsterdam), 12 April 1994.

15. See Peter Hillmore, 'Rent-a-faces 'twixt fame and famine', the *Observer*, 9 April 1995.

16. John Longhurst, 'Famine Pornography. Relief and development community must share blame for Africa's negative image', *The Ottawa Citizen*, 3 March 1995.

17. *Mensen in Nood* Director Jaap van Soest, quoted in Jan Landman, 'Tussen Marketing en Inspiratie', *BijEEN*, October 1994, p. 6.

18. Dutch Red Cross spokesman Bas Kuik, quoted in 'De "Top-Tien"', *BijEEN*, October 1994, p. 4. In 1995 the Dutch Red Cross failed to gain official recognition of its broader identity when it was denied eligibility for government co-financing for development programmes, despite a strong political lobby.

19. J. Benthall, 1993, *Disasters, Relief and the Media*, I.B. Taurus, London, p. 210.

20. Charity Know-How is a consortium of agencies largely set in motion by the British Foreign and Commonwealth Office in 1991. The British government provides one-to-one matching grants to British agencies in support of NGO projects in eastern Europe, Russia and the former Soviet republics.

21. M. Duffield, 1995, 'Protracted Political Crisis and the Demise of Developmentalism. From Convergence to Coexistence', draft discussion paper, University of Birmingham, p. 15.

22. C. Smith, 1994, 'The New Corporate Philanthropy', *Harvard Business Review*, May–June, p. 112.

23. Raymond Bonner, 'Compassion Wasn't Enough in Rwanda', *New York Times*, 18 December 1994; see also Russ W. Baker, 'The Cross and Croatia. AmeriCares Has Odd Priorities in the Balkans', *Village Voice*, 17 August 1993.

24. R.M. Kramer, 1981, *Voluntary Agencies and the Welfare State*, University of California Press, Berkeley.

25. See, for example, H. Baitenmann, 1990, 'NGOs and the Afghan war: the politicisation of humanitarian aid', *Third World Quarterly*, 12:1; B.H. Smith, 1990, *More than Altruism. The Politics of Private Foreign Aid*, Princeton University Press, especially Chapters 2 and 3; L. Mason and R. Brown, 1983, *Rice, Rivalry and Politics: Managing Cambodian Relief*, University of Notre Dame Press, Indiana.

26. M. Robinson, 1995, 'NGOs as Public Service Contractors' in M. Edward and D. Hulme, *NGOs, States and Donors: Too Close for Comfort?*, Macmillan, London.

27. For a country-by-country review see Smillie and Helmich, *Non-Governmental Organisations*.

28. In 1993 in Britain, private aid agency salaries for chief executives were said to be between £20,000 and £40,000, that is,

US$30,000–$60,000 (possibly averaging £32,000, or $48,000); and for chief financial officers between £15,000 and £35,000, that is, $22,500–$52,500 (possibly averaging £28,000, or $42,000). These figures appear in a letter from an executive of World Vision UK to *Third Sector* (issue 7, 14 January 1993) responding angrily to an article in the magazine's issue of 3 December 1992. That article, 'Charity pay gains on national average', was based on a survey showing rapid narrowing of the pay gap for senior charity managers. The survey found that a median basic salary of a chief executive of a charity in Britain as £42,000, versus a national (mainstream) median of £ 45,000 per annum.

Private aid agency salaries in Germany and The Netherlands are probably somewhat higher than those in Britain, while those in Belgium may be somewhat lower.

The average US non-family foundation (which gives away $7 million a year) pays its Chief Executive Officer an annual salary of US$134,000. ('Gina Graham', 1995, 'Foundation Culture', *Left Business Observer*, No. 70, November, p. 4.) Most, but perhaps not all other private aid agencies in the US would pay their CEOs much less.

29. Ms Yumi Kikuchi, quoted in 'Japanese NGOs Leaders See Canadian and American NGOs in Action' *Kokoro, Newsletter of Japanese NGO Center for International Cooperation*, 3:3, October 1991, p. 4.

30. See, for example, E. Waeterloos and H. Couderé, 1990, *De professionaliteit van medefinancierde niet-gouvernementele organisaties in België*, Centrum Derde Wereld, Universiteit Antwerpen, paper 90/133. For an overview, see J. MacKeith, 1993, *NGO Management: A Guide Through the Literature*, Centre for Voluntary Organisation, London School of Economics, London.

31. See Joseph Rowntree Foundation, 1995, 'Managing the voluntary sector', *Findings: Social Policy Research*, No. 76, based on a 1995 report by Diana Leat, *Challenging Management*, from VOLPROF, City University Business School, London.

32. The Dutch and German official aid agencies, whose local representatives can act with considerable flexibility, were highly praised. USAID, on the other hand, was roundly criticised: 'It is widely regarded as administratively incompetent, lacking in responsibility and understanding, and aggressive in its dealings with people.' From D. Hallowes, 1995, 'Of Partners and Patrons: NGO Perceptions of Funders', Olive Information Service, (Durban), Avocado Series No. 5/95, p. 4.

33. Waeterloos and Couderé, *De professionaliteit van ...*, p. 61.

34. This is not to underplay the real difficulties non-profits face in measuring performance. These are reviewed succinctly in R.M. Kanter and D.V. Summers, 1987, 'Doing Well while Doing Good: Dilemmas of Performance Measurement in Nonprofit Organizations and the Need for a Multiple-Constituency Approach', in W.W. Powell (ed.), 1987, *The Nonprofit Sector. A Research Handbook*, Yale University Press, New Haven.
35. R. James, 1994, 'Strengthening the Capacity of Southern NGO Partners. A Survey of current Northern NGO Approaches', *INTRAC Occasional paper Series*, Vol. 1, No. 5, April, p. 32.
36. See Ian Smillie, 1993, 'Changing Partners', in Smillie and Helmich (eds), *Non-Governmental Organisations*, p. 24 and passim.
37. The Dutch private aid agency efforts always to give their stories a happy ending is described in van der Velden, F., 1994 'Tien Dilemma's bij Particuliere Ontwikkelingssamenwerking', in *Particuliere Ontwikkelingssamenwerking op de Helling*, Occasional Paper Nr. 43, Derde Wereld Centrum, Katholieke Universiteit Nijmegen, Nijmegen, p. 55.
38. See P. Quarles van Ufford, 1988, 'The Myth of a Rational Development Policy: Evaluations versus Policy-Making in Dutch Private Donor Agencies', in P. Quarles van Ufford *et al.* (eds), 1988, *The Hidden Crisis in Development: Development Bureaucracies*, Free University Press, Amsterdam, pp. 75–98.
39. *Responsive Philanthropy*, Newsletter of the National Committee for Responsive Philanthropy, Washington DC, Fall 1994, p. 10.

Interlude:
The Rise of the Transnational Agency[1]

Ian Smillie

Some of today's best-known private aid agencies began as wartime or post-war relief efforts: Save the Children (SCF UK); Foster Parents Plan (now PLAN International) Oxfam UK, CARE and World Vision. These five organisations and a handful of relative newcomers, such as Médecins sans Frontières, dominate the scene in terms of their size, and in terms of the messages they provide to their supporters at home about development issues and developing countries. Collectively, their budgets are probably greater than all the rest combined. And these organisations – transnational private aid agencies – are emerging as a distinct class of organisation, very different from other Northern agencies.

A transnational corporation is one which operates in several countries at once. For shareholders, their greatest asset is their ability to move capital quickly in response to national conditions, and their general lack of accountability to any particular national government. Criticised for the stimulation of inappropriate consumption patterns and the production, through capital-intensive technologies, of inappropriate products, transnationals exert considerable political and economic leverage in the South, often damaging or suppressing local entrepreneurship with their superior knowledge, global contacts, support services and – through transfer pricing – their ability to raise and lower costs to suit local tax situations.

To compare well-respected private aid agencies with transnational corporations will be regarded by some as heresy, but there are many real similarities between the two entities – in corporate behaviour and global ambition, and in the exercise of trust and control.

In the Beginning

During the mid-1960s, Oxfam UK began its Northern outreach by investing £60,000 in the establishment of the new branch, Oxfam-Canada. By 1970, Oxfam-Canada had sent £1.2 million overseas, of which half was channelled directly through Oxford.[2] The Oxfam start-up in Canada has parallels in Europe, Japan and Australia. The American World Vision, for example, sponsored the Canadian organisation, which in turn begat the Australian body, which then begat World Vision New Zealand. CARE established a successful fundraising branch in Toronto in the late 1940s, and later in Ottawa, and the payoff was phenomenal. CARE Canada's 1994 income (in cash and kind) was C\$75.3 million.[3] CARE made similar investments in the early 1980s in Germany, Norway, Italy and France, and later Austria, Denmark and Japan. A 1987 start-up investment from CARE International proved hugely successful in Australia; within five years, its new affiliate had already become the third largest agency recipient of Australian government assistance.[4]

World Vision, with 20 offices in Europe, North America and elsewhere, demonstrated even more spectacular growth, spending US\$261 million world-wide in 1993.[5] In Canada alone, between 1991 and 1994, its total revenue from individuals, corporations and government rose by 31 per cent to a total of C\$95 million – all in Canadian *cash* contributions. In Australia, World Vision raised A\$66.9 million in 1991, an increase of almost 20 per cent over the previous year.[6] The support it received from the Australian government was more than double that of the next largest agency. A relative newcomer, the French agency Médecins sans Frontières, had at least seven national affiliates within a dozen years of its start-up in 1979.

Salient Features of the Transnational Private Aid Agency

The transnational pace of growth, especially during a recessionary period when the incomes of other agencies have been stagnating or reversing, is surprising. Some of the reasons for this growth are perhaps obvious; others are not.

A Strong Relief Emphasis

Most transnationals devote a significant part of their fundraising effort and their expenditure to emergencies (PLAN International stands out as the exception). In recent years this has proven the only way for the biggest fundraising agencies, SCF UK and Oxfam UK, to maintain and expand their market share. It has also proven the most successful way for newcomers to enter established markets. CARE Australia, for example, has focused extensively on refugee and emergency situations

(Sudan, Iraq, Somalia, Indochina), rapidly surpassing more established organisations such as Austcare, UNICEF and SCF Australia.

Child Sponsorship
Alan Fowler suggests that child sponsorship is one of the most effective means of shortening the gap between giver and beneficiary: 'Identification with an individual in the South is one way of making a distant obligation more immediate.'[7] Child sponsorship has been one of the most enduring success stories in private aid agency fundraising. Despite widespread criticism, child sponsorship continues to grow.

It is the bedrock of several of the older organisations (Save the Children USA, World Vision, Plan International) and has been the key to their expansion into new countries. Foster Plan Japan has become – in ten years – one of the biggest and fastest growing fundraisers in the country, supporting 57,000 foster children and families in 1994 (more than the UK and Germany combined), an increase of 60 per cent in three years.[8] Between 1986 and 1991 the income of *Stichting Foster Parents Plan Nederland*, more than doubled to about US$70 million.[9] By 1994, 44 per cent of PLAN's world-wide child sponsorships were being funded from Holland alone.

Economies of Scale
Larger agencies can avail themselves of the best consultants and managerial talent, as well as the newest and most effective fundraising methods. They have large workforces which mean that gaps can be filled relatively easily and emergencies answered quickly. They can afford research, policy and publicity departments, things which are beyond many smaller organisations. They can also absorb mistakes, poor investments and political ructions in a way that smaller organisations cannot.

Global Reach
Most transnational agencies work in scores of countries in Asia, Latin America and Africa. They not only look professional, they usually *are* professional. This makes them attractive to the individual donor, but it sometimes also makes them *essential* to bilateral and multilateral donor agencies. When an emergency erupts in Rwanda, Haiti or Bangladesh, it is often these organisations that have the infrastructure in place, and the experience to deal with it.

Perhaps as important from a financial point of view, whenever a new funding window opens in a bilateral agency, the transnational will have (or can soon make) programmes to suit the funding criteria:

generic issues such as human rights, the environment, democracy or women in development; special geographic interests such as Southern Africa or the Philippines.

'Transfer Pricing'

This term is used for dramatic effect rather than precision. The agency equivalent of transfer pricing, however, is in some ways comparable to the corporate approach:

- *Transfer programming*: An established British, French or American agency opening a fundraising office in a new country can demonstrate very quickly that it is a going concern, because it already has field operations that can be 'transferred' into brochures and fundraising programmes. This, and hiring Norwegians, say, can quickly make a French or an American organisation look very Norwegian. Japan has been viewed as a potential gold mine in this regard. CARE, Save the Children, World Vision and PLAN International all opened offices there after 1983. World Vision has been very successful raising funds in Taiwan.

- *Transfer emergencies*: The transnational agency can demonstrate quickly and effectively to several donor constituencies at once that its people are 'on the ground', responding to an emergency. CARE, for example, demonstrated simultaneously to television audiences in Britain, the United States, Canada and Australia that it was operational only days after the 1993 disaster 'broke' in Somalia – simply by changing the face and the accent in front of the camera. World Vision Hong Kong sent cameras, on behalf of WV International, to a 1993 Chinese flood disaster. Oxfams in Canada, the United States and elsewhere have benefited repeatedly from the international media publicity earned by Oxfam UK workers in Bangladeshi, Sahelian and Ethiopian disasters. This, plus economies of scale and access to increasingly sophisticated communications technology give such organisations considerable advantage over the lone German or French agency operating on its own, regardless of the quality of its work.

- *Transfer fundraising*: Most Northern governments provide matching grants based on an agency's domestic fundraising. The terms and conditions of the matching formula vary greatly, from 50 per cent or less to well over 90 per cent. A transnational agency can take advantage of a better ratio by opening offices in countries with good matching ratios, investing heavily in fundraising, and requesting a match for the resulting income. This practise is becoming especially fashionable in the European Community as national borders blur.

- *Transfer financial assistance*: When a transnational affiliate has financial difficulties, others are able to provide assistance of a type that is completely unavailable to other agencies. In the mid-1970s, when CARE USA faced a liquidity problem, CARE Canada came to the rescue with a loan. When CARE Britain faced a major cash-flow crisis in 1994, it was the turn of CARE USA to provide a financial rescue package.

The impact of these techniques can be dramatic. PLAN International, for example, raised US$28 million in cash in the United States in 1991. In the same year, it raised US$58 million in The Netherlands. On a per capita basis, this represents about ten cents per person in the US, and US$3.89 in Holland. Similar calculations show that World Vision raised less than a dollar per head in the United States in 1991, approximately US$1.50 in Australia and US$1.78 in Canada.[10] With differentials like these, it is little wonder that new markets are so aggressively tackled.

Shallow Programming Roots
Since the mid-1980s, Northern agencies have faced a growing identity challenge. Once the confident purveyors of development projects which they designed, managed and evaluated themselves, it was logical, when Southern NGOs began to emerge, that their Northern counterparts would turn from self-managed projects to support of Southern partners.

Surprisingly, however, of the major transnationals, only Oxfam and SCF UK have worked to any extent with Southern NGOs. While Oxfam and its affiliates made the transition well, most of the other transnationals have actively rejected this approach. World Vision, CARE, PLAN International and some of the larger members of the International Save the Children Alliance have, in fact, tended to reinforce the approach that Northern agencies took to development in the South in the 1960s, continuing to devise, manage and evaluate their own projects directly.

High Cost
Overheads are a thorny subject for agencies because of the powerful public myth that development is cheap. True overheads for transnationals are as hard to discover or decipher as for any other agency, and they may not be any higher than for other organisations of similar

size and complexity. Where they *are* higher, it may have to do with the increasing cost of running sophisticated fundraising and advertising departments aimed at maintaining or expanding the organisation's market share. The Dutch version of Médecins sans Frontières, for example, *Artsen zonder Grenzen*, spent 37 per cent of its 1990 gift income on publicity and fundraising.[11]

Higher costs are a common characteristic of the child sponsorship agencies. World Vision Australia spent 32 per cent of its gross 1991 income on fundraising and administration,[12] and the high cost of its German operations became the target of television and print journalists in the late 1980s. Save the Children USA, which prides itself on overheads of about 18 per cent, came in for a media drubbing at the end of 1995, which showed that real overheads were perhaps in excess of 40 per cent.[13]

Government Support

The one area where there is no common denominator among the transnationals is their attitude towards government support. Oxfam America will take no funding from government whatsoever. CARE and World Vision, on the other hand, have no limits on government support: CARE US, for example, received 56 per cent of its 1991 income in the form of cash, kind and freight contributions from the US government.[14] World Vision's global income includes about 20 per cent in government grants. SCF UK's government income hovers around the 16 per cent level, SCF US receives almost 50 per cent of its support from government, while *Radda Barnen*, the SCF affiliate in Sweden, limits government intake to 50 per cent. PLAN International probably receives less government funding than any of the transnationals – less than 4 per cent in the United States and less than 2 per cent in Canada.[15]

Devolution

Oxfam and CARE

The original idea of an 'Oxfam International' was all but dead by 1974, with completely independent Oxfams in the US, Canada and Quebec. The same sort of thing happened to CARE, although a 'CARE International', with headquarters in Paris, was formed in 1980 to act as a clearing-house for its affiliates. Relations between these CARE affiliates and their connection to overseas programmes vary. Some, such as Canada and Australia, have become 'lead agencies' for certain country programmes. Most continue to be run and staffed by CARE

USA, however, with affiliates such as CARE Britain contributing money and staff to general field operations, or 'buying' projects which they can 'sell' to donors in their own country. There is no CARE affiliate, however, in any Southern country.

Oxfam UK is in the process of making itself 'more European and more truly international'. Part of this has to do with strategic positioning in the rapidly evolving European scene, part with a recognition that independent programming overseas can be counter-productive. The re-creation of a more centralised Oxfam International, however, coincides with a move in the opposite direction in India, where efforts to create an independent member of the Oxfam family have been debated half-heartedly by the Northern members for years.

World Vision

Although overall control is exercised from the organisation's headquarters in California, World Vision has probably devolved more than others. Headquarters staff numbers fell dramatically, from almost 500 in 1989 to fewer than 150 in 1994. The organisation is responsible to an 86-person council, elected from advisory councils and boards elsewhere, and is more or less equally divided in makeup between North and South. The Board, which is considerably more powerful than the boards of most other transnationals, is made up of representatives from World Vision operations worldwide. Today, roughly half of the Southern operations, including Thailand, India, Kenya, Tanzania and Zimbabwe are in a category which includes provision for a local advisory council or board of directors, and eligibility for representatives to serve on the international Council and Board.

The International Save the Children Alliance (ISCA)

ISCA is a loose grouping of 24 organisations with similar aims and objectives, collectively supporting a small secretariat in Geneva. The secretariat's main activities are liaison with the EC, UN agencies and other NGO bodies, the coordination of information between member agencies, and lobbying within the international system on issues related to the rights and welfare of children. Its 1993 budget was US$285,000.

But the ISCA 'family' of organisations is considerably less than a family. Communication between the Northern affiliates is limited, and except in emergencies, there is little or no coordination at field level. Two, three, or even five different member agencies will set up and operate their own programmes in a country, with as much communication between them as might exist between CARE and Oxfam.

A unique feature of the official SCF grouping is that nine of the 24 affiliates are Southern organisations, with Southern Boards, staff and programmes. Of the transnationals discussed so far, SCF is the only one to have encouraged, or even to have allowed truly independent Southern affiliates. Several of these were fostered by SCF US in the late 1970s and early 1980s, but there is considerable apathy towards them in some parts of the network. SCF UK is not a funding agency and therefore maintains its own staff in the field – because it is 'accountable to its donors'. In Lesotho, for example, it works with government, not SCF Lesotho. Ultimately the biggest devolutionary issue within the International Save the Children Alliance – as with CARE and Oxfam – has to do with trust and control.

Conclusions

The Transnational Impact on Development

Undoubtedly, transnationals are setting new standards of professionalism for private and governmental agencies in some areas of endeavour, namely food aid, emergencies and refugee situations. Transnationals can move quickly; they have decades of relevant experience; they have a core of professionals who are willing to take great personal risks and who know what to do under fire. Some are carving out particular niches. CARE has developed a reputation in logistics; Oxfam has built expertise in the provision of water supplies in emergency situations. Médecins sans Frontières has obvious expertise in health.

In development programming, however, the transnationals have considerably less, and probably declining impact. The most innovative and influential work in participatory development today, in job creation, in the environment, rural banking, gender and human rights, is being done by Southern NGOs, not by operational Northern agencies. A survey of current development literature reveals few references to the work of the transnationals.[15]

Impact in the North

Will the transnationals crowd out other Northern agencies? The answer is almost certainly yes, especially in the field of emergency relief. It is not yet clear from the statistics, however, whether transnationals are poaching *development* donors from other agencies, or whether they are expanding the market. The answer is probably a bit of both.

The impact of transnationals on public attitudes in the North is hard to gauge. Some, such as Oxfam UK and SCF UK have active and internationally respected development education and campaigning programmes. The development education work of most others is so small that it rarely warrants a line item in the annual report. Many actively thrive on pictures of starvation and of desperate children. These, most favoured by child sponsorship agencies, foster a general image of helplessness in the South, suggesting that Africans and Asians make irresponsible parents. To the extent that public opinion polls show falling support for official development assistance, it should be asked how much the more rapacious fundraising agencies have contributed to public cynicism and dismay.

Transnational agencies of course do not all operate in the same fashion. Unlike transnational corporations, they rarely move staff between their Northern affiliates. A dictat from the international head-quarters would most likely be ignored. While many of the affiliates may be excellent performers, some are not, and headquarters can usually do little about it. Some transnationals, however, have traded long-term development impact for short-term child sponsorship and emergency donors. This does not deny the commitment of their workers to development. But at a corporate level, many transnational private aid agencies bear uncanny similarities in opportunistic behaviour to transnational corporations. Like many transnational corporations, they have maximised growth through the successful international manipulation of inputs, pricing, marketing and product. Unlike most transnational corporations, however, they have been largely unsuccessful in extending the definition of 'international' South of the development Mason-Dixon line.

Transnational agencies have done something else, however. They have demonstrated that there is still an enormous fund of goodwill in the North, that even in the 1990s, the pool of people willing to try to understand, and to help in the South can be expanded. The transnational success may flow partly from high-powered fundrais-ing and advertising. But it is also the product of an obvious but inexplicable *vacuum*, inexplicable because despite the 3000 other agencies raising funds and awareness in the North, international giving and international *thinking* still remain resolutely at the bottom of the Northern priority list. If the growth of transnationals provides any lesson, it may be that the private aid community's enormous tolerance for amateurism contains the seeds of its own destruction.

Notes

1. This section has been adapted by the author, with permission from his publisher, from Chapter 11 of *The Alms Bazaar: Altruism Under Fire – Non-Profit Organizations and International Development*, IT Publications, London, 1995.
2. M. Black, 1992, *A Cause for Our Times: Oxfam, The First 50 Years*, Oxfam, Oxford, p. 170
3. CARE Canada Annual Report, 1994
4. CARE Australia Annual Report, 1991/2; AIDAB/NGO Cooperation Program Annual Report, 1991/92.
5. World Vision Annual Report, 1993.
6. *Childview*, World Vision Canada, February/March, 1995.
7. A. Fowler, 1992, 'Distant Obligations: Speculations on NGO Funding and the Global Market', *Review of African Political Economy*, No. 55, p. 15.
8. *Worldwide Annual Reports*, PLAN International, 1992, 1994.
9. See also Fowler, 'Distant Obligations'.
10. Sources: Annual Report, World Vision Australia, 1991; *Childview*, World Vision Canada, Feb/March 1993; *Voluntary Foreign Aid Programs, 1993*, USAID; Fowler, 'Distant Obligations'.
11. See also Fowler, 'Distant Obligations'.
12. Annual Report, World Vision Australia, 1991.
13. *Money* magazine (December 1994) reported an SCF (USA) figure of 17.9 per cent, but a dramatic exposé in *Penthouse* (December 1995) attacked this claim, placing the actual at well over 40 per cent.
14. USAID, 'Voluntary Foreign Aid Programs, 1993', Washington, 1993.
15. These figures have been calculated from 'ballpark' figures in the Plan 1992 Annual Report; from USAID, *Voluntary Foreign Aid Programs, 1993*; and from the 1991–2 Annual Report of CIDA, Ottawa, 1993.
16. Farrington and Bebbington refer to only one transnational in their extensive 1993 study, *Reluctant Partners? NGOs, the State and Sustainable Agricultural Development*, Routledge, London, 1993. The 1994 UNICEF *State of the World's Children* contains one bibliographical reference out of 137 from a transnational – Oxfam UK. In the World Bank's 1990 *World Development Report* on poverty, none of the 261 references in the bibliography can be traced to a transnational. Of the 394 bibliographical references in the 1993 *World Development Report* on health, only one is from a transnational (SCF UK).

4

Do Private Agencies Really Make a Difference?

Alan Fowler and Kees Biekart

'Uncontrolled hobbyism' was once the stick used to beat private aid agencies in the past. Today, it is the 'report on failed projects'. A variety of critical voices – academics, government officials, journalists and those working in the field – are repeating the same message: the effectiveness of (private) foreign aid should be carefully assessed. Now that political justification of aid is vanishing with the demise of the Cold War, its developmental impact is becoming more important. Implied is the suggestion that private foreign aid is probably not as effective as was generally assumed in earlier years.

To move toward objectively assessing the agencies' effectiveness, however, is to embark on a path full of pitfalls. First, the distinction between individual project effects and the wider development impact of combined projects is not often explicit. What do the success stories presented in fundraising campaigns to the public tell us about the overall achievements of private agencies? Second, the theoretical and practical difficulties of impact assessment are so substantial that it is almost unrealistic for agencies to say that they can verify what they do achieve in terms of impact on people's lives. Are agencies honest, therefore, about what they present as the results of their work? Or is exaggeration and mystification the name of the game, with the funding public unable objectively to distinguish between the wheat and the chaff?

Claims: What Do Private Aid Agencies Say They Achieve?

Over the past few years, private aid agencies have become more cautious about saying what they have achieved or will achieve. Instead of emphasising results, they now tend to list the problems they tackle. In other words, they concentrate on the justification for their programmes in a particular country or sector, elaborating on the kind of priorities and goals they are striving for. This has educational as well as fundraising value, but offers little more that an implicit notion and 'contract' that the problem will in fact be mitigated or eradicated, to what degree, over what time scale and how. Without explicit measures on offer, other sources are needed to determine what sort of impact private agencies say that they are making.

Examination of their public messages, analysis of agency annual reports listing their projects and reviews of other documents show two common types of results being sought by private agencies: alleviation of poverty, and strengthening civil society through enhancing participation of grassroots organisations, in short, economic and political change benefiting the most needy and disadvantaged. They further claim that they are often better than governments trying to do the same thing.

Alleviating Poverty

Private aid agencies all claim that they contribute to tackling poverty: 'Structural poverty eradication in the South, directly, as well as by contributing to social changes in the North and the South that enhance a more just distribution and sustainability.'[1] Work on basic needs – drinking water, health care, education and housing – continues, especially in Africa during the numerous recent emergencies. But this intervention strategy is being superseded because of its paternalism and poor performance. Nowadays, the focus is on 'structural aid' in which 'causes of poverty are addressed, instead of only the results'.[2] Oxfam UK speaks of the need to 'secure sustainable livelihoods'. That is, private agencies claim that their interventions will not be needed in the long run since the poor will have reached a level of sustainable development in which external aid has been replaced by local resources and economic surpluses. Current programmes therefore often aim at production and income generation for the poor: small enterprise, credit for (rural) cooperatives, or training programmes for professionals.

This strategy, however, sidesteps a fundamental issue. Without control over the wider context by which these projects' progress are determined, the perspectives for securing sustainable livelihoods by the poor are obviously rather low. Small-scale and community-based often means insignificant, and limited gains made at this level can simply be reversed by policy choices at higher levels, such as structural adjustment. Hence agencies have been obliged to think also about macro-level strategies of change. Some call this evolution a third generation strategy of 'sustainable systems development', while others see it as an effort to address political issues of public policy choice and power within a development-oriented strategy.[3]

Enhancing Participation and Empowerment

The notion that 'poverty is more than the absence of material means ... It is also the lack of access to power'[4] leads agencies to consider development as a process of change in which (poor) people identify common goals and work together to empower themselves and acquire more equal access to resources. To achieve this, human rights have to be guaranteed and the poor must gain the space and capacity to organise themselves, thereby strengthening civil society.

Private agencies claim that they are able to contribute to this structural change, both by defending people's rights and by enhancing the levels of participation and organisation of the poor, that is, through empowerment. But empowerment cannot be 'delivered' by Northern agencies; it is a process and depends more on local people than on (external) resources.[5]

Private aid agencies thus are confined to playing an indirect role of supplying financial resources to grassroots-level groups trying to organise themselves. As these groups are still in a process of building up organisational capacity, agencies channel resources through local partners such as churches or Southern NGOs. Although a substantial amount of private aid is still administered directly by large 'operational' agencies like PLAN International, Catholic Relief Services, World Vision, ActionAid, and Médecins Sans Frontières, complex 'aid chains' have emerged between Northern donors, Northern private agencies, local intermediaries and beneficiaries. Southern NGOs are assumed to stand closest to the poor and are able to promote a collective sense of responsibility. This, it is claimed, could lead to a strong civil society acting as a countervailing power to (undemocratic) governments.[6]

Despite the obvious need for democratisation and participatory development, agency use of these terms is often highly rhetorical. Official agencies including the World Bank have also started referring to participatory development, albeit through top-down approaches. Although viewed with some scepticism, the creation of supportive national and international environments is probably a necessary complementary condition for empowerment strategies to be successful beyond grassroot levels. But again, it limits the role of Northern private agencies to that of remote suppliers of resources to the South. Only a minority of agencies choose to complement the project machinery with other inevitable action: to apply pressure on their home governments to favour these supportive environments by changing their policies.

Comparative Advantages Over Official Agencies

Increasing self-criticism and self-doubt, as well as recent impact studies, have made private aid agencies more modest about their performance. Still, they continue to claim to perform better than average official aid programmes. The claimed comparative advantages of private agencies may be summarised in roughly six areas: better reach, innovation, low cost, speed and flexibility, inclusiveness and higher probity:

- *Better reach*: Agencies claim that they reach the poor and vulnerable, such as female heads of households and the landless, more directly than governments. This is due to their smaller scale of operation that offer easier, better tailored access to communities and grassroots organisations at micro-level. By working closer to the poor (today they seldom talk about the 'poorest of the poor', whom they seldom reach),[7] private agencies contend that they use more appropriate participatory methods as well as understanding and responding to immediate and longer term needs. (In the Interlude following this chapter, a Senegalese social scientist examines the meaning of these terms in actual agency practice in his country.)

- *Innovation*: Being creative in looking for new solutions to old problems is one thing which agencies say they have brought to the development community. Private agencies argue to have led to innovation in (official) development co-operation by introducing new issues (gender, sustainability, primary health care) and new techniques (participatory evaluation and monitoring, appropriate technology). They also act as pioneers in pushing for alternative approaches to privatisation or structural adjustment policies. This capacity partly results from shorter and better communication paths between the organisations that work with the poor and those who can translate this experience into practical inventions and techniques.

- *Low cost*: One of their most durable claims is the use of fewer resources than official aid agencies to achieve the same results. In the market of development projects, private aid is more competitive than official aid, largely due to the smaller size of operations combined with more dedicated staff willing to work for lower salaries.

- *Quick and flexible*: The speed and flexibility of private agencies responding to sudden emergencies is praised as one of their main advantages over government bureaucracies who often are hampered by more complex decision-making procedures and diplomatic obstacles.[8] Agencies are in general also quick to start up fundraising campaigns. However, speed can lead to poor judgement, as the 1994 drama in Rwanda demonstrated, and flexibility can mean that an agency is too easily convinced to change plans that have not been well conceived or negotiated. Or it could mean agencies respond too quickly to changes in local circumstances that might be irrelevant in the longer run.

- *More inclusive*: A condition for successful implementation of development programmes is the involvement of its beneficiaries in all stages. Past experience has shown that projects are unproductive or even counter-productive if the people who benefit are during this process are only passive consumers of aid.[9]

- *Higher probity*: Inhabiting the moral high ground in development leads to the conventional wisdom that private agencies are upright, honest and likely to act with high principles in what they do. Paradoxically, rather than trusting NGOs more, official donors tend to set more stringent, dedicated accounting requirements than they can do to governments.

Driven by Values

The advantages of private aid compared to official aid are inter-related and come down to the virtues of being small, independent, enthusiastic, and allergic for bureaucracy. But small in size does not mean small in ambitions. Private agencies and their partners in the South see that they have a distinctive and strategic role to play for: 'other than the state or the market, civil society doesn't run on power or profits, but on values; they [agencies and Southern partners] can provide the ideal platform for the realisation of solidarity networks between citizens in North and South, conscious of the need for a sustainable development model'.[10]

Appearing to be value-oriented gives private agencies special status in public opinion, a status carefully used in campaigns to raise money. Agencies need this magic image, even if it is over-stated. Seldom do they object to it, for to do so might affect private donations. The danger of not rectifying exaggerated profiles and unwarranted perceptions, however, is that they may create expectations that are impossible to fulfil, leading to inevitable public disillusionment and a perpetual fear of being found out. And that fear leads to defensive attitudes, lack of transparency and a filtering, bending, or glossing over of the truth.

This brings us back to the start of the chapter, namely that the concern of private agencies to maintain a bright reputation as 'virtuous Davids fighting the Goliaths of famine, government inequity, slavery and oppression'[11] calls for an assessment of their claims.

Proofs: How Do Agencies Justify What They Claim?

Making claims about achievements in alleviating poverty and strengthening civil society is one thing, backing them up with evidence is another story altogether. For while assessing impact is simple in theory, it is difficult in practice. Ideally all an agency needs to do to support its claims is to identify what has changed in the lives of people it assists and link this change to the assistance given. Unfortunately for the agencies, these steps are deceptively hard to carry out.

There are three reasons for this. One has to do with the position agencies hold within the aid systems. The second relates to finding out what has actually changed in reality, as opposed to what was intended. Third is an incompatibility between the basic principles of the aid system and accomplishing sustainable development on the ground. This inconsistency produces a paradox when agencies try to ensure, and hence be able to show, that their assistance has caused the changes found.

Problem 1: Agencies and the Aid Chain

Figure 4.1 shows how agencies are part of a chain of organisations which move resources from providers to those in whose name resources are raised, the poor of the world.

Many, but not all, Northern agencies identify and form partnerships with like-minded Southern NGOs which, in their turn, work with community level organisations comprising the people they are trying to assist. Novib, Danchurchaid, and WaterAid work in this way. Other agencies, especially those dealing in child sponsorship such as World Vision, PLAN International and ActionAid, combine the function of Northern and Southern NGOs within themselves. They raise money from individuals in the North and with their own staff work directly with poor communities. However, for most agencies it is very difficult to prove its own performance because they must rely on others to achieve their organisational goals.

The second problem in justifying agency claims has to do with the complexity of the situations they try to affect. Most private aid is packaged as 'projects'. Descriptions usually sketch the existing situation and the problem to be addressed, define the intended beneficiaries and the expected impact on their lives, the sequence of

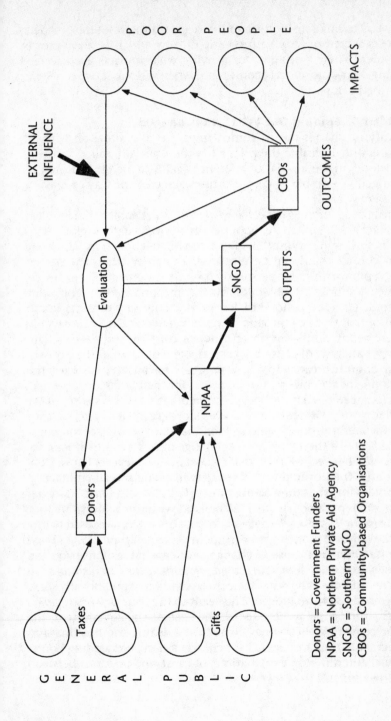

Figure 4.1 Agencies in the Aid Chain

Donors = Government Funders
NPAA = Northern Private Aid Agency
SNGO = Southern NGO
CBOs = Community-based Organisations

activities to be done by different parties and the resources needed. Projects therefore provide the basic unit by which performance is measured. Their limitation for proving what impacts agencies are making on people's lives becomes clear when we look at two problems described below.

Problem 2: Finding Out What Has Changed

Identifying change means comparing a previous situation with an existing one. Defining the prior situation is usually called 'creating a baseline', that is a point of reference against which the future can be judged. A number of complications stand in the way of making this an easy affair.

First, the agency has to decide *what issues are relevant* to the problem to be tackled, for example, poor health or low levels of literacy. This entails sorting out symptoms from causes, relationships which are often complex and can be disputed, especially when the parties involved have different perspectives on development. For example, is poverty simply a problem of low income, and is low income due to people's laziness, ignorance, low productivity, lack of assets, unfair terms of trade, or exploitation by money lenders? Each cause would require a different solution and hence content of a baseline. An agency's analysis of cause is a critical element in what the organis-ation communicates to its supporters because it justifies the development activities and approaches for which funds are requested. Very few agencies have an explicit statement about the causes of the problems they are seeking to solve. More often than not, all they describe are symptoms, such as food insecurity or lack of income.

The lack of a theory of cause or change makes it more difficult for agencies to be precise about what they want to achieve and how. Con-sequently, their overall objectives remain vague and all-embracing. Rationales for what they do are flimsy. Policy choices and strategies are incoherent or poorly justified beyond symptom alleviation. And inconsistencies between means and ends are seldom realised before it is too late and money has been spent. Ask any agency to send you their statements of cause or change and see what response you get.

A second issue is *choosing appropriate indicators or measures*. In other words, deciding what factors are significant and how they are to be recognised and judged. This leads to the issue of *whose opinion counts* – the people to be assisted, the agency, the government, the donor providing the money, who? Establishing the baseline and project plan often forces difficult choices among contending points of view, and differing explanations of cause and relations between the powerful and the powerless.

Tangible indicators, such as a lack of water, health or education services are reasonably easy to define. Levels of poverty become more difficult to specify and the notion of community strength or empowerment even more so. How do you recognise a strong, but poor, community when you see one? Of necessity, indicators of change are usually chosen on the basis of logical inference, common sense, best guess, speculative assumption, or plain wishful thinking. Further, some important indicators or measures of the human condition take place over time, and cannot be determined at one instant – for example, the rate of infant mortality. A final challenge is to ensure that indicators are relevant to the poorer sections of the community – the landless, women, children, the elderly – in other words accurate disaggregation and targeting. The measures eventually chosen effectively define the content of the 'contracts' made along the chain and for the basis for assessing performance.

The third dilemma in creating a baseline is *knowing where to stop*. How wide must an agency cast its net in detailing factors relevant to the community it works with? This issue is important because it sets the boundaries or draws a line around what the agency decides to negotiate and tackle. For example, deteriorating terms of trade, currency devaluation, rampant inflation, government corruption and fraudulent political systems may all contribute to the plight of the poor, but an agency is seldom in a position to redress them. Because causes of problems nest within one another from (inter)national to local levels, the agency has to (a) set a practical limit to what it can address and (b) provide supporters with a frank appraisal of what is beyond its reach.

The technical difficulties inherent to creating baselines are equally present when it comes to establishing the situation during and after an agency's assistance.

Although there are signs that things are changing for the better, most agencies seldom master these problems because they cost money and time, increasing overheads which funders do not want to pay for. It can be argued that these difficulties explain why so few impact studies have been undertaken: the agencies have claimed that it is so complex to create a baseline, that no impact study is better than a bad one.

This, then, takes us to the reason why independent performance assessments are done at all. It is because they are generally undertaken to counter critique; they are seldom used as lessons for future policies. Tom Carroll, wondering why critical analyses of NGO performance mostly come from scholars and hardly ever from donors, points at the dependency relationship between donors and their principal clients: 'All donors have to perform in a manner that their own boards and funding sources find satisfactory if they want to stay in business.'[12] Exposing the real difficulties of performance assessment to constituents hence raises the question of how do agencies know and manage what they are doing? How can they, in fact, enter any 'contract' and be held accountable by those with a legitimate interest in them (see Chapter 2). On what is accountability ultimately based?

In the infrequent circumstance where a good baseline is constructed and change accurately charted, agencies face yet another problem in substantiating their claims, that of determining what has made the difference.

Problem 3: Linking Cause and Effect

Like almost everyone else in aid institutions, agencies portray development as a linear process where, from good intentions, money and technical skill serve as inputs which are transformed in a logical sequence to outputs which, in their turn, give rise to positive predetermined impacts on people's lives. That is, there is assumed to be a known one-to-one relationship between inputs and sustainable human change. This assumption is hardly ever true, but is central to convincing donors and taxpayers that the organisation is making the difference with their money.

The linear assumption does not hold true because as assistance moves further down the aid chain it becomes subject to more and more external influences that cannot be controlled or countered, but must be accommodated. Agency achievements are always contingent on other factors. At the end of the chain, all agency-supported changes taking place among the target population have become dependent on a whole range of other determinants including the weather, a functioning infrastructure, people's attitudes, political stability, inflation, exchange rates, organisational self-interest, government policies, behaviour of donors, shift in international terms of trade and so on. Being relatively small actors on the development stage, the proportional influence of agencies on people's lives within all of these other factors is often not very significant at all. Yet, while some of the more professional agencies recognise the limitations of their contribution to alleviating poverty, the need to present an image of significance and impact means that the reality of contingency is not accorded its true weight.

By shielding assistance from external influence, agencies could try and make a stronger and more direct link between their work and change in people's lives. But, paradoxically, doing so would virtually ensure that the benefits of their support would not last because sustainability occurs when benefits or other impacts can be maintained from within the society without the agency's ongoing assistance. Put another way, unless an agency's activities eventually link into the wider environment in which people live they will not produce lasting change.

Sustainable development requires that agencies integrate their work into the wider context. Thus to be effective, their level of influence must diminish over time. This demand runs counter to a pressure to convince the general public of the agencies' central role, control on outcomes and significance in the development enterprise.

Notions of complexity, dependency and the art of integration and withdrawal – all implicit to sustainable development – do not figure highly in agency claims. Fundraising messages still make a donation appear to be the linear magic bullet which kills poverty.

In the mainstream agency approach, projects are the building blocks for development. But just as you can't define the characteristics of a wall by looking at one brick, you can't define sustainable development and improved well-being as the sum of individual projects. Project achievements contribute to but do not equal development impact. This means that assessing a agency against its overall function in the world, usually called its 'mission', is not the same as and cannot be reduced to evaluating its projects. This distinction is seldom made clear in messages to the public.

Agencies can justifiably argue that providing hard evidence about what they achieve is technically difficult and often costly. In such a situation they can either err on the side of modesty, honesty and caution or be tempted to misuse the difficulties to exaggerate or mislead. Which stance do agencies tend to adopt? One way of answering this question is by examining the few published evaluations of agencies work, together with our own experience and research.

Do Agency Claims Stand Up To Verification?

Impact Studies

Independent evaluations of agencies are relatively recent and few in number. While relying on projects, these studies attempt to look at the performance of agencies overall.[13] In Europe, these 'impact studies' have been carried out by analysts recruited for their independence and familiarity with development and agencies. In all cases the stimulus for these appraisals has not come from the agency community in question. Rather, it has come from outside pressures.[14]

Impact studies differ from evaluations of specific projects or programmes which periodically take place where public funds are involved. In only a few cases, such as the Dutch, Finnish and the Swedish studies, are these made available to the public as a matter of policy. And, despite the involvement of external evaluators, close scrutiny of these studies suggests that they are slanted towards the more successful locations and activities. In terms of hard evidence about the overall achievements of agencies they must be treated with caution, if not a pinch of academic salt. The boxes show the principal features and findings of the publicly available information about agency performance.

Box 4.1: The Danish NGO Evaluation (1988–89)

Scope: Case studies and 17 project evaluations of Danish private agencies in India, East and West Africa and Central America.

Main findings:

Strong points
- Danish NGOs are qualified partners in international development cooperation. They supplement and often complement official aid programmes and are sometimes able to work in alternative ways.
- Danish private agencies are not able to reverse or change negative developments created by weak economies, inefficient governments, falling commodity prices or debt problems. But they can, however, stimulate small-scale development and facilitate local NGOs with resources despite their difficulties.
- The private agencies can play an important role in development education as 'awareness creators' in Denmark and in the North.

Weak points
- The agencies have acted too much as 'owners' of successful local projects, thereby affecting sustainability and hampering local integration.
- Too much competition between agencies for funds in Denmark and good projects in the South, and lack of coordination.
- Unclear delegation and priorities, rigidity and poor communication leading to delays and frustrations.
- Danish agencies have no explicit policies or strategic plans on gender issues.

Data on impact in terms of who was actually reached, their improved well-being, degree of poverty reduction, cost-effectiveness and so on was not provided, despite being explicit objectives of the study. This shortcoming is partly attributable to the lack of baseline information and poorly defined objectives against which effectiveness could be measured, a common shortcoming but a prerequisite for both judgement and effective management.

The study carried out on British NGOs was initiated by the government. It wanted to know about the effectiveness of its co-funding for economic activities. Box 4.2 provides a summary.

Box 4.2: British impact study (1990–92)

Scope: Independent evaluation of 16 rural poverty alleviation programmes of British private agencies located in rural areas and explicitly engaged in poverty alleviation through income generation in countries of South Asia and Sub-Saharan Africa.

Main findings:

- Three-quarters of the projects appeared to meet their objectives and had an impact on the population concerned.
- The level of success was related to: (a) level of participation of beneficiaries in all stages of the project, (b) quality of management and (c) skills and commitment of the staff.
- Agencies and NGOs have paid little attention to cost-benefit analysis; costs are generally higher than expected.
- NGOs often underestimated the wider environmental context in which they are operating.

Assessment of the effects:

- *Reaching the poorest*: most projects fail to do so.
- *Poverty alleviation*: little evidence of improvement of the economic status of the poorest.
- *Sustainability of projects*: few projects would be financially self-sustaining.

When set against their modest achievements, weaknesses in terms of engaging with the very poor and supporting sustainable processes which improve their economic status leave few grounds for concluding that these agencies live up to expectations.

In the late 1980s, a growing chorus of doubt amongst politicians, academics and critical specialists about the performance of Dutch private aid agencies prompted the agencies concerned to instigate an independent review of their work. The work took some 18 months to complete at a cost of about 1.5 million Guilders (nearly US$1 million).

Box 4.3: The Dutch impact study (1990–91)

Scope: Evaluations of 19 programmes of the four Dutch co-financing agencies (Cebemo, Hivos, ICCO, Novib) in six of the 104 countries they work in; focusing on results in income-generation, provision of social services and consciousness raising. Included country studies to provide a national-level assessment of agency impact.

Main findings:

- NGOs are important catalysts in processes of change, but they should not replace the role of grassroots organisations. NGOs are generally too dependent on external aid. Dutch agencies should act more as advisers (transfer of knowledge) and less as financial institution.
- Dutch private agencies are often acting too quickly without prior reflection on real needs. Too little attention is paid to effectiveness and sustainability of interventions.
- Both donor agencies and partners are hampered by a lack of professionalism, pay little attention to cost-effectiveness and strategies directed at increasing financial independence. Mechanisms for accountability of NGOs *vis-à-vis* beneficiaries need to be improved.

Assessment of effects:

- Due to vague or absent initial programme objectives, it was impossible to assess in detail the impact of Dutch co-financed activities. The study could not pretend to evaluate, but only gives a more *superficial assessment of results*.
- Programmes for *income generation* are indeed directed at the very poorest, but it is not proven that they actually benefit from them. The reach of these programmes is limited and sometimes benefits the less poor.
- Programmes providing *social services* (education, health, drinking water) have generally been effective.
- It is doubtful that *conscientisation* programmes generated a significant change in power relations or influenced decision making. Gender-oriented projects have not yet shown fundamental changes.

As an attempt to counter scepticism about the work of the Dutch co-financing agencies, this study did not provide the intended unequivocal confirmation of high performance. The final summary report in English was printed using grey ink. This was probably an unintentional signal that the findings themselves were grey and ambiguous; the case for greater agency effectiveness in development was just not proven. Again, vague starting points and poorly defined objectives worked against finding the evidence needed to prove the agency case. The question thrown up again is how do agencies know what they achieve and on what basis can and do they manage to ensure effectiveness?

Box 4.4: The Swedish impact study (1994–95)

Scope: Thirty-seven development projects located in Bolivia, India, Kenya and Zimbabwe. Assessment against nine broad criteria associated with development impact: poverty focus, degree of people's participation; gender characteristics; contribution to environment and environmental awareness; sustainability; utilisation of Swedish personnel; innovativeness, flexibility and replicability; extent of pre-project appraisal, monitoring and evaluation; the function in promoting democracy and human rights.

Main findings:

- Some 90 per cent of projects were assessed as being likely to reach their immediate, direct objectives.
- However, projects did not correspond to 'good development performance' judged against the nine criteria, although projects may have scored well on one or two.
- Swedish agencies are not very successful in promoting viable income generation projects.
- Poverty impact was generally lower than was claimed; impact was better when social relationships underlying poverty were addressed.

The authors again note the common limitation of vague project objectives in carrying out their work, as well as the complexity of what was intended and a significant lack of transparency and openness in two particular cases. Moreover, its generally positive assessment was tempered by the rider that '... the projects selected were almost certainly biased towards those more likely to be amongst the successful'.[15]

Yet, typical of many studies, the final conclusions do not seriously take the agencies to task for not achieving their organisational goals. The evaluators offer a number of exit routes for agencies by stressing that development is '... a complex, and usually difficult undertaking', '... especially where addressing poverty means addressing power relationships within a community and across communities'; which is almost always the case and has been so since development began.[16] Further, they note that the criteria they applied were not those adopted or negotiated by The Swedish International Development Authority (SIDA) when the grants were made.

What, then, does this observation tell us? Little more than if you move the goal posts, agencies will probably not score many goals. An easy evasion of the real issue of agency effectiveness. Development, again, is not easy – why should it be? But professional, competent agencies will surely have got this right after so many years of trying without evaluators having to tell them what development criteria are? The truth is that, despite strong personal commitment of staff, most agencies are not that professional or competent. They are just not found out.

All these concerned agencies are subsidised by government. The studies were either initiated or pushed by governmental donors. Hence only the agencies receiving public funds face this type of scrutiny. The others have been able to tell their supporters what they want them to know without any independent validation of their stories. Occasionally, agencies, such as Oxfam Quebec, World Vision and War on Want, have faced a hostile press, but the source is often information leaked by disgruntled (ex-)employees. Articles by journalists, critiques by respected academics and public expressions of concern about the value of aid can lead to studies of agency performance. But if and when these appear months or years later, the heat has generally died down, the audience is not so attentive and the staff involved have moved on.

Independent and publicly accessible impact evaluations covering agencies which raise the majority of their funds from the general public, such as PLAN International, World Vision, and Oxfam, are seldom carried out. And if carried out, they are seldom published. Where agencies decide to invest in such an undertaking a common incentive is the prospect of generating positive publicity from the findings. This has been the case with Band Aid's far-reaching evaluation of its assistance during the drought in the Horn of Africa and an independent assessment of World Vision's approach in moving from relief to sustainable development in southern Ethiopia (to be published as a monograph). These initiatives remain, unfortunately, exceptions.

As people involved with agency evaluations and as informed observers of impact study processes, we cannot escape the conclusion that the reasons for undertaking these exercises are not to inform or learn, but to control and justify. Evaluations are still a tool for policing contracts and relationships along the aid chain. Impact studies are an instrument to justify continued governmental funding to agencies in the interest of both the agencies and the aid bureaucracy. Surely the purpose of these efforts must be to learn in order to improve, which means including the embarrassing project failures and blunders that we all make; none of these experiences feature in impact studies. Why not? Private agencies and their donors are still in the mode of negating rather than embracing failure as a source of new knowledge and learning.

Additional Perspectives

In addition to impact studies there is other evidence about agencies' work which paints an even less positive picture about both their direct and indirect effects, the latter being an area ignored in the impact studies. Some examples can be mentioned here. In Mozambique, agencies were found to function as almost a shadow government.[17] They effectively divided up the country between them and determined what services would be provided to which groups, undermining rather than reinforcing the government's own attempts to set priorities. Support for the importation of second-hand clothing in Africa, certainly put shirts and dresses on men and women but at the cost of strangling the livelihoods of local tailors and producers.[18] The copious documentation on food aid, calls into question its long-term benefit to recipient countries but constitutes a substantial source of revenue for the big agencies such as CARE and World Vision, which they are loathe to give up. Indeed gaining a high public profile in emergency provision of food and relief supplies is becoming an important factor in mobilising public support for long-term development work.

This takes us into the area of agency work in conflict situations where their role can perpetuate the very situations they want to stop. The Ethiopian famine in 1985 first brought to light the Mengistu regime's diversion of food aid to its own army, thus sustaining its war effort. Similar experiences are to be found in Somali, Sudan, Liberia and in Rwanda where perpetrators of genocide residing in refugee camps enjoy food distributed by agencies on behalf of UN agencies such as UNHCR and the World Food Programme.[19] Some observers argue that under the flag of humanitarianism an unhealthy symbiosis is emerging between agencies and the UN peace-makers and peace-keepers. 'Something is terribly wrong in the provision of humanitarian aid in Africa', was the comment of African Rights, 'There is little in the last fifteen years that relief agencies can look upon with pride.'[20] The moral dilemmas faced by agencies in conflict situations should not be discounted, but the tighter link between relief profile and development income is tilting the grounds of decision making towards organisational survival and retention of market share, albeit couched in the terms of ensuring continuity in development work.

In making up the balance about agency performance, four areas of agency claims detailed in the first part of this chapter merit particular attention: poverty alleviation, democratisation, being better than governments and being driven by values.

Poverty Alleviation

At best, agency socio-economic impact is modest, but is just as likely to be negligible. It is certainly not able to counter the structural nature of poverty and in Africa, for example, as most of the continent slides into economic decline, private aid only helps people get poorer less quickly. Moreover, agencies' limited economic successes are mostly to be found with people who already have assets and education and hence are unlikely to be the poorest to start with. The poorest are seldom reached.

Improvements in living conditions and people's physical well-being does occur, but this is achieved where agencies act as substitutes for decreasing government provision of social and welfare services such as health, water and education. Little, if any, of this type of assistance is sustainable without continued external funding. The SIDA study found that, in common with others, Swedish agencies could show little lasting impact in Bolivia, one of Latin America's poorest countries. One explanation is the use of a project-oriented approach that '... even if these projects have the goal of initiating learning or organisational processes, they have not been able to create a sustainable and permanent capacity within Bolivia to finance and support civil society initiatives'.[21] What we are looking at, especially in the poorest countries and economies, is not greater self-reliance but a shifting dependency to private aid agencies.

As already seen, an important dimension of agency work are unintended and negative effects. These are seldom noted because they are not being looked for. For example, a project in Kenya introduced zero-grazing with an improved breed as a way to increase productivity of milking cows while reducing pressure on the environment through over-grazing. While indeed generating greater income, the stalling of cattle at the homestead meant that they no longer walked to water, the water had to be brought to them, eight buckets per cow per day. This is women's work. So, while men, who controlled cash income from sales of milk were better off, women became totally overloaded by demands on them as water carriers. Their health deteriorated as a result. This aspect was not seen by the planners whose project had no remedy for the hardship caused.

The situation need not necessarily improve where women are assisted to generate income for themselves, which is presently a high priority for agencies and their donors. For instance, lack of insight as to how households work meant that in Zimbabwe a project

---

Box 4.5: Do Private Agencies Contribute to Poverty Alleviation? (A Selection from Recent Evidence)

'Addressing symptoms of poverty is one thing, addressing its causes are quite another, and in this regard Finnish NGO-supported projects (like those of most NGOs) have not performed so well.' (Finnish evaluation of NGO programme 1994, p. 132)

'Most projects failed to reach the very poorest, and even in cases where poverty alleviation occurred, improvement in economic status was modest. There was little evidence to suggest that many beneficiaries had managed to escape from poverty on a permanent basis'. (British impact study 1992, p. 8)

'Most (Danish) NGOs succeed to some degree, and some to a high degree. It is not difficult to find examples of NGOs working under very difficult conditions in co-operation with some of the world's poorest.' (Danish NGO evaluation 1989, p. 95)

'All economic programmes (of the survey) indeed were directed at the poorest sectors of the population. However, it is hard to acknowledge whether a part of the benefits directly reached the poor. In some cases, it can be confirmed that also non-poorest sectors benefited from the profits.' (Dutch impact study 1991, p. 31)

'The direct beneficiaries [of the 30 evaluated NGO programs] tend to be the 'middle poor', those at the third and fourth quintile of the income-distribution spectrum. (...) Even the highest rated [NGOs] have relatively few direct beneficiaries among the poorest rural households.' (Carroll's study of 30 Inter-American Foundation (IAF) programmes in Latin America, 1992, p. 67)

---

designed to empower women economically meant that as women's income grew, men started to reduce their contribution to financing family needs, instead investing in themselves as well as the brewery. For women it was a negative sum game: they gained little from their new endeavours but were saddled with an additional workload. Turning around these undesirable outcomes is not simply a question of starting another project or modifying the existing one – the causes lie deep within cultural practices and attitudes which are not simply amenable to change because an agency says it should be different. It is as if eradicating male chauvinism in the West can be achieved simply by decree of the women's movement.

Other unwelcome results are to be seen in the weakening of government by attracting away the most competent staff, in the growth of an unsustainable voluntary sector which bears little relationship to the potentials of the local economy, and the growth of tensions within the sector because of a competitive scramble for funds among Northern and the growing number of Southern NGOs. In

Zimbabwe, stress between local NGOs and international agencies has led to the latter being excluded from the national NGO representative body.

The message arising from impact and other studies is that agencies are not as consistently gender sensitive or as able to reach the poorest and most deprived strata of society as their claims would suggest. Existing evidence also raises questions about the scale of agencies' outreach: current, optimistic estimates indicate that they may at most be assisting some 20 per cent of the world's poor, hardly the impression one gets from today's publicity.[22]

Participation and Empowerment: Promoting Democracy

In terms of democratisation, agencies have been shown on occasion to increase the likelihood that people and groups excluded from processes of government will participate and exert themselves. And, in times of political repression or conflict, for example during the imposition of apartheid in South Africa, or during the Pinochet regime in Chile and the Philippines under Marcos, agencies can and do help nurture and keep alive local organisations and leaders who would otherwise succumb to state pressure. Private aid has probably been most effective during stages of political transition, a stage in which official donors often are reluctant to establish relations with the (outgoing) authoritarian regime.

These positive findings must be tempered, however, with equal and more common evidence of agency assistance leading to complacency and dependency rather then assertion and empowerment. It can also produce 'disempowerment', as was the case with a Honduran federation of peasant organisations that, in the late 1980s, suddenly received massive amounts of private foreign aid from a dozen agencies pleased to see the fragmented Honduran peasant movement getting unified. Without time to build the capacity to manage the sudden inflow of new funds, the federation actually collapsed as a result of corruption, infighting over money and inadequate mechanisms to ensure accountability. The peasantry in Honduras are now as fragmented as before. A similar story is told about collective cooperative movement in Zimbabwe in the mid-1980s. And so on.

It is not uncommon to encounter situations where the first question a rural community asks – if they haven't seen the name or symbol on the door of your vehicle – is 'what are you bringing'. The starting point is that agencies are providers rather than enablers or facilitators of the communities' own development initiative and efforts.

Our own experience and available documentation show that the vast majority of agencies are not primarily concerned about better governance and democracy, but with delivering services to satisfy people's needs and with organisational survival. Why? Maybe because Board members are usually far from radical; more often than not they are from among the 'great and the good', possessing a social conscience or a hankering for social status or they are chosen because of useful links to the regime in power. Another explanation could be that leaders and most staff are from the educated middle class where work in an agency presents an opportunity for livelihood rather than a personal expression of solidarity with the plight of the poor and marginalised. Fortunately, there are still a number of exceptions to this trend, particularly in those agencies trying to provide new opportunities for alternative North–South power relations in the 1990s.

Agencies have been known to take on the voice of the people they are meant to serve. Meetings and fora are common arenas where this happens, with agencies being invited to explain the needs and situation of the poor in their countries. This talking by proxy weakens the role of elected leaders and the foundations of democratic process. Profiling on behalf of other people, usually without a mandate, also helps agencies to attracts funds. Other people's poverty and marginalisation become a resource to be exploited rather than a struggle to be won.

The influence of agencies can extend to the point where local institutions are relegated to the back seat or where external support is captured by the existing elite to reinforce their positions. Leading figures in the current and previous Chilean governments all have vast history of running NGOs during the opposition period of the 1980s.[2?] However, today the NGO community in Chile has almost ceased exist. Throughout Africa you can find local committees named af the agency which instigated them as 'owners' of their projects old man in East Africa was proud to announce during a ch meeting on a remote rural road that he was the Chairman of International, a status probably unknown to the Internationa located in Europe. While in Ethiopia, Tanzania and Zim agency support through churches was found to reinforce auth top-down structures.[24]

By offering services where government fails and by artic needs of people who are poor, agencies can and do un growth of forces by which people will assert thems own interest. The current priority to provide credit to than pressuring for public policies which will rever ing skewing of incomes towards the rich is but agencies buying into an amelioration rather than strategy. This is particularly the case where the be productive endeavours of poor people are appropr economic systems.

Box 4.6: Do Private Agencies Enhance Participation and Empowerment? (Indications from Recent Research)

'There are no examples of principle change in power relations, nor of an essentially changed way of decision-making.' (Dutch impact study, 1991)

'In some projects the beneficiaries have quite genuinely been empowered; in others any empowerment remains nebulous both in concept and practice.' (Finnish evaluation of NGO programme, 1994: 140)

'[NGO] strategies that provide tangible benefits in the short run are often used to stimulate the process of participation but do not automatically lead to long-term growth in participation.' (Carroll 1992: 92)

'[NGOs] may be closer to the rural poor than are public agencies, but their claims to be allies of the grassroots are being questioned by those they allegedly represent: an indicator that their own actions would need to be democratised in order to enhance their contributions to the alternative development based on empowerment (...).' (Bebbington and Thiele 1993: 205)

In sum, the record of agencies directly impacting on wider democratic processes in countries or regions is not encouraging. Governments have more than enough ways of keeping agencies and their local intermediaries in their place – as welcome substitutes for public services and placators of what might otherwise be a potentially destabilising mass of people who are poor and politically marginalised. For example, a study of the political impact of Latin American NGOs in the 1970s and early 1980s found little evidence to support the widely held view that they had been particularly instrumental in helping overthrow the military regimes common throughout the continent.[25] The experience of Nicaragua and El Salvador has shown that competing private foreign aid agendas helped polarise emerging civil societies there, thus obstructing democratisation.[26] A study in Kenya found that agencies were more likely to maintain the status quo than alter it in favour of the poor.[27] Overall, despite the misleading but politically correct use of the term 'empowerment', the bulk of the agency community is developmentally conservative and unempowering, happily fulfilling traditional roles of social support and welfare provision. The vocal advocating a different position in development do not correspond the mainstream of agency activity.

Better Than Governments

t and other studies did not look for and hence do not provide ce about the comparative merits of governments and private aid agencies as agents of poverty alleviation and forces for social justice. This is because it is virtually impossible to make a fair comparison between governments and private agencies; government can legislate and control many of the conditions under which it works, while agencies are not in a similar position. In addition, it is difficult to identify and attribute overhead or indirect costs to an activity or output, like installing a well or running training programmes. How much of a Ministry's administration should be taken into account? Without precise norms of judgement, hard, undisputed, comparative figures will not be generated. In terms of poverty alleviation, therefore, we are set to remain in the realm of logical inference and common sense when assessing comparative advantage.[28]

When it comes to social justice, the prospects of making firm statements about agencies versus governments are almost as remote. That is because not all private agencies are progressive and assertive in terms or people's rights and not all governments are conservative and bent on maintaining the status quo. However, one place to look for the impact of private aid agencies on justice in society is the area of public policies: do they work for or against the poor and excluded? Analysis on this area in Africa, suggest that agencies have a long way to go when it comes to shifting policies in pro-poor ways. By and large, they lack the necessary analytic capacity, contacts, points of leverage, fora for exchange, necessary mandates and financial resources to exert significant influence.[29] Exceptions occur when governments want or need agency inputs, such as when trying to formulate policies in new areas such as prevention and treatment of HIV and AIDS, enabling the informal sector or choosing appropriate technologies. But pushing on an open door is not the sort of situation agencies portray when talking of their role in advancing social justice for the poor. Reality suggests, however, that willing-buyer-willing-seller is the more likely scenario than winning a struggle when agencies do make an impact on the public arena.

Even the much-publicised achievements of agencies in influencing official policy statements drafted at international conferences, such as on environment at Rio de Janeiro, on population in Cairo and on human rights in Vienna, seldom translate into similar impacts within the countries signing such agreements. Back on home ground, agencies must take more care lest they invite the unwelcome attentions of security services or a hostile press.

Driven by Values

All organisations are driven by values of some sort. The for-profit sector values money, on occasion tinged with a concern for social resp sibility. Public bureaucracies value and strive for order, consistency and stability. Political parties value and aspire to power. For agencies today, as preceding chapters show, there is little doubt that rapid expansion in number and size, driven by official aid, is pushing their values into areas of, at best, altruistic ambiguity and at worst naked commercialism within a cloak of charity.

Agencies with a strong identity and constituency face serious dilemmas about what they stand for, how they should respond to the age of contracting, how to retain and reward competent staff, how to stay true to their principles and so on. Others, and it looks like the majority in North and South, in the name of survival and increasing the scale of their mission will set their sails to catch the donor breeze, becoming contractors in all but name. Juggling with these dilemmas make the values of some agencies appear full of contradictions. For example, they criticise emergency assistance for not being a solution, while simultaneously boasting about the resources they mobilise for this. Could it be that the contribution to public profile, organisational overheads and annual turnover of emergency aid tilts the balance against consistency of message and the beliefs which underlie them?

Yes, as the rest of the 1990s unfolds, agencies will remain driven by values, but given the scramble for aid contracts these will probably not be the values of civicness and social calling in the name of the voiceless.

Conclusions

While uneven in scope and quality, none of the independent studies available gives unequivocal support to the claims and images created by agencies. Up until the late 1980s, as marginal actors in development, agencies enjoyed the benefit of the doubt about their performance along the lines of 'good intentions are enough'. With the dramatic growth in their numbers and funds available to them, agencies no longer enjoy the 'security of obscurity' and a simple public *a priori* belief in their effectiveness. Increasing external and critical scrutiny of agencies over the past few years means that the jury is no longer out. Indeed the jurors appear to be re-entering the court of public judgement wearing a sceptical face.

It is only in exceptional cases, such as Danchurchaid's investigation of Alan Boesak's NGO in South Africa, that agencies are strong enough to make misuse of funds openly known through the press. Seldom are cases of misappropriation pursued in the courts or made public in other ways. For to do so would shatter the moral myth, which is not seen to be in anyone's interest, apart from the donor, that is, who stays in the dark.

Setting claims against reality shows that being an agency does not simply and assuredly equate with being a cost-effective agent of sustainable, equitable, effective and gender-sensitive development. It is the lack of freely available objective information which hides this fact and inhibits the general public's ability to separate rhetoric from reality and the wheat from the chaff. And, because all agencies face the same difficulties and vulnerabilities when it comes to proving their worth, none is inclined to rock the boat by suggesting that they alleviate poverty or enhance democracy better than 'brand X'. This leads to a bizarre situation of agencies competing in a donor market-place where buyers cannot reasonably compare the products on offer or their relative value for money; they must still choose by an act of faith.

By not making public their internal assessments of performance allowing comparison with others, agencies engage in a subtle form of market manipulation, a novel type of conspiracy. From this per-spective, a consumer's guide to agencies, produced by an independent entity, is long overdue. Agencies not wishing to collaborate in such an undertaking could be readily questioned about their motives, trans-parency and even honesty.

Agencies have, more through omission and careful phrasing than through straight dishonesty, not presented a fair picture of their per-formance, nor made it clear that it is virtually impossible for them to do so. They have not been inclined to allow outsiders to openly examine their work and make their findings known. They err on the side of exaggeration about their roles and impact, overstating accom-plishments and their power to affect poverty and injustice. This does not mean that they do not have a crucial role to play in shaping how the world evolves, but they must adopt a different, more humble and honest stance towards those supporting them. Failure to do so will only set agencies up for a fall as more and more information about their work inevitably enters the public domain. Going by their past record, however, its looks unlikely that agencies will take the step towards open public scrutiny unless it is forced on them.

What can we say overall about agency performance on the basis of the impact studies and other evidence? First, if we hold to the dis-tinction made between performance in projects on the one hand and performance in sustainable development, poverty alleviation and democratisation on the other, agencies can show some modest success at the first but can take little or no credit for the second. Yes, some projects do reach the poorest; yes, lives have been saved in emergencies; yes, trees have been planted, wells sunk, incomes raised, children educated, groups have been formed, women better protected and their rights respected. But remember, the studies have been biased towards success stories like the Grameen Bank and Bangladesh Rural Advancement Committee (BRAC) in Bangladesh, *Se Servir de la Saison Sèche en Savane et au Sahel* – Using the Dry Season in the Savannah and the Sahel (Six-S) in West Africa and Organisation of Rural Associations for Progress (ORAP) in Zimbabwe, so often held up as examples. These are still to be replicated and become the rule rather than the exception.

The developmental impact of agencies in terms of lasting solutions to poverty, exclusion and injustice have yet to be found. And this is not because the investigators of the studies did not try. The hard truth is that the goals they set and aspire to are beyond them. The problems they address are too complex. The agencies' size and institutional position does not give sufficient leverage on the larger forces and systems which keep the poor poor. And their financial dependence on government does not allow them the autonomy to challenge the self-interest of Northern countries that stand in the way of change. As we know them, most agencies are essentially a product of colonialism and the Cold War.[30] Through their existing development and relief projects on the ground, they are not going to be the catalysts and force for poverty alleviation, inclusion and social justice in the new world order.

Notes

1. Joint press release by Cebemo, Hivos, ICCO, Novib, reacting on the publication of the Dutch impact study (GOM: Oegstgeest) 28 January 1992, p. 4.
2. ICCO, undated, *Participation in Development, General Guidelines of ICCO*, (Netherlands).
3. The evolution of private agencies (and/or Southern NGOs) is often characterised as a three-stage transition process, suggested by Elliott, (in 'Some Aspects of Relations Between the North and South in the NGO Sector'): from welfare to development, to empowerment. Korten (in 'Third Generation NGO Strategies: A Key to People-centered Development') calls these stages generations of programming strategy and identifies relief and welfare (1st generation), small-scale self-reliant development (2nd generation) and sustainable systems development (3rd

generation). Both articles in A.G. Drabek (ed.), 1987, Development Alternatives: The Challenge for NGOs, *World Development* (Supplement), Vol. 15.

4. Oxfam UK and Ireland, 1993, *Mission Statement*, p. 1

5. Elliot, 'Some Aspects of Relations ...', pp. 57–8; Rowlands, J., 1995, 'Empowerment examined', *Development in Practice*, Vol. 5, No. 2, pp. 101–7.

6. J.P. Thérien, 1991, 'Non-governmental organizations and International Development Assistance', *Canadian Journal of Development Studies*, Vol. 12, No. 2, p. 272.

7. G. Griffiths, 1987, *Missing the Poorest: Participant Identification by a Rural Development Agency in Gujarat*, Discussion Paper No. 230 IDS, University of Sussex, May.

8. D. Rondinelli, 1994, *Development Projects as Policy Experiments: An Adaptive Approach to Development Administration*, Methuen, London.

9. There is substantial writing on participation in development. All of it points to a positive relationship between people 'owning' development processes, and the effective use of resources and sustainability of benefits. This causation is seen normally to hold true for all levels and types of development actors: from communities to senior government officials and international policy makers. See, for example, P. Oakley, 1991, *Projects with People: The practice of participation in rural development*, ILO, Geneva; and, World Bank (1994), *The World Bank and Participation*, World Bank, Washington DC. See also, in this volume, I.-P. Lalaye, 'Practicing Democratic Development: Cases from Senegal', pp. 136–43.

10. Ekstermolengroep, 1994, *Naakte keizers of volwaardige partners? Rol en plaats van de NGO-beweging in de internationale samenwerking*, NCOS (National Centrum voor Ontwikke-lingssamenwerking), NCOS, Brussels, p. 16 (authors' translation).

11. J. Clark, 1991, *Democratizing Development*, Earthscan, London, p. 52

12. T. Carroll, 1992, *Intermediary NGOs: The Supporting Link in Grassroots Development* Kumarian Press, West Hartford.

13. Evaluations of individual agencies projects or programmes are more common, but findings are seldom made public. Our analysis is based on the following impact studies of agencies: Denmark: DANIDA, 1989, *Danish NGO Report, Synthesis*, Ministry of Foreign Affairs, Copenhagen; United Kingdom: R. Riddell *et al.*, 1990, 'Judging success: Evaluating NGO approaches to alleviating poverty in developing countries', *Working Paper*, No. 37, Overseas Development Institute, London; R. Riddell and M.

Robinson, 1992, 'The impact of NGO poverty alleviation projects: Results of the case study evaluations', *Working Paper* No. 68, ODI, London; Netherlands: GOM, 1991, *Betekenis van het medefinancieringsprogramma: een verkenning* (Significance of the co-financing programme: An Overview), GOM, Oegstgeest; Finland: FINNIDA, 1994, *Strengthening the partnership: Evaluation of the Finnish NGO support programme*, ODI/Ministry of Foreign Affairs, Helsinki; Sweden: R. Riddell, A. Bebbington and L. Peck, 1995, *Promoting Development by Proxy: An Evaluation of the Development Impact of Government Support to Swedish NGOs*, SIDA Evaluation Report, No. 95, Swedish International Development Authority, Stockholm.

14. In the case of The Netherlands the agencies concerned chose to finance the work from their own resources, which was not the case in Great Britain or Denmark.

15. Riddell *et al.*, *Promoting Development by Proxy*, p. 62.

16. Riddell *et al.*, p. 63.

17. J. Hanlon, 1991, *Mozambique. Who Calls the Shots?*, James Currey, London and Indiana University Press, Indianapolis and Bloomington.

18. Marc Van Laere, 'Oude kleren, stof tot nadenken', *Wereldwijd*, No. 246, 1994, pp. 4–11.

19. African Rights, 1994, *Humanitarianism Unbound?: Current dilemmas facing multi-mandate relief operations in political emergencies*, Discussion paper No. 5, African Rights, London; M. Duffield, 1995, 'Protracted Political Crisis and the Demise of Developmentalism: From Convergence to Coexistence', Discussion paper presented at International Seminar 'Aid under Fire' at Sussex, April.

20. African Rights, *Humanitarianism Unbound?*, p. 36.

21. A. Bebbington and A. Kopp, 1995, *Evaluation of the Swedish NGO Support Programme: Country Case Study Bolivia*, ODI, London, January, p. ix.

22. UNDP, 1993, *Human Development Report*, Oxford University Press, Oxford.

23. K. Biekart and A.E. Fernández Jilberto, 1991, 'Europa y la socialdemocratización de la política en América Latina: La renovación ideológica de la izquierda en Chile', *Revista CIDOB d'Afers Internacionals* (Barcelona), No. 20, pp. 5–27.

24. M. Schmale, 1993, *The Role of Local Organizations in Third World Development: Tanzania, Zimbabwe and Ethiopia*, Avebury, Aldershot.

25. B. Smith, 1990, *More than Altruism: The Politics of Private Foreign Aid*, Princeton University Press, Princeton.

26. K. Biekart, 1994, 'La cooperación no-gubernamental europea hacia Centroamérica: La experiencia de los ochenta y las tendencias en los noventa', *Documento de Trabajo*, No. 3 (San Salvador: Prisma), Noviembre.

27. A. Fowler, 1993, *Non-Governmental Organisations and the promotion of democracy in Kenya*, Doctoral thesis University of Sussex, December.

28. A. Fowler, 1988, 'Non-Governmental Organisations in Africa: Achieving Comparative Advantages in Micro-Development', *Discussion Paper*, No. 24, Institute of Development Studies, University of Sussex, Brighton.

29. M. Bratton, 1990, 'Non-Governmental Organisations in Africa: Can they Influence Public Policy?', *Development and Change*, Vol. 21, pp. 87–118.

30. Of course, there is a small minority of agencies (usually the ones not subsidised by government, and often harassed by government) representing the spirit of citizen concern – call it solidarity – that is often so sadly missing in the world of private aid agencies.

Interlude: Practising Democratic Development: Cases from Senegal

Issiaka-Prosper Lalaye

Editor's Note

The preceding chapter painted issues of claimed results, including partic-ipatory, democratic institutions, on a broad scale. The following text complements that chapter's broad canvas as a miniature. Yet for its micro-cosmic focus, it is no less illuminating of universal patterns.

In Africa, especially since the end of the Cold War, official donors have begun tying their aid more strongly to performance in what they term 'good governance'. They also mandate the involvement of local people in aid project implementation, even to the point of conjuring up acceptable forms of 'community-based organisation' where such things had not hitherto existed. For their parts, private aid agencies and their Southern NGO branches or intermediaries now hold high the banners of 'participatory development'. They assert the primacy of transparency and 'ownership' of programmes by 'the communities involved'.[1] For them, democracy is not merely a pre-condition but an essential *precondition of authentic development.*

But how do the aid agencies go about putting this rhetorical resolve into practice? The following article considers some cases in Senegal. As in many other African countries, various local-interest groups have welcomed private aid agency/Southern NGO programmes. Similarly encouraging is the Senegalese government as it disengages from social development tasks, thus fulfilling what one close observer describes as a 'fundamental objective: the World Bank's desire to push ahead with its policy of transferring gov-ernmental responsibilities – and burdens – to peasant organisations'.[2] Private aid agencies in Senegal thus enjoy a certain protected status, if not unreserved admiration.

This modest inquiry, commissioned specially for this book, reflects Southern researchers' views of Northern intervention in their country.[3] It is a condensed and translated version of a longer paper[4] synthesising the results of the study in 1995 coordinated by the author.

Presuppositions

Why should we look to agencies/NGOs for evidence of democratic practice? There are several reasons. In general they operate with fewer constraints than government agencies, and work at closer proximity to ordinary citizens, where they become more intimately aware of needs and obstacles to fulfilment of need. They must respond not with words but with deeds, thus making local participation indispensable to achievement of aims.

Indicators of Democratic Practice

We chose to probe the realities of democratic approaches along five dimensions: knowledge, strategy, means, results and critical evaluation:

- *Knowledge* confers power. This power may be used in democratic or anti-democratic ways with respect to those who do not possess it.

- The *power over strategy of action* is a key indicator. What is to be done? Who should do it when, and in regard to what overall process? How such concrete questions of action are answered can reveal much about the democratic content of agency/NGO intervention.

- Among the means needed to bring about action, money plays an unparalleled role. *Attitudes and behaviour with respect to money* provide insight into democratic conduct of NGO/agency activities.

- Results of NGO/agency interventions provide a fourth means of analysing the democratic content of 'the developers' as well as 'those to be developed'. *Who participates* in the gains and the losses of collective action may be considered a key indicator of democratic content.

- Finally, participation cannot be complete if those involved are denied the *right to criticise*. Criticism allows for improvements, a concern of all actors, not just the directors.

Units of Analysis and Context

Selected for study were two transnational private aid agencies operating in a region of Western Senegal through locally-registered branches. One of them, which we call Agency A, is a church-based body active in the zone since the early 1970s. The other, a secular organisation which we call Agency B, has worked here since the early 1980s. They were chosen because of their relative accessibility and prominence. The precise degree of autonomy of the branches from central agency authority could not be determined. But in neither case is one dealing with wholly autonomous 'NGOs', although the branches may present themselves as such in Senegal.

Four micro-projects of Agency A and five of Agency B were selected for attention. These projects are based in seven rural or semi-rural villages within an 80-kilometer range of a major Senegalese city. Here Islam is virtually universal, and the position of the village *marabouts*, the male politico-religious leaders, is strong. All the projects aim to boost participants' income, such as through fattening sheep, sewing garments, gardening vegetables and raising fruit trees. A few additionally provide chances to gain literacy skills. Eligibility for benefits depends on membership in groups set up specially for the projects. One project group is composed entirely of young men, while one (a sewing workshop) is composed entirely of women. All others are mixed groups of men and women. With the exception of one village, all project participants belong to the same ethno-linguistic group.

Under supervision, four Senegalese researchers, sociology students at the University of Saint-Louis, visited project sites and interviewed key informants. These included intended beneficiaries organised in project groups, village notables and representatives of the branch of the private aid agency.

The following summarise main findings, grouped according to the five dimensions of democracy sketched above.

Democracy in Knowledge

In every project studied, local people had to state their need for it. Such collective expressions suggest that people know how to define and articulate their needs.

This sounds promising, but it does not guarantee democratic management throughout. Our findings suggest that agency attitudes toward local knowledge is anything but democratic. Some of their projects ignore good local practice. Women in the sheep-fattening project said they could fatten their animals with better foodstuffs and at a faster rate than that recommended by the agency's extension officer. The young gardeners said they could harvest their onions better according to their own schedule – something the agency representatives had refused to accept. And the women's sewing workshop had to give up their traditional tie-dye methods in order to 'meet modern preferences'.

If democracy implies valuing local knowledge on an equal footing with imported knowledge, then the practice of the agencies is not democratic. Even where agencies pay lip-service to local good practice, their agents are surrounded by a halo of power that reproduces inequality in their relations with participants. The abandonment of traditional know-how is the price paid in order to 'develop'.

Democracy in Setting Strategies

Agency A says that it will only finance a project if the request has been drawn up by groups whose officers are selected democratically. Similarly, Agency B holds that project requests must come from the people themselves. In short, intended beneficiaries are the initiators of strategies, at least in principle.

Yet to the outsider, it appears at first glance to be the agencies, not the people, who are the masters at the game. It is the agencies' prerogative to set the path and the activities to reach project goals. Project groups, for example, are often artefacts of agency intervention, not of spontaneous local initiative.

However, these are merely appearances. Local factors weigh heavily on every project's orientation, modifying strategy. Chief among these factors is the local elite, and what its members do to remain in charge or to influence everything in their communities. Traditional leaders, not necessarily elected through democratic processes, lay claims on the projects meant to meet needs of the populations at large, especially the least advantaged. Another factor is the local market. Price fluctuations do not allow a 'linear' application of plans. Good faith and good planning are not enough; project participants must be able to adapt to continually changing circumstances and forces.

Participation in setting strategies has to be understood in this context. Strategic choices have to be made not only at the outset, but along the way, sometimes over several phases impossible to project in advance. Among the nine projects studied, only the sewing workshop showed evidence of continual participant control over strategies. This was the only case in which participants learn to cope with the turbulence of the economic environment.

Democracy in Financial Means

For Agency A, local financial participation is usually minimal, being at most 4 or 5 per cent of total project costs, or even nothing at all. Agency B on the other hand, requires that at least 25 per cent, and sometimes 35 per cent, of project cash outlays be borne by local participants. They must also provide free labour or food, such as to feed the bricklayers' building project construction works.

However, when it comes to money management, things remain in the hands of the agencies themselves.

Agency A states that the leaders of local groups enjoy full rights to inspect the books. But our findings suggest that this is purely a nominal right. No villager has ever exercised it. In general, benefits local populations are supposed to receive are not assessed in figures. Participants do not know exactly what they give and what they get. The leader of a garden project group supported by Agency B refuses to inform other members of the total weight of the groundnuts she takes to market on behalf of the group. On those rare occasions when they are told about such matters, villagers are genuinely astonished to learn the (for them) enormous amounts of money that donors apply to these projects.

In such circumstances, it is hard for beneficiaries to assume any responsibility over project means, especially money. Contrary to the case of inequalities in knowledge, unequal power over money automatically confers a hierarchy that is hard to correct. It is only in fables that the rich share their fortunes equally with the poor. The inequalities introduced by money appear to be indestructible. Nevertheless, even a situation of inferiority *vis-à-vis* the agency as a donor does not necessarily jeopardise internal group discipline to prevent an individual from monopolisation or siphoning off of benefits – as illustrated by the sewing workshop group and one of the gardening groups.

The groups studied all state that they lack confidence in their agency 'partners'. However, in matters of money, the problem is usually more complex. 'The community', as if it were one homogenous thing, turns out to be an agency illusion. For to the degree that the agencies wish to aid the poor, they find that these are the least accustomed to handling large sums of money. Especially when these sums seem to 'fall from the sky', they exercise a powerful attraction. It is not so surprising, therefore, that when groups are formed, even without outside interference, monies collected will commonly be entrusted to a few 'rich' villagers rather than to the poor.

Democracy and Results of Collective Action
Strikingly, the projects studied make little if any profit. Financial returns to beneficiaries are minimal. Added to that, virtually none of them is ever seriously evaluated.

Where there are profits, prominent families monopolise most of them. Once again, only those groups with strong internal structures, such as the women's sewing workshop, manage equitably to redistribute what little profit there is. Yet agencies generally take a *laissez-faire* approach in matters of distributing the fruit of joint effort. Similarly, where there is no democratic management, members can end up shouldering losses they had not directly incurred. In one project, an individual from the group had convinced Agency B to give him a loan for a business venture. It failed, and the other members were saddled with the debt.

In sum, the study turned up evidence suggesting agency indifference in regard to results and to the distribution of gains and losses.

Democracy and the Right to Criticise

Although senior officials of Agency A say that they are ready to take seriously any critique, every village group involved in the nine projects studied holds the firm view that 'they (the agency representatives) do not wish to take account of what we say'. Villagers find it deplorable that there are no gatherings or meetings to allow them to express their views, counsel and criticisms. But at the same time, they told researchers that whenever a gathering does take place, they had never seized the chance to make known their concerns. That is because such meetings have been ritualistic moments to ratify the status quo. What villagers would like are meetings in which the atmosphere allows for open expression of what everyone really thinks.

This is not easy. Local cultural habits, and the mutual wish to preserve tranquillity, and to repress the urge to draw attention to shortcomings, create major barriers. Thus whenever a moment to take stock of the agencies rolls around, consensus among intended beneficiaries is more apparent than real. In the presence of agency officials and their local extension agents, who are strangers to the local communities, no villager will be crazy enough to express publicly an opinion likely to create animosity with a neighbour. Such brazen behaviour in a village would, after the strangers had departed, demand unacceptably large efforts to soothe feelings and patch up relationships.

Thus, to elicit public criticism in an African village that is frank, consistent and effective, measures have to be taken to organise it, nourish it and above all to protect those who are supposed to generate it and benefit from it. For critical African intellectuals, of course, things are different; as urban dwellers they tend to be less vulnerable to the constraints faced by villagers.

Can Development Be Democratised?

To answer the question, Do agencies democratise development?, we examined the practice of two of them, noting acts and omissions along five dimensions. The results force us to answer the question in the negative. Doubtless they would like to do so, but for the moment these agencies are not yet succeeding in rendering development *democratic*, that is, *participatory, accountable and egalitarian*.

But rather than resign oneself to further trials of good intentions, let us ask whether development is at all democratisable? For if, by its very nature, development cannot be done democratically, how can agencies or their Southern NGO branches or partners achieve in the Third World something that more powerful actors have not managed to achieve elsewhere?

In industrialised countries, which are so assured of being developed, is development so democratic as it seems? Do all development actors there work in participatory, accountable and egalitarian ways?

If everyone participates, what do we say about the unemployed and excluded? If development actors are accountable to each other and the broader society, what do we say about the persistence of poverty and the enormous environmental problems created by development in these countries? And what should equality mean if the developed countries of today's world are supposed to represent egalitarian development?

Despite their good intentions and all the good that they do, Northern agencies working in the South do not yet succeed in democratising development, not even in the way development in the North projects itself as democratic. For this development is fundamentally non-egalitarian and unaccountable – toward the environment and toward that 'underdeveloped' part of humanity.

To develop is never easy, especially if development should be not of the privileged but of everyone, regardless of race, sex, age or skin colour. *To develop democratically*, for the time being, is merely a slogan. As such, it elicits a lot of hope. But who would dare to say that hope is worthless?

Notes

1. See, for example, International Council of Voluntary Agencies, undated, 'Relations between Southern and Northern NGOs: Policy Guidelines', ICVA, Geneva, mimeo. These guidelines were among the points of reference used in framing this study.

2. B. Lecomte, 1992, 'Senegal: the Young Farmers of Walo and the New Agricultural Policy', *Review of African Political Economy*, 55, p. 88.
3. For other recent cases, reaching conclusions similar to those presented here, see N. Nelson and S. Wright (eds), 1995, *Power and Participatory Development: Theory and Practice*, Intermediate Technology Publications, London.
4. Prof. Issiaka-Prosper Laleye, 1995, 'Les ONGs et le développement démocratique', Saint-Louis, typescript. Fieldwork reports were prepared by Mr Abdou Ndao, Mr Khadidjatou Sam, Mr Oumar Ndiaye, and Mr Amadou Sarr Diop.

5

Northern Lights

David Sogge

They may still be fragile beings, but in these neoliberal times, most private aid agencies and their Southern NGO associates have enjoyed the protection of a favourable political climate in the North. After all, they represent *private* initiative, which can be the next best thing to private enterprise. Funding authorities and much of the media have decked agencies in the cloak of love – as long as they don't begin making unreasonable political noises, that is. Agencies should be seen but not heard.

But that's where the trouble begins: some non-governmentals, including a few private aid agencies, decline to be docile. The ones who start sounding alarms about global apartheid find themselves increasingly exposed to attack. They risk getting smeared as 'special interests'. Conservative hostility toward outspoken organisations is growing. Today, in North America at least, there is talk of a 'war on nonprofits'.[1]

And these are not their only difficulties. From the South, agencies are also feeling pressure. Their Southern 'partners' are politely declining to be spoken for any longer. Southerners are tiring of agencies which busy themselves with the problems of people far away while pertinently ignoring the same kinds of problems at home in the North.[2] Some have begun bypassing their would-be agency allies, sending their own persuaders to Brussels and Washington. As one Central American small farmer leader put it, 'Others always used to speak in our name. That's now changed.' And about the non-profit groups which try to speak for smallholders in Central America, and have absorbed most private aid flows, he expressed himself bluntly: 'We don't need all those NGOs.'[3]

These are strong words from the South. They add a counterpoint to hostile noises from the North. Private aid agencies are not used to such attacks on their *bona fides*. The criticism after all, is of established hierarchies and roles: the chain of help from Northern donor via Southern NGO to 'beneficiaries', and the prerogative to lobby on behalf of others.

Such tensions are not new. Since the time of Dickens's Mrs Jellyby and her charitable campaign on behalf of the natives of Borrioboola-Gha, the helpers' communication practices have touched but also annoyed people both in the South and in the North. Trying to be helpful for some, they can end up just being *trying* for others.

And yet the agencies' most powerful assets are in persuasion, not in delivery. By putting across telling messages matching their principles, a few have helped change policy and thus achieved far more (for far less money) than many hundreds of mini-projects and relief aid ambulances. That other agencies ignore these triumphs and cling all the more firmly to their soup ladles of benevolence is itself a telling message.

Shifting Pressures, Shifting Paradigms

Voices from the South have for years called on Northern agencies radically to change their communication policy on home ground: first, to stop patronising and stereotyping people in the South, especially by portraying them as helpless objects of pity. A main request is: Get the poverty pornography out of agency advertising. Second, to apply pressure on Northern centres of power to stop practices – war, support of dictatorships, economic bullying and other forms of domination – that actively disadvantage people in the South, and, incidentally, make a nonsense of much development aid there.

Ironically, the founding impulse behind several groups that later became private aid agencies was to do precisely that: to take a stand against official Northern arrogance or indifference toward peoples in distress. Christian Aid, Catholic Institute for International Relations (CIIR) and Oxfam are examples in Britain; Novib is an example in The Netherlands. *Private* charity was perhaps useful to generate interest and make symbolic gestures, but it was originally a *secondary* motive. To mobilise shame and apply public, political pressure (in some instances to prise loose aid from *government*) was the main task.

Today, that task has been taken up by another type of non-profit group mentioned earlier in this book: knowledge-based NGOs, including those actively campaigning through action and information. Amnesty International and Greenpeace are foremost examples, but even less well-known NGOs like the World Development Movement in Britain or the Third World Network based in Malaysia are forces to be reckoned with in North–South policy battlefields.

These NGOs generally do not command the large resources of the agencies. Because most do not advertise, they are poorly known to the public. But with their command of facts, tenacity, and flair for pushing their arguments, they have been setting the pace in debates ranging from food policy to the arms trade to the aid business itself.

Together with environmental and poverty action groups, these pushy types of organisations – sometimes with help from a few progressive private aid agencies – are challenging a central tenet of the aid paradigm, namely, that The Problem is 'out there' on a poor periphery of the world, whose misfortunes have no connection with acts and omissions by the powerful in the wealthy core of the world.[4]

Most aid agencies look at the North as the source of money, goods, and knowledge for transfer abroad – an activity logically demanded by the conventional attitude, and the assumption of Northern superiorities. Some in those mainstream agencies would agree that the North also has its problems, and wields unaccountable powers. But they usually get shouted down by managers and owners who argue that those things have little to do with underdevelopment and besides are not the province of a private aid agency.

Today, however, while such views may match commonplace public sentiments, they are no longer tenable for some private aid agencies, even those not known for antipathy to the established order. Take for example what a prominent article in the magazine of *World Vision International* had to say in 1995:

> Not only has the model of economic growth failed globally as a means of ensuring a just distribution of the earth's resources, it also is failing in the North ... [T]he challenge to World Vision, as well as other NGOs, is to be committed to a process of learning and education that will challenge prevailing expectations and consumption patterns. This focus on unsustainable consumption expresses Mahatma Ghandi's observation that 'there is enough for everyone's need, but not for everyone's greed'.[5]

Startling words, given their source. They suggest that even agencies steeped in the politics of the religious Right and the Cold War can reach the point – at least in their rhetoric – of smashing their icons and rejecting old orthodoxies. A culture of contentment may dominate the age, but notions of fairness and redistribution are refusing to go away. From them arises a new discourse with themes markedly different from those backing standard remedies of aid and economic growth.

Timidity and Temerity

Yet most agencies, even those without any roots in anti-communism or religious fundamentalism, shy away from talking about causes and taking stands on public issues. Call it prudence or call it timidity, inhibitions still rule. What are the chief inhibitions, and how valid are they?

Upsetting Public Givers

Agency managers usually have to cope with an understandable fear of biting the hand that feeds them. By their lights, the North is where you raise money, not where you pose awkward questions about institutions in the North itself. Agency communication strategists tend to be riveted to matters of agency growth or survival: how to gain or retain contributors in a tightening charity market, how to gain or retain friends in high places – who are themselves on the defensive as official aid budgets are slashed.

Inside the agencies, struggles around basic purposes and strategies loom large.[6] In the 1990s, emergency aid factions retook ground lost in the 1970s to the structural anti-poverty camp. Where hostile media and nervous constituents are seen to lurk outside, and strong compartmentalisation and weak management beset the inside, managers may elect simply to keep their heads down, making only perfunctory gestures toward education and advocacy. They have evidently asked themselves why begin raising the complex matter of causes, let alone loaded issues of over- and under-consumption in the North, where there are handsome and blameless results to be gained from straightforward appeals for charity?

But fears of upsetting public givers may be exaggerated. A recent study by an 'apolitical' child-sponsorship agency in the US suggests that contributor loyalty and donations in fact go up where fund appeals go beyond images of pitiful children to include explanations of socio-economic issues and community-wide approaches to poverty.[7] In mounting political pressure, high-profile environmental NGOs have long demonstrated that active, even combative campaigning can attract supporters and improve balance-sheets; some aid agencies now claim similar results.[8] Many contributors favour agencies 'with attitude'. There is evidence, in short, that development education pays. Even political pressure can pay.

Displeasing Funding Authorities in the Official Aid System

As private aid agencies have become favoured public service contractors, authorities in the official aid system make a point of seeking

private aid agency opinion. They set up consultative forums for policy dialogue; on occasion they pay for agency participation at international gatherings and special governmental events. World summits on food, the environment, population and poverty can afford agencies, usually in the company of knowledge-based NGOs, with chances to make a difference in policy – or at least in policy utterances. Their participation has sometimes meant that conferences end not with a mealy-mouthed statement of wishful thinking but a forceful document with staying-power as a global point of reference; the work of Oxfam UK and Ireland in respect to the 1992 UN Conference on Environment and Development illustrates this.[9]

But where the policy-makers' chief aim is to 'get them into the tent', risks increase that instead of doing the leveraging, the agencies themselves will be leveraged. In the early 1990s, the former head of Canada's official aid body Canadian International Development Agency (CIDA) said repeatedly, 'The [agencies] have to get on the policy trail; the Government will just have to learn to live with criticism.' However, such signals are often mixed with other, hardly welcoming signs; on macro economic or weapons issues, agency opinion is commonly ignored. Policy dialogue is then exposed as pseudo-consultation.[10] Southern 'partners' of aid agencies usually spot co-optation when they see it; in the late 1980s, South African NGOs receiving money from the European Union (all of it by way of Northern private agencies) threatened to refuse further funds because the Europeans were failing to follow their promised complementary policies of pressure on the apartheid government.[11]

Agency fears of cooptation by official aid funding authorities may be just as valid as fears of being punished by them. Lacking an explanation of causes and their own clear strategies and social bases, agencies risk remaining the soft, cuddly face of what is often ugly geopolitical calculation.

Agencies are Paid 'Not to Think but to do'[12]
Most agencies shrink from challenging powerful and reputedly well-informed aid bodies with their own findings. Few agencies have built up capacity for policy research. The humiliating supposition is that, 'with their hugely greater resources, agencies like the World Bank can develop [counter-arguments to agency critiques] at a speed and a level of sophistication which no NGO can match'.[13]

Yet campaigners North and South, often operating with fewer resources than the private aid agencies, have challenged these powerful institutions' analyses, whether on debt, dams, or the real significance of 'development'. Not infrequently, they have found them wanting. Knowledge-based NGOs such as the New Economics Foundation in London and Redefining Progress in San Francisco question the validity of conventional indicators of national well-being, such as GNP per capita; they put forward alternative indicators that match public intuition more closely.

Would the World Bank and IMF enjoy their reputations for intellectual invincibility if media gatekeepers bothered to check their claims? Recent evidence about aid approaches in the Sudan and Lesotho suggest that they should. In those countries, and probably many more, the IMF and others largely overlooked the unregistered economy, especially remitted wages. Their mental models scarcely resembled economic reality. Policy prescriptions based on such travesties turn out not merely off-target, but perverse.[14]

Falling Foul of Agency Minders

Custom, national statute and the agencies' own charters can often limit what they can say and do in public. Those enforcing tax laws, sometimes prompted from behind the scenes by political interests, are the source of ultimate sanction in many lands. However, the means of skirting statutory rules are many, and the official watchdogs often prefer to avoid confrontation; an agency determined to put across a strong message can usually do so with impunity from statutory authorities. In 1991, that most salient instance of Western governmental control, the Charity Commissioners for England and Wales, rapped Oxfam on the knuckles for its campaigns on southern Africa and Cambodia. But close students of the subject think that even this watchdog poses no serious threat to the prudent activist aid agency.[15]

Self-regulation and self-censorship are probably far more common, and effective, modes of control. Today, those closest to funding authorities tend to wield decisive powers over public utterance. But subtle control occurs through peer pressures and formal trade associations. Codes of conduct of those associations tend to discourage only the worst excesses of advertising, however, and not to prescribe modes of education and advocacy.

Educate and Advocate in Whose Interest?

Even if credibility is high and social standing firmly rooted, agencies must still cope with other obstacles arising from interests within and outside themselves which steer communication practice along accustomed paths.

Self-promotion

On the face of it, private aid agencies approach the public and decision makers to inform and influence them about the problems and potentials of others. To summarise one broad strategy of the mid-1980s,[16] agencies aim to convey information and analysis, promote humanitarian values, and motivate citizen action chiefly with regard to poor people in poor countries.

Promotion of one's self – the pursuit of revenues and reputation – is merely a prerequisite, goes the rationale. Agencies do it only to make the rest possible. But as Chapter 3 notes, many agencies find it hard to get the genie of the market back into the bottle. Self-interest and selflessness are together in the saddle, and ride agency communication strategists over a publicity steeplechase.

This drives communication practice toward ambiguity or silence. Most hesitate, and make careful calculations before taking a stand on disputed public policies, such as free-market fundamentalism, or a popular military crusade. Despite some surprising shifts, such as the radical utterances cited above from a World Vision publication, few private aid agencies take such stands.

A common response is simply to blur the vision. The charitable project gets subtly conflated with development itself. Self-publicity comes to masquerade as 'raising awareness'. This approach has evidently reached such alarming proportions in the United States that recent codes of conduct of a main agency trade association explicitly call on every member to 'make a clear distinction between its fundraising and development education efforts'.[17]

On the policy advocacy front, it can be asked if the situation in the mid-1990s has moved fundamentally beyond that of the mid-1970s, when an agency researcher based in Europe hypothesised that 'Voluntary agencies are most likely to resort to pressure activities when their own operations or immediate organizational interests are jeopardized ... and least likely to speak out on issues that touch on the political and economic self-interest of the high-income countries';[18] or beyond that noted in the mid-1980s by a well-informed observer of US agencies: 'Much of the existing NGO public policy activity tends to be directed toward the rather limited objective of assuring more government resources for NGO programmes.'[19]

The Big Tent of Official Aid

Defence of official aid is a broad tent. Few agencies omit it from their public education and advocacy efforts, and many seem to take it as a moral duty. Across Europe, for example, agencies have spearheaded campaigns to raise official aid allocations, with the symbolic 0.7 per cent of GNP as the target norm. Yet over the content and quality of official aid, agencies are usually much less vocal.

Defending official aid comes naturally to most agencies, not only because many depend on state revenues for their overseas work, but also because governments give them money to raise that defence. Legislation enabling government subsidies for development education is commonly justified by needs for a domestic constituency for official aid. Especially in smaller, export-dependent states with strong traditions of social welfare – Canada, Sweden, Denmark, Norway, The Netherlands – building public sentiment for foreign aid is deemed a public service, and agencies are among those 'contracted' to provide it.[20]

Subsidies to development education and advocacy are just one way official aid agencies help build a constituency for aid, and often not the most significant. Getting other institutions into the tent has also been important. A 1994 survey of national advisory bodies on foreign aid or North–South relations in 17 European countries showed that scientific and policy research institutes are most commonly represented in official aid advisory councils, while private aid agencies are the second most commonly represented, with business and trade unions in third place. However, business interests are anything but marginal actors. Advisory councils free of agency or research interests exist in some countries, such as Germany, where the Working Group on Developing Countries, chaired by the Federation of German Industry, provides a formal channel for corporate influence on North–South issues.[21]

Since the 1970s, local governments and chambers of commerce, professional and academic associations, trade unions and the environmental NGOs, and now the military and police, have acquired a stake in official aid, joining an already well-ensconced coterie of lobbyists representing agribusiness, manufacturing, trade and transport interests.[22] Choirs singing the praises of foreign aid are small but gaining more voices; especially now that aid budgets are under pressure, the repertoire seems more confined than ever to the old fundamentalist hymns.

Getting more people to pay attention to North–South issues can of course be a good thing. When a police trade union or a city council or a women's group discovers that international cooperation is not the complex affair they thought it was, and begin engaging across borders, the gains in both the South and the North can be important. But successful twinning and linking does not depend on congruence with official aid agendas; indeed freedom from those agendas often yields more promising outcomes.[23]

The end of the Cold War brought neither a clear re-centring of official aid policy on poverty alleviation, nor the peace dividend to make it possible. More common was Western triumphalism, louder claims for neoliberal remedies, and more intense downward pressure on aid budgets. Agency managers may privately acknowledge the waste, corruption and uselessness of much official aid, but find themselves rallying to defend it all the same. No wonder, then, that coherent strategies for education and advocacy continue to elude the private aid agencies.

The Interventionist Spin: 'Rwanda was the best thing that's happened to us in years.'

The urgency and drama of humanitarian crises have a compelling power. Indeed agencies may position themselves strategically: stationing sentinels in field offices, stockpiling emergency supplies, and keeping media contacts warm in order to gain logistical and publicity advantages when crises arise. As noted in Chapter 3, agencies face irresistible pressures to make acute human suffering, and dramatic interventions, the very core of advertising. The impact on revenues can be spectacular, often in direct proportion to the enormity at issue. At 1994 year-end review meetings on both sides of the Atlantic, agency staff heard their fundraising colleagues remark, 'Rwanda was the best thing that's happened to us in years.'

Communication practice can also affect practice on the ground, often to prolong crises – often making them, unintentionally, more lucrative. The imperatives of media-led marketing reinforce a type of 'humanitarianism' whose logic requires the presence of Northern 'helpers' to rescue passive locals in quite controlling ways, such as camps.[24] From Biafra to Cambodia to Somalia to Rwanda, a pattern of cascading decisions has repeated itself. The humanitarian cart is placed before the political horse. The intention was to save lives but the cumulative effect was to block peace initiatives, and probably prolong and even increase the agonies of many.

Relief agencies now say it would be better to prevent humanitarian crises from occurring in the first place. But the public exposure of the roots of these crises remains a low priority. In part that is understandable. Even if an agency has the capacity to make them (and few have bothered to build such capacity), explanations are complex and speculative. Moreover, they can often lead to damning indictments of official aid bodies which offer agencies large contracts – as, for example, in the cases of American meddling in Somalia and French military aid to Rwanda. In those countries, the diktats of Northern powers helped produce the extreme economic stress and social friction that brought catastrophe to those countries.[25] In short, preventive whistle-blowing is obviously the better humanitarian option, but that by no means guarantees its popularity with funding authorities and those they contract to manage crises.

Agencies can spend years striving for balance between messages often logically difficult to reconcile:

- They are strong people coping well!
  - They are needy victims unable to cope!
- Self help works!
  - Help works!
- Let local priorities rule!
  - Let today's donor criteria rule!

Market-driven humanitarianism is throwing agency communication strategists off-balance. Respect for self-determination and people's capacities to resolve their problems, traditional themes of advocacy and public education, get drowned out in a drumbeat of calls for 'humanitarian' (military) intervention.

Such calls are nothing new. To promote its role in Vietnam in the 1960s, CARE suggested to the US military, 'The CARE Relief Campaign offers every American a way to take a personal part in the winning of this war.'[26] Some 30 years on, CARE's President was calling for troops to 'move in and run Somalia'.[27] Boundaries between humanitarian and military action are breaking down. Agencies with a flair for the bold and decisive stand to reap handsome rewards. The often perverse outcomes, after the humanitarians have departed, are much less well-reported, as the sanguinary cases of Somalia and Rwanda show. Public education in such a climate can be a thankless business.

Mediatised Passivity
Portrayals of crisis and need in faraway places carry effects beyond those of evoking empathy or jingoism. They are also about things close to home in the North, in particular, self-regard and identity. The interdependence of the media and private aid agencies for their mutual advantage illustrates this. A British anthropologist has treated at book-length the perils and paradoxes of media manipulation by agencies.[28] He offers many cases of television's powers to enchant and distort, to reproduce heroic narratives as 'news' and thereby to satisfy Northern audiences' needs for myth. Such rehearsals of self-confirming sagas are nowhere more evident than in the case of agency intervention in the South, particularly at moments of crisis.

Marking this pattern is the preponderant role of outsiders – the agencies, governments and media – as noble rescuers. Local people, on the other hand, are often portrayed as helpless victims or bystanders, or mischievous troublemakers.[29] The self-congratulatory story line of trouble-helplessness-rescue is thus repeated again and again.

The interplay of agencies and media generates images (and realities) of passivity and irresponsibility. At another level, the interplay of televised media with their audiences in the North poses curiously similar problems. The bombardment of reports of horrific events has a levelling effect: the one is as gruesome and hopeless as the next. Feelings of compassion may follow, but also, perhaps more powerfully, passivity and self-abnegation. For those who are themselves excluded the feeling arises, 'Can I complain, me, a mere unemployed person with nothing, in the face of these unceasing catastrophes on the planet? How could I dare to protest at "my" reality?'[30] Agencies wanting to elicit solidarity rather than charity must swim against powerful streams.

Media gatekeepers and the businesses that run them hold considerable powers to stereotype people in poverty and poor countries. This can be done with respect for their cultures but with subtle messages that reassure the comfortably-off. Running parallel to public education efforts, and in the US at least with far greater impact, is the magazine *National Geographic*. This national institution, edited near the corridors of power in Washington DC, reaches 37 million people each month with images of 'an idealized and exotic world relatively free of pain or class conflict, a world stumbling or marching on the path to modernity ... What this style shows is at stake is an American national identity that is rational, generous, and benevolent.'[31]

Conclusion

In the charity market-place, an official aid system, now increasingly allied with security establishments, and a media industry eager to produce more 'infotainment', are powerful interests that push and pull at agency communication practice. Given current rules of the game, agency managers may quite rightly want to keep communication strategies pivoting on the attraction in the near term of resources for agency self-perpetuation and growth. But to avoid talking about causes – issues of pain and class conflict – in communication strategies is no necessary guarantee that an agency will continue to attract resources. Indeed the longer-term impact may be contrary to such expectations.

Impact

What are the effects of agency communication efforts, especially those termed 'education' and 'advocacy'? The short answer is: No one really knows.

There are two main reasons for this ignorance: First, to gauge impact beyond, say, the simplest costs:returns ratio of a television commercial, is a tricky and complex undertaking. Agencies often lack clarity about what, beyond 'raising awareness', they aim to achieve. Where many other influences are at play, it is difficult to attribute an achievement or failure to a given agency that uses a given approach at a given moment.

Second, conceptual frameworks about the impact of non-state actors, and research within any frameworks, are poorly developed. Two close observers of the influence of the 'poverty lobby' on British domestic policies conclude that 'the question of interest group effectiveness is probably the least adequately researched aspect of the study of pressure groups.'[32] In the mid-1980s, 15 years after it had become a standard piece of aid agency furniture, there was still 'conspicuously little' evaluation of development education.[33] By the mid-1990s, little had been done to fill that gap.[34]

In short, knowledge of what has worked and why is poorly developed. Practitioners are assembling some notions slowly, mainly through case studies, anecdotes, and trial and error. The following pages review some findings by students and practitioners of agency public education and advocacy – the latter sometimes also referred to as lobbying or political pressure. For some, it is strategically important to keep the two firmly apart; for others, it is precisely of strategic importance to gear the two closely together in for mutual reinforcement. They are treated separately here chiefly to ease presentation, not to sharpen the distinction, which is generally overdrawn.

Effects of Development Education

With no fixed curriculum, discourse, or pathways to professional credentials to be followed, and with audiences, scope of content, duration, methods and aims almost as diverse as the agencies promoting it, development education takes highly amorphous, non-comparable forms which resist easy assessment.

As managers in the 1980s addressed problems of agency isolation, short-term and erratic funding, ad-hoc staffing, poor organisation and conceptual weaknesses, there began to emerge something resembling strategies and programmes. Some of these have been reviewed in depth.

Reaching European Farmers and Trade Unionists
In one of the broadest studies to date,[35] a team of eleven researchers from three European universities reviewed 33 of the 410 development education projects promoted by 22 aid agencies and other types of NGOs in nine European countries in the period 1984–8 with subsidies from the European Commission in Brussels.

About half the projects aimed at organised publics in rural areas where the content pivoted mainly around North–South aspects of agrarian issues, particularly the impact of European farm policies and surpluses on rural life in the South and North. The other half were concerned with urban publics and pivoted on North–South dimensions of industry and labour, such as the shift of industry to low-wage zones, effects of European trade policy and the Social Charter, industrial development in the South, labour markets and migration, and the interplay of peace, environment and industrialisation.

Overall, the 17 farm-focused education projects did help organisations of farmers, students, and consumers take the issues on board, moving some of them to press for shifts of farming practices. However, they brought only a few participating groups to take action, such as one group's helping press parliamentarians on GATT negotiations and the issue of animal fodder imports from the South.

The other half – 16 industry-focused education projects – generally helped members of participating unions to gain a better grasp of where they, and workers in the South, stood in the world economy. In some cases they strengthened special units in unions to address Southern/global issues and helped them exchange information across borders about multinational corporations. But as with the farm-centered projects, they generally failed to lead groups to take concrete action. A major lesson was: the leap to macro-issues is a long one; the more concrete and relevant to union members (at a time of crisis for many of them) the more interested they will be.

More significant was the impact on the agencies and NGOs themselves. Most of them gained in skills, motivation, capacities to plan and execute programmes. They also gained credibility and ties with community-based organisations of farmers, consumers and trade unionists. Two development education-action networks emerged as a result: IRENE (International Restructuring Education Network Europe) and RONGEAD (Network of European NGDOs on Agri-Foodstuff and Development). Both have complemented the work of trade unions and farmers' organisations in Europe, and, as noted later in this chapter, have helped private aid agencies score successes in European policy battles.

Awareness-Raising in The Netherlands: High Output, High Consumption
In 1970 the Dutch government created the National Commission for Development Education (NCO) as an independent statutory body to draw public attention to Southern and North–South issues. It has functioned chiefly as a subsidy window for a broad range of Dutch groups, media projects, special events and a few private aid agencies. With an annual budget in the mid-1990s of about US$11 million (and rising) it funds around 500 projects each year.

These subsidies have for years been under right-wing parliamentary attack. In 1992, the Minister of Development Cooperation ordered a review of the work of the NCO. The resulting report[36] helped account for the Dutch support across a broad political spectrum for North–South activities, including foreign aid.[37] It noted that NCO-supported projects annually reached more than 5 million people. But the impact on Dutch schools, churches, municipalities, trade unions and other institutions proved to be even stronger than the impact on the public at large. Its most significant effect, then, has been the creation of a substantial social infrastructure for communication and a tradition of debate about Southern and North–South issues. The report concluded, however, that it is impossible to isolate the effects of NCO-subsidised activities from the many other influences on Dutch policies toward poor countries.

After 30 years, what have been the concrete outcomes of this effort by activist NGOs and some private aid agencies? In 1993 a leading figure in this 'Third World movement', whose activities depended to no small extent on the NCO for twenty of those years, ventured an assessment that in The Netherlands

> ... general opinion about the origins of poverty [has] changed. In social organisations and political parties the problem of poverty has become an important theme for discussion and policy. Finally, at the governmental level, the Third World Movement managed in a number of cases – especially where it concerned violations of human rights and political oppression – to turn policy around.[38]

A 1994 opinion survey confirms the scope of active Dutch public concern about problems in the South. The Dutch express it mainly through charitable giving; eight out of ten say they give something toward poor country causes. The strongest support for private charity comes from the centre of the political spectrum; those with party-political preferences on the Left favour official foreign aid ahead of private aid. There is a strong hint of a guilty conscience: almost half of all Dutch adults think that 'we' (better-off Northerners) are partly to blame for the problems of poor countries.

However, the survey indicated that the public is losing faith; a mere 27 per cent felt that aid monies are well spent while 35 per cent considered them badly spent; 32 per cent thought they were partly well spent, partly not. Eight years earlier, the Dutch had been more sanguine about aid: in 1986, 38 per cent considered aid monies well spent, a mere 16 per cent poorly spent and 39 per cent in between. Such disenchantment was described as 'a time-bomb under readiness for future support'.[39]

It would be virtually impossible to attribute any of these trends to private aid agencies' communication strategies alone. However, it is plausible to assume that their overall contributions have been relatively modest. More important have been the efforts of the government-supported regional Centres for International Cooperation (numbering 16 in 1995), and beyond them the hundreds of church fellowships, action committees, youth wings of political parties, trade unions, municipalities and film makers constituting the 'Third World movement' just noted.

The Dutch national investment has also paid off handsomely for aid agencies active in the Dutch charity market, now one of the most lucrative in Europe. Several transnational aid agencies with only shallow roots in The Netherlands moved up rapidly in this market in the 1980s, yet they have contributed little to public education about development issues.

Development Education in the US: Sobering Conclusions

If public education efforts in The Netherlands spring up in a lush and well-watered garden, then those in the United States cling to their niches for survival in a howling desert. Subsidies are minimal and tend to be narrowly focused on school-based and adult education. Churches, action groups, unions, some private aid agencies and knowledge-based NGOs do what they can with modest resources and highly ambiguous signals from central government.

Perhaps typical of many was an effort by the educational arm of Church World Service to promote 'global education' in mainstream Protestant churches through a series of two- to four-day seminars in the period 1985–8. Despite deliberate efforts to recruit 'new learners', the 371 participants of ten seminars were mainly lay activists and pastors, that is, people already alert to the issues. As planned, the chief outcomes were tested methods and materials for use within the wider circuit of affiliated churches. However, an evaluation of the effort produced not the predictable recommendation for more and better booklets about African poverty, but rather a proposal to make development education pivot on first-hand exposure to poverty and exclusion at home: 'We need not travel overseas to have this experience. The "other" lives next door! "Third World" realities exist in our cities and towns. Refugees, farmers, and welfare recipients, as participants in seminars, repeatedly challenged the impression that global injustice happens to someone else somewhere else.'[40]

In 1983–4, a working group representing about 20 private aid agencies drew up *A Framework for Development Education in the United States*. Described as an unprecedented commitment by US private aid agencies 'to press beyond overseas programs to address structural aspects of global hunger and poverty',[41] its results have never been formally evaluated. However, in a series of workshops ending in June 1991, more than 300 people, many of them staff of mainstream private aid agencies, met to reflect and to draw together a plan 'even more powerful and persuasive for the 1990s as the *Framework* had been for the 1980s'.[42]

Assessing the results of the *Framework* was not the chief aim. But in reference to it, and to aid agency efforts of the intervening seven years, workshop participants reached some sobering, even damning conclusions. They felt that development education had 'played at best a marginal role'. Most of it was:

> ... concerned more with short term tactics than overall vision or strategy ... Even the non-governmental organizations specifically concerned with the plight of the poor often consider their development education activities as little more than an add on to an institution founded for other purposes ... Many NGOs still see their educational efforts like a village project: preparing curricula for a specific school or program ... Many NGOs appear to be looking for donors, not constituents; to deliver services rather than to work for transformation.[43]

Participants concluded that while the 1984 *Framework* had many merits, 'development education' was an outmoded concept, keeping agency activities apart from those of other related groups, restricting thinking about what is possible, and appearing too narrow or ambiguous to others outside the development education community.

Against the kind of marginal incrementalism and puny scale of conventional development education, the group proposed an alternative *Agenda for Action*. At its heart is the concept of transformation.

Its three key objectives, each linked with specific strategies and action plans, are:

- Shifting thinking and action among US private aid agencies, especially to enlist them in advocacy and constituency building;
- Gaining a place for global education in schools and universities not as one more special interest, but 'as a concern that permeates education generally', and
- Mobilising support for a global, transformative approach by linking with other affinity groups, knowledge-based NGOs, non-US organisations and especially popular movements.

The *Agenda* introduces a key proposition: 'Only when individuals and organisations become active participants in grassroots movements with a common agenda will we be successful.'[44]

Conclusion: From Self-Promotion to Transformation?

Development education efforts have been modest relative to the resources potentially available to them, especially from private aid agencies whose turnovers run into tens of millions. So too their outcomes. Exceptions, such as in The Netherlands and Scandinavia, arise where the investments have been large and sustained enough to create something like a critical mass of institutions. But even there, and probably everywhere else, it is hard to rebut the trenchant American (self-) critique and counter-proposal. A real breakthrough – general acceptance that it is in most people's mutual interest to achieve transformation, and thus to educate and advocate for it – has yet to be made. The environmental movement may have achieved such a breakthrough, but in the agency-dominated sector of development, there is as yet no North–South common agenda.

Impact of Policy Advocacy

From the British and Foreign Anti-Slavery Society in the 1840s and the anti-imperialist circles in the 1890s to domestic anti-colonial movements through the mid-twentieth century, private organisations have applied public pressure to shift Northern policy toward non-Western countries. One reason for their continued reappearance is that they sometimes succeed. Today, at the urging from social movement leaders in the South and from their own constituencies, private aid agencies are asked to do more.

Voluntary groups have usually spearheaded such efforts. But certain types of private aid agencies have made substantial contributions.

Foremost among them, although curiously absent in most writings on aid agencies and policy influence, are the endowed foundations.

Endowed Foundations and Policy Leverage
Because of their association with policy-making elites, the old endowed foundations might be better portrayed as objects of lobby and pressure, not as active agents practicing those arts. Given the many revolving doors connecting some foundations with big government and big business, this is a reasonable objection to considering them here. It is hard to dispute one liberal observer's broad conclusion, repeated in two book-length surveys, that ' ... the profile of their activity is clearly conventional, not reformist. They are over-whelmingly institutions of social continuity, not change'.[45]

Yet they do operate with formal autonomy, often far more than some not-so-private aid agencies, and address issues common to other private aid agencies. Their frequent success in influencing public and private policies of many kinds, including those affecting poor countries, means that there is something to learn.

Foundation grants account for only a small fraction of overall private aid agency flows. And although the large old foundations have clearly enjoyed privileged access to governing and opinion-forming elites, those advantages cannot explain all of their enormous influence. Shrewd strategies explain more: All the key foundations active inter-nationally have pursued systematic, long-term investment in the South and the North to generate ideas and the institutions to translate them pragmatically into policy measures and technologies. They consult extensively among themselves. Their joint efforts to steer the course of policy are sometimes exposed with embarrassing effect, as recently occurred in the United States, where the Rockefeller-led consultative group, the Environmental Grantmakers Association, was 'frankly plotting to shape the agenda of mainstream environmentalism'.[46] Using such approaches, Ford, Rockefeller and Carnegie have helped set the trends and the tempo in aid and development thinking for more than 50 years.

Foundation investments in key universities and research centres have yielded many of the concepts and methods underpinning official and private thinking about economic development, governance and other poor country issues. Some of the key outcomes have permeated discourse and practice in aid and other aspects of North–South relations:

- 'Modernisation' theory, and an ideology of developmentalism emerging in the 1950s from support to behaviouralism in the social sciences, especially political science research focused on Asia, Africa and Latin America (Ford Foundation);[47]

- Area studies programmes at US universities (Ford) and various social science disciplines, notably anthropology, in British universities (Rockefeller foundations);[48]
- 'Community development' models of intervention, forerunners to integrated rural development approaches of the 1970s, were in essence designed politically to counter the Communists; India was a main testing-ground in the 1950s, where projects took place in close collaboration with early US aid programmes (Ford).[49]
- 'Green revolution' technologies to boost crop yields (Rockefeller);
- 'Human resource development', especially in Africa, aimed mainly at creating technocratic elite cadres to lead modernisation processes, pivoting on support to universities and institutes of public administration and, through scholarship programmes, to universities in the US and Britain (Carnegie, Ford);[50]
- 'Law and development', an effort led by US legal professionals acting as 'missionaries' to transmit US legal norms and methods, gained official backing and reached perhaps its greatest scope in Latin America in the 1970s; but was overtaken in importance by grants toward human rights NGOs and networks (Ford);[51]
- 'Community development corporations', semi-public authorities set up chiefly to rehabilitate housing and restore some economic life to US inner cities; begun in the 1960s, and later supported by government, the model now being exported to the South with some success (Ford).

Like other private aid agencies, the foundations have financed tangible projects for poverty alleviation in poor countries. But unlike the others, they tend to invert the priorities: short-term gains for beneficiaries are merely auxiliary objectives; the chief aim is experimentation for long-term policy purposes.

A crucial complement to these policy experiments, however, has been strategic emphasis on the 'knowledge industries' of higher education, research, publishing, media and on interchange among policy makers. Institutions in both the North and South are involved. The timelines tend to be long, sometimes stretching over decades. They pivot on intellectuals and elites (including disenfranchised elites) and do not stray far from conventional paradigms.

The anti-poverty impacts of these concepts, and the institutions to convey them, may be open to serious question. But there can be little doubt that as ideas in good currency among decision makers and opinion formers, they have commanded wide and respectful attention. Having set the agenda and the discourse, the foundations achieved that crucial power of leverage, making their relatively modest grants go a long way. Other private aid agencies, and the official aid system, abetted by universities, think-tanks and the media have all put money, talent and energy over long periods toward programmes shaped by these ideas, however flawed. That, after all, is what the foundations set out to do.

Few foundations and other private aid agencies have moved beyond elite-centred (conservative or Fabian socialist) approaches to include contact with new social movements and other sources of countervailing norms and power. The challenge to the foundations is to make their enormous policy influence available to those movements – or at least to clear channels for the movements to do it themselves. A few private funders, such as the Wiebolt Foundation and the Woods Charitable Fund in the United States make community organising a major part of their domestic grant portfolios. A challenge to other private aid agencies is to learn from the foundations' example.

Campaigns on the Issues
A number of 'policy successes' surface repeatedly in writings on private aid agency and NGO efforts in advocacy and pressure.

Challenging Corporate Practices
At the top of several writers' lists of achievements[52] are the international curbs imposed on the sale of powdered baby milks. At the outset, this could have been dismissed as a non-starter: it meant a head-on confrontation with multinationals where millions in profits were at stake. Yet a coalition of organisations took on the food giants, mobilised shame, and over years of well-publicised skirmishes, kept on succeeding. The effort also led to permanent changes in public health practices. For example, in besieged Sarajevo in 1992, health-workers intervened with a public education campaign to prevent the unhygienic use of the breastmilk substitutes.

At least 140 citizen groups in 70 countries now monitor developments on this front. The number of infant lives thus saved due is not known, though it may be in the tens of thousands every year. Diarrheal diseases make up about one-sixth of the world's 'burden of illness', accounting for 1.3 million infant deaths in 1990.[53] The accumulated cost of the world-wide campaign and current monitoring on the issue (not counting the funds which the multinationals used to fight it) might approach US$10 million over 20 years. In cold cost:benefit ratios, few conventional development projects can touch this one in efficiency and impact.

Adoption by the UN's Food and Agriculture Organisation of an International Code of Conduct on the Distribution and Use of Pesticides is another instance of public pressure on large vested interests. Like the International Code of Marketing of Breastmilk Substitutes, it is not legally binding on companies, and few have complied with it officially. NGOs and trade unions are key sources of follow-up and further pressure. The global 'burden of illness' reduced due to this campaign is not known, but the main point is this: If well done, concerted public advocacy can yield greater positive effects for far less money than any health project to treat the victims of pesticide misuse.

Citizens' groups and knowledge-based NGOs were vital to these triumphs, but what roles did private aid agencies play in them? In the case of breastmilk substitutes, perhaps the most strategic one was to seize upon the issue (in this case identified in a 1973 advisory report for the United Nations) and call attention to it. Here credit is due to War on Want, an agency whose political vision predisposed it to look for vulnerable places in the armour of large corporations, and whose policy it was to make public pressure a top priority.

Thereafter, after some years of hesitation, other private aid agencies took up the issue. The bulk of the work fell to specialised groups and a coordinating body. The world campaign on pesticides arose through NGOs and trade unions, and received start-up finance and publicity from Oxfam UK. But it operated on its own. This suggests an organisational key to success: an acceptance of a division of labour. Agencies supply the funds, and where they can, access to information and policy makers; so doing, they should then let the specialised, knowledge-based NGOs get on with the job.

Questioning Official Aid Policies

Criticising official aid is not something any agency does lightly, for reasons suggested earlier in this chapter. A misplaced word can put its survival, and that of the whole enterprise of aid, in jeopardy. Yet some have shown great zeal, especially where the issue touches their interests and principles are thwarted. Sometimes they succeed, usually where governments have blocked aid flows and are therefore vulnerable to shame.

During the Second World War, the Oxford Famine Relief Committee challenged the British government's blockade of relief supplies to Belgium and Greece; the protest was rebuffed but the Committee set up its own relief effort to the Greek Red Cross; thus did a pressure group became an aid agency, Oxfam.[54]

Toward the end of the Vietnam War years, the Board of the American Friends Service Committee (AFSC) defied the US administration's embargo by shipping humanitarian aid to North Vietnam; the administration later backed down.[55]

When the South African government sought in 1988 to impede the flow of funds reaching domestic anti-apartheid groups from abroad, a consortium of European private agencies channelling EC funds mobilised, together with their South African church and NGO grantees, a public campaign to stop the South African measure. As those funds were a main pillar of European official policy toward South Africa at the time – in a classic illustration of the political uses of foreign aid, they clearly helped European states resist pressures to apply tough sanctions – governments readily complied with the private aid agency protests, and quietly but firmly forced the South African government to withdraw their embarrassing legislation.

Such confrontations and moral victories may be heartening, but they have been few. Indeed they put into relief the limits as well as the strengths of private agency challenges to governmental use of aid as a political tool. Agency efforts to lift official aid embargoes of Cambodia (1979–90), Nicaragua (1979–90), Cuba (from the 1960s onward), and Iraq (1990 onward) have failed to budge any US-dominated institution. And their efforts to circumvent them have been, in the United States at least, an invitation to government harassment and obstruction. Humanitarianism does meet razor-wire-and-floodlight borders when big-power interests want them.

Most private aid agencies respect those lines, mainly in silence. A number of them, formally or informally contracted by government for operations on the ground (or genuinely driven by ideological fervour), join in the chorus of voices orchestrated by the administration in power. This often meant siding with unsavoury Cold War clients of the United States, from Angola's Unita and Afghanistan's Mujahidin to the Khmer Rouge and the Nicaraguan Contras. Both 'new Right humanitarians' as well as mainstream agencies participated. Médicins Sans Frontières (France) actively aided such movements as Unita in Angola.[56]

Opposing the cynicism behind the embargoes, though not addressing the issue within their ranks of *realpolitik*/Cold War manipulation of private aid efforts, small consortia, mainly of European aid agencies mounted lobby efforts and public campaigns. Private aid agency cooperation with knowledge-based NGOs and the media in these cases were slow to develop, despite the needs and potentials there, especially in the case of US church-NGO action regarding Central America.

The campaign led by Oxfam UK and other agencies to end European participation in the US-led embargo of Cambodia generated active public protest in 1989, but European governments only dropped their boycott of Cambodia with the definitive end of the Cold War.

These episodes illustrate the ease with which genuine humanitarianism can be strangled in the crib and pressure deflected for years, especially where agencies are vulnerable to manipulation as public service contractors.[57]

Other cases, chiefly having to do with official aid policy on food for emergencies, could also be cited. These adjustments in policy such as establishing emergency food reserves may be helpful reforms. However, some of these 'Third World lobby' successes look strikingly like 'trade association' successes for some agencies, given their long-standing roles as food aid contractors. It is therefore not so surprising that critical questions about the damage food aid has inflicted on poor countries get posed not by private aid agencies but by knowledge-based NGOs, academics and journalists.[58]

Breakthroughs on Meso- and Macro-Policies?
As noted earlier, official donors, including the World Bank, have long sought to bring private aid agencies 'into the tent' with perfunctory invitations to furnish policy memos, sit on consultative bodies, and especially participate in certain development projects. But on issues of macroeconomic importance, where the stakes run into billions, private aid agencies (like other NGOs) are considered out of their depth, generally meeting condescension and closed doors. A recent study underscores the limits to agency involvement and cosy policy dialogue as a strategy to change World Bank practice. It concludes:

> In participation as with infrastructure lending and adjustment policy, NGO efforts have yielded ambiguous results ... In none of these areas have the NGO campaigns achieved their objectives: reworking the intellectual or policy framework for adjustment lending; sharply reducing infrastructure lending and reorienting energy sector lending; and opening the Bank's operations to a participatory and learning approach that would shift the Bank away from development plans set by a technocracy.[59]

However, multilateral banks have had to pay increasing attention to what is happening *outside* their tent. Activist and knowledge-based NGOs have been working assiduously, sometimes with help from progressive agencies, to assemble material illustrating harmful effects of donor dogmas. Outcomes of these efforts have been modest, but not negligible. Evidence from the UK suggests a direct link between public campaigning and advocacy and the British Government's decision in 1987 to begin softening the debt burden of a number of poor countries. In 1995, even the World Bank had softened its traditional hard line on the issue.[60]

As Northern governments continue to write off poor country debts against a background of public pressure coming from campaigning NGOs supported by a few private aid agencies, evidence of advocacy effectiveness continues to mount. In Switzerland, an agency/NGO-led effort to keep Switzerland out of the World Bank failed, but the follow-up effort to avoid diversion of bilateral aid funds to the World Bank was successful, as was a petition signed by a quarter of a million people to write off a large part of poor country debt to the Swiss Government.[61]

Important incremental victories also can be won at intermediate levels. In 1993, a consortium of European private aid agencies, Eurostep, mounted a campaign to end European Union subsidies to beef exports to West Africa, a policy obviously damaging for local producers, and for European official aid programmes designed to promote livestock in West Africa. Embarrassed by the absurdity of their position, European Union policy makers promptly cut back the subsidies.

This successful advocacy effort had been no lucky bet, but the fruit of years of careful, professional research and consultation in Africa and in Europe under the aegis of a knowledge-based NGO network established in 1980 in France, Solidarités Agro-alimentaires (SOLAGRAL), part of the RONGEAD network mentioned earlier in this chapter. For its part, the private aid agency consortium used its acquaintance with national and European Union policymaking, and skilfully orchestrated media attention. To combine the knowledge-based NGO and private aid agency was a winning formula, and could serve as a model for work on other policy terrains.

Environmental deterioration and poverty form one of those terrains. With the environmental movement showing the way, establishing the local contacts and nailing down the facts, a few private aid agencies have swung in behind them with grants for action-research to contest, for example, mega-projects in the Amazon basin. The results are promising. The World Bank and others have had to rethink their lending policies toward mega-projects such as dams and forest exploitation, with ripple effects through state planning offices and corporate boardrooms.

Conclusions

> The definition of the alternatives is the supreme instrument of power.[62]

Late twentieth-century movements for women's equality, for environmental progress and for civil and political rights have achieved stunning successes because they have kept insisting that there *were and are alternatives* to business as usual. Of course these movements all meet setbacks, but outcomes thus far show clear trends: issues once dismissed without a hearing as dangerous nonsense are now becoming the stuff of laws, norms and valued institutions. That is, the effectiveness of those once-ridiculed social movements stems from their power to show that there are choices and to structure public attention and policy agendas accordingly.

The case is rather different on matters some private aid agencies want to address – the North–South dimensions of poverty and exclusion. On these issues, citizen movements and their allies in political parties seem cowed and divided. Big corporations, and especially global financial institutions and their tribunes, define the alternatives and set policy agendas. The triumph of their dogmas stems from the simple expedient of insisting, with little fear of concerted opposition, that *There Is No Alternative*.

Why do so few private aid agencies challenge this arrogance of power and insist, like their environmental and other NGO counterparts, that alternatives deserve a hearing? Much of this book has suggested that many private aid agencies, despite their apparent strategic advantages of money and opportunities to become acquainted at first hand with some raw realities of poverty and injustice, find it undesirable, if not unthinkable, to challenge today's orthodoxies.

There is one salient difference between mainstream agencies and the human rights, environmental and women's organisations with whom they are sometimes compared. It is that many agencies have come to look, sound and behave like ordinary for-profit businesses. Classic exchange – cargo to the South, images of misery-and-rescue to the North – remains for most the heart of the circuit. As they become ensnared in the logic of institutional growth, and seduced by the opportunities and urgencies of the short run, agency managers ally themselves more closely with funding authorities, whether public givers in the charity market, endowment holders, or controllers of the 'market' for official aid system contracts. Constituents, the social backbone of some agencies, become less important.

A Common Agenda?

Yet some agencies – even a few conceived and raised in the hothouse climate of the Cold War and neoliberalism – are struggling gamely against these currents. They talk about causes and are broadening the lens to include the North as well as the South – sometimes with cautious official blessing. In Germany, for example, official thinking now favours development education's task as 'increasing the understanding of the public for the structural causes of development and underdevelopment and the whole complex of inter-related problems behind these terms'. Moreover, it should make 'the urgency of development problems clear by demonstrating the direct repercussions they have on [German] society'.[63]

Some agencies have come to attach such importance to education and advocacy that both have been made integral to basic agency purposes. CUSO and Oxfam Canada ratified these shifts in the early 1990s. As a result, in-house distinctions between North-centred educational work and North–South resource-transfer work are disappearing. The Dutch technical assistance agency SNV decided in 1992 to drop 'awareness-raising' as a separate objective, putting in its place an approach termed the 'international dimension'. It abolished the department responsible for education. The point was to integrate public education and policy into the heart of the organisation's work.

Some do so out of their own traditions and moral leadings. Others, such as church-based agencies linked with progressive currents in their wider community are simply compelled to broaden their scope on the insistence of their Southern counterparts and movements in the North. In The Netherlands the regional Centres for International Cooperation, whose focus was once exclusively on problems abroad, now integrate them with hometown issues of immigration, racism, environment, peace and security. Drawn into paying attention to poverty and exclusion in their own backyards, a few seem ready to communicate more forcefully about common agendas, North and South.

Practical South–North reciprocity can help. Southern evaluations of Northern aid agencies, as in the case of USA for Africa and some Norwegian church agencies, are simple, but instructive steps. As savings and credit schemes invented in Bangladesh catch on in the ghettos of Chicago, as African urban activists help community officials in the *banlieus* of Paris cope with social decay, and as local government officials from Europe make pilgrimages to Curatiba, Brazil to see how cities can be made more sustainable, fresh policy ideas will get transmitted at low cost, and know-how created in 'poor' countries will be revalued.

Broadening the terrain of activity to include one's own country should be a decisive step toward the common agenda. In 1996, a Christian aid agency, Tear Fund, announced that it is to use a third of its resources at home in Britain, convinced that 'poverty in some inner cities may be as bad as in the Third World'.[64] Two years earlier, Oxfam UK and Ireland gained front-page attention for its decision – in the face of bitter criticism, including that of other aid agencies – to make anti-poverty grants 'on its own doorstep'. Although still in early, experimental stages, engagement on home ground is forcing Oxfam to think more profoundly about its own society, and about itself.[65] As of early 1996, Oxfam's General Director could say that, because his organisation now has to listen closely to what poor people in Britain are saying, it is coming to realise that it could do a much better job of listening to the poor in Asia, Africa and Latin America.[66]

However, a number of mainstream private aid agencies such as CARE and Save the Children USA have long worked both on home ground and abroad, yet they show little interest in transformation, or a common agenda. It will take more than the shock of recognition – such as that Oxfam UK and Ireland seems to be undergoing – to bring about a redefinition of an agency as a progressive social actor in its own society. Among other things, alliances will be needed.

Making common cause with kindred organisations and movements can help. Practical alliances between private aid agencies and knowledge-based NGOs have, as noted earlier in this chapter, proved effective on a number of fronts, from trade policies to tribal peoples. Practical and effective innovations are emerging where agencies, on behalf of Southern counterparts, help broker the services of specialist groups, from electricity cooperatives to inner-city development corporations to local government management teams. One healthy side-effect here is a certain demystification of 'aid'. Links with environmental think-tanks and pressure groups are, given the broad awakening to planetary risks, are especially promising.

Such trends are gaining momentum. A red thread running through them is that an agency can choose to gain better roots and legitimacy and thus of 'reinventing' itself – not as just another kind of business or special interest group, but as a genuine alternative, a civic institution responding to social injustice wherever it finds it. The trends pose the possibility that in the first decade of the new millennium, the themes of charity and benevolence in agency communication may begin giving way to the themes of mutual interest and no-nonsense solidarity.

Notes

1. National Committee for Responsive Philanthropy, 1995, 'The War on Nonprofits', *Responsive Philanthropy* (newsletter), Washington DC, Spring issue.
2. See, for example, Joao Bosco Feres, 'Holle frasen uit het Noorden' (Empty phrases from the North) *InZet* (Amsterdam), No. 7, April 1993 pp. 4–6; and B. Pouligny, 1993, 'Dificile et utile apprentissage pour les ONG', *Le Monde Diplomatique*, 1993, p. 5: 'Many participants [from Northern NGOs at the Vienna Human Rights NGO Forum] showed weak representation ("semi-absence" some said) in debates and silence on the reality of human rights in their own countries, in particular regarding economic and social rights (with the crucial themes of extreme poverty and exclusion.) Most are in effect entirely oriented toward other regions of the world. Their counterparts from the South wonder about the nature of this civil society of the North, which is put forward to them as a model.'
3. H. van de Veen, 'Wilson Campos uit Midden-Amerika: "Wij hebben al die NGO's niet nodig"', *Onze Wereld* (Amsterdam), June 1993, p. 18. The article cites Campos's criticisms of the NGOs: 'inefficiency, competition among themselves, bureaucratism, corruption, lack of democracy (the paternalism) of many of these organisations'.
4. Jorgen Lissner's formulation in 1977, cited ten years later by Lemaresquier, and restated in various ways by others, still seems valid for most of the aid business:

   > ... the one lasting image coming across to the public from the mainstream agencies is this:
   > The development problem is all 'out there'. It is caused by endogenous factors inside the low-income countries. We in the high-income countries are outside spectator; our present standard of living is the result of our own efforts alone. The only, or most important, thing we can do to reduce poverty and human suffering in the Third World is to provide more aid resources.

   J. Lissner, 1977, *The Politics of Altruism. A Study of the Political Behaviour of Voluntary Development Agencies*, Lutheran World Federation Department of Studies, Geneva, p. 158; cited in T. Lemaresquier, 1987, 'Prospects for Development Education:

Some Strategic Issues Facing European NGOs', *World Development* vol 15, Supplement, p. 191.

5. Greg Thompson, 1995, 'The Rich, the poor and the earth', *Together, A Journal of World Vision International*, No. 45, January–March, p. 4.

6. In social sector non-profits, departments tasked with fundraising and communication are commonly at odds with those responsible for programming, the 'service-providers'. Struggles about communication can be bitter, provoking internal trench warfare for years. See J. MacKeith, 1992, 'Raising Money or Raising Awareness: Issues and Tensions in the Relationship Between Fund-raisers and Service-Providers', Working Paper 12, Centre for Voluntary Organisation, London School of Economics and Political Science.

7. Jaya Sarkar, Global Education Coordinator, Childreach (USA), 27 February 1995; as noted from a telephone conversation.

8. A. Van Rooy, 1994, 'The Altruistic Lobbyists: The Influence of Non-Governmental Organizations on Development Policy in Canada and Britain', D. Phil. dissertation, Lincoln College, Oxford, p. 164, citing staff of the British agencies Christian Aid and War on Want.

9. Van Rooy, *Altruistic Lobbyists*, Chapter 13.

10. As noted in Canada for example. See T. Brodhead and C. Pratt, 'Paying the Piper: CIDA and Canadian NGOs', in C. Pratt (ed.), 1994, *Canadian International Development Assistance*, McGill-Queen's University Press, Montreal and Kingston, p. 114.

11. See Carmel Rickard, 'European funds "an excuse for inaction"', *Weekly Mail* (Johannesburg), 30 June–6 July 1989.

12. Alan Fowler, interview, cited in Tjitske Lingsma, 'NGO's in het zuiden geen afspiegeling van onze idealen', *Viceversa* (The Hague), November 1993, p. 1.

13. M. Edwards, 1993, '"Does the Doormat Influence the boot?": Critical Thoughts on UK NGOs and International Advocacy', *Development in Practice* 3:3, p. 166.

14. R.C. Brown, 1993, *Public Debt and Private Wealth. Debt, Capital Flight and the IMF in Sudan*, Macmillan, London; and J. Ferguson, 1990, *The Anti-Politics Machine. 'Development', Depoliticization and Bureaucratic State Power in Lesotho*, Cambridge University Press, Cambridge.

15. See P.J. Burnell, 1991, *Charity, Politics and the Third World*, Harvester Wheatsheaf, Hemel Hempstead, p. 8; J. Lissner, 1977, *The Politics of Altruism: A Study of the Political Behaviour of Voluntary Development Agencies*, Lutheran World Federation Department

of Studies, Geneva, pp. 112–19; and Van Rooy, *Altruistic Lobbyists*, pp. 169–70.

16. Joint Working Group of Development Education, 1984, *A Framework for Development Education in the United States*, Private Agencies in International Development (PAID)/American Council of Volunatry Agencies for Foreign Service (ACVAFS), New York.

17. InterAction, 1993, *InterAction PVO Standards*, Washington DC, point 7.7.3, p. 12.

18. Lissner, *Politics of Altruism*, p. 224.

19. L. Minear, 1987, 'The Other Missions of NGOs: Education and Advocacy' *World Development*, Vol. 15 Supplement, p. 209.

20. The dangers of dependence on state subventions were brought home dramatically in 1995 when the Canadian Government cut virtually all funds flowing through its Public Participation Programme and other channels for public education on North–South issues. This hit about 90 development education organisations across Canada, especially those outside the Toronto-Ottawa-Montreal triangle, forcing most to fold up. Having shifted from being among the most generous nations to among the least in matters of public education, the government assumed that private aid agencies like Oxfam-Canada and CUSO (also cut back) would fill the gap. (John Saxby, personal communication.)

21. A. Kooij and R. Mevis, 1994, *Cooperation of Advisory Structures for Development Cooperation Policy: A Survey in Seventeen European Countries*, Nationale Advies Raad, The Hague.

With only ten members, Finland's consultative council is the smallest in Europe; also exceptional in this council is the presence of journalists.

22. Official discourse about foreign aid varies from political culture to political culture and from epoch to epoch. One researcher has identified four categories of national role conception governing discourse on aid: the Good Neighbor, the Activist, the Merchant, and the Power Broker. For public education and advocacy, private aid agencies will usually avoid the latter two roles, although those conceptions are among the most consistently used in arguing the merits of foreign aid in national official discourse. See M. Breuning, 1994, 'Why Give Foreign Aid? Decision maker perceptions of the benefits to the donor state', *Acta Politica*, No. 2, pp. 121–44. (As Dutch official rhetoric about its aid turned decisively toward the 'merchant' role in 1995, after years of domination by 'activist' discourse, the transience of these roles bears emphasising.)

23. See Institute for Policy Studies, 'U.S. Sister Cities and Development Cooperation – A Report Card', *Global Communities*
(newsletter of Institute for Policy Studies, Washington DC),
Spring/Summer 1992.

Somewhat more positive trends have been observed in The
Netherlands, where municipalities have enjoyed both central
government subsidies and independent, voluntary initiative
to undertake often useful cooperation programmes with
municipalities in the South. See L. Heijlman, 1994,
Ontwikkelingssamenwerking: Doet Onze Gemente Daar Iets Aan?
Doctoral Thesis, Vrije Universiteit, Amsterdam.

24. The demerits of refugee camps is a central theme of an exhaustive
study based mainly on agency operations in the Sudan and
Uganda by Barbara Harrell-Bond, 1986, *Imposing Aid*, Oxford
University Press, Oxford.

25. See M. Chossudovsky, 1994, 'Les fruits empoisonnées de
l'adjustment structurel', *Le Monde Diplomatique*, November, p.
21; and M. Chossudovsky, 1993, 'Dépendance alimentaire,
ingérence humanitaire en Somalie', *Le Monde Diplomatique*, July,
p. 16.

26. R.R. Sullivan, 1968, *The Politics of Altruism: A Study of the Partnership between the United States Government and American Voluntary
Relief Agencies for the Donation Abroad of Surplus Agricultural Commodities 1949–1967*, PhD dissertation, Johns Hopkins University,
cited by Lissner, *Politics of Altruism*, pp. 99–100.

27. Letter to The *Guardian*, 15 September 1992, quoted in 'Military
Intervention and the role of NGOs' by Alex de Waal, letter in
Third Sector, 3 December 1993, p. 8.

28. J. Benthall, 1993, *Disasters, Relief and the Media*, I.B. Taurus,
London.

29. For fuller discussion of these morally complex matters see African
Rights, 1994, 'Humanitarianism Unbound?' London, mimeo; W.
Shawcross, 1984, *The Quality of Mercy: Cambodia, Holocaust, and
Modern Conscience*, André Deutsch, London; and Benthall,
Disasters, pp. 92–121.

30. F. Brune, 1993, 'Néfastes effets de l'idéologie politico-médiatique'
Le Monde Diplomatique, May, p. 4.

31. C.A. Lutz and J.L. Collins, 1993, *Reading National Geographic*,
University of Chicago Press, Chicago, p. 46.

32. P.F. Whiteley and S.J. Winyard, 1987, *Pressure for the Poor: The
Poverty Lobby and Policy Making*, Methuen, London and New
York, p. 111, quoted in Van Rooy, *Altruistic Lobbyists*, p. 16.

33. Lemaresquier, 'Prospects for Development Education', p. 198.

34. A concerted effort for this chapter to find in-depth evaluations of development education in Germany, a country where government subsidies run to DM 5–6 million a year for this purpose, yielded nothing.

35. Drawn from C. Carracillo (ed.), 1994, *Educating for Development. The Other Form of Cooperation*, ITECO, Brussels, and Institut d'études du Développement, Univ. Catholique de Louvain; Peace Research Centre, Katholieke Universiteit Nijmegen; Economie et Humanisme Centre de recherche associée à l'Université de Lyon II, 1991, *Evaluation des Projets d'éducation au Développement Co financés par la Communauté Européene, Rapport de Synthese, 3eme Phase.*

36. B&A Groep, 1992, *Beweging Gewogen*. Rapport van de door de Minister voor Ontwikkelingssamenwerking op 5 maart 1992 geinstaleerde Commission, 'Impactstudie Nationale Commissie Voorlichting en Bewustwording Ontwikkelingssamenwerking', The Hague.

37. In 1994 an opinion research bureau survey showed that 84 per cent of Dutch adults would like to see Dutch aid stay at the same level or be increased. Only in 1970 was that proportion higher (91 per cent); in 1980 it had reached a low point (62 per cent) but by 1982 it had started climbing again (75 per cent).

   Only Norway, where the government is also a major subsidiser of development education, shows equivalently high levels of public support for aid as of the early 1990s (see German and Randel (eds), *The Reality of Aid 95*, pp. 110–11). In Finland, where public support for aid has traditionally been high despite minimal government subsidies for development education, a sharp recession saw a decline in that support; 76 per cent of Finns polled in 1994 were satisfied with Finnish aid at its current levels, or thought it was too low. (Liisa Laakso, University of Helsinki Institute of Development Studies, personal communication, 1994.)

38. H. Beerends, 1993, *De Derde Wereldbeweging. Geschiedenis en toekomst*, Jan van Arkel/Novib, Utrecht, p. 350.

39. T. van Veen, 1994, unpublished research paper commissioned by NCO and *Onze Wereld*, Team Vier BV, Amsterdam, typescript, pp. 5, 11, 18. Thanks are due to Alan Fowler for access to this document.

40. Office of Global Education, National Council of Churches, USA, 1988, *Global Education Seminar Project. Final Report*. Baltimore, p. 27. Thanks are due to the report's author, Thomas B. Hampson, for having kindly provided a copy.

41. Minear, 'The Other Missions of NGOs', p. 201.
42. T.B. Keehn, 1991, 'Introduction: The New Context', in Inter Action Development Education and Constituency Building Committee, *Education for Global Change, A New Framework and Program Plan for a Just and Sustainable Future*, Washington DC, p. 3.
43. S. Arnold, 1991, 'Our Global Vision: Development as Transformation', in InterAction Development Education and Constituency Building Committee, *Education for Global Change. A New Framework and Program Plan for a Just and Sustainable Future*, Washington DC, pp. 12–13.
44. InterAction Development Education and Constituency Building Committee, 1991, 'An Agenda for Action', in *Education for Global Change, A New Framework and Program Plan for a Just and Sustainable Future*; Washington DC, p. 3.
45. W. Nielsen, 1985, *The Golden Donors*, Truman Talley/E.P. Dutton, New York, p. 423.
46. 'Gina Graham' (pseudonym), 1995, 'Foundation Culture', *Left Business Observer*, No. 70 (November 4), p. 4.
47. P.J. Seybold, 1980, 'The Ford Foundation and the Triumph of Behavioralism in American Political Science', in R.F. Arnove (ed.), *Philanthropy and Cultural Imperialism. The Foundations at Home and Abroad*, G.K. Hall & Co. Boston, pp. 269–303. See also R. Bellah *et al.*, 1992, *The Good Society*, Vintage Books, New York, Chapter 7, Part IV 'America and the World. "Modernisation" as Policy and Theory', pp. 232–5.
48. D. Fisher, 1980, 'American Philanthropy and the Social Sciences: The Reproduction of a Conservative Ideology', in Arnove (ed.), *Philanthropy and Cultural Imperialism*, pp. 232–60.
49. L. Holdcroft, 1982, 'The Rise and Fall of Community Development in Developing countries 1950–1965: A Critical Analysis and Implications', in G.E. Jones & M.J. Rolls (eds), *Progress in Rural Extension and Community Development*, Vol. I, Wiley, London, pp. 207–31.
50. E.H. Berman, 1980, 'The Foundations' Role in American Foreign Policy: the Case of Africa, post 1945', in Arnove (ed.), *Philanthropy and Cultural Imperialism*, pp. 203–32.
51. A. Gardner, 1980, *Legal Imperialism. American Lawyers and Foreign Aid in Latin America*, University of Wisconsin Press, Madison. The author was for many years an official of the Ford Foundation.
     On Ford and its leading role in human rights funding in Latin America see K. Sikkink, 1993, 'Human Rights, Principled Issue-

networks and Sovereignty in Latin America', *International Organization*, 47:3, pp. 410–41.

52. For example, Clark, *Democratizing Development*, pp. 157–9, Edwards, 'Does the Doormat Influence the boot', p. 166 (repeating Clark's list and adding others); Burnell, *Charity, Politics* ..., pp. 256–7.

53. World Bank, 1993, *World Development Report 1993. Investing in Health*, Oxford University Press, New York, p. 224.

54. B.H. Smith, 1990, *More than Altruism: The Politics of Private Foreign Aid*, Princeton University Press, Princeton, pp. 42–3.

55. Lissner, *Politics of Altruism*, pp. 210–11.

56. In 1984 the President of MSF France, Rony Brauman, is quoted as having said that Unita had built 'the most impressive village public health programme in black Africa'. *The Economist Development Report*, July 1984, p. 2. When asked how MSF would substantiate such an astonishing claim, an MSF official suggested that any queries had to be directed to Unita.

    See also T. Barr, D. Preusch and B. Sims, 1986, *The New Right Humanitarians*, Inter-Hemispheric Education Resource Center, Albuquerque; and H. Baitenmann, 1990, 'NGOs and the Afghan war: the politicisation of humanitarian aid', *Third World Quarterly*, 12:1

57. On Cambodia see J. Pilger, 1989, *Heroes*, Pan Books, London, pp. 385–459. For an early review of Cold War manipulation of private aid, and the continuing trend to break down the boundaries between the military and private aid spheres, see Inter-Hemispheric Education Resource Center, 1988, *Public and Private Humanitarian Aid. Legal and Ethical Issues*, Albuquerque. For a swingeing anti-imperialist analysis from observers in Dutch-speaking Belgium, see M. Vandepitte *et al.*, 1994, *NGOs: Missionarissen van de Nieuwe Kolonisatie?*, Uitgeverij EPO, Berchem, Belgium, esp. pp. 98–103.

58. One exception is the Unitarian Universalist Service Committee (UUSC), which sponsored research, later used in NGO lobby efforts, on US food aid to Central America. See UUSC and Inter-hemispheric Education Resource Center, 1989, *Food Aid in Central America: Feeding the Crisis: A Policy Report to Congress*, Albuquerque. Although supported by some aid agencies, it was the UK-based World Development Movement, whose 1986 lobby efforts with the encouragement of Tory Minister of Overseas Development led to reduced pressures to dump European Union surplus foodstuffs via European aid programmes. See Burnell, *Charity, Politics*, pp. 260–1.

59. P.J. Nelson, 1995, 'The World Bank and Non-Governmental Organizations. Political Economy and Organizational Analysis', mimeo, January, p. 5. Thanks are due to the author, as of 1996 at the Center for Global Change, University of Maryland, for providing a copy of this paper.

60. Burnell, *Charity, Politics*, pp. 261–2, citing John Clark of Oxfam.

61. M. de Goys, 1993, 'Switzerland', in Smillie and Helmich (eds), *Non-Governmental Organisations and Governments: Stakeholders for Development*, OECD, Paris, pp. 276–77.

62. E.H. Schattschneider, 1975, *The Semisovereign People*, Dryden Press, Hinsdale, IL, p. 66, quoted in P.M. Haas, 1992, 'Introduction: epistemic communities and international policy coordination', *International Organization*, 46:1, Winter, p. 16.

63. From an unnamed 1992 paper by the German aid ministry BMZ, cited in M. de Goys and H. Helmich, 1993, 'Germany', in Smillie and Helmich, *Non-Governmental Organisations and Governments*, p. 150.

64. Madeline Bunting, 'Charity to begin at home', *Guardian Weekly*, 21 January 1996.

65. Conclusion drawn from statements by Chris Hudson, Board member of Oxfam UK and Ireland, as interviewed by Edgar Pieterse, Copenhagen, March 1995.

66. David Bryer, General Director of Oxfam UK and Ireland, in a talk given at a gathering organised by Novib on 11 January 1996 in The Hague.

6

The South: Three Perspectives

[T]he idiocy of Western diplomacy has possibly been surpassed only
by that of Western non-governmental organisations.

> Tomaz Mastnak, Slovenian philosopher,
> regarding former Yugoslavia, 1994.[1]

Editor's Note

*Private aid agencies evoke strong feelings not only in those parts of the world
normally termed the South; in Europe, as the quotation above makes clear,
their presence can also elicit highly charged responses. The 'South' in
today's usage connotes situations of North–South asymmetry, of giver and
receiver roles. Skewed, and often tension-ridden relations are of course not
confined to Northern interventions in Africa, Asia and Latin America. They
can arise wherever the 'helper' meets the 'helped'.*

*The following three articles offer perspectives on private aid agencies as
observed at the 'receiving end'. These three by no means exhaust the
issues, but they bring forward views that private aid agencies cannot
dismiss as trivial or secondary.*

An African Perspective

Yash Tandon

The Recent Past

Development died in Africa during the 1980s. As the World Bank noted
in 1989, Africa south of the Sahara 'witnessed almost a decade of falling
per capita incomes, increasing hunger, and accelerating ecological
degradation ... Overall Africans are almost as poor today as they were
thirty years ago.'[2]

Throughout the 1980s and 1990s the World Bank and IMF
persuaded the whole of Africa to go through Structural Adjustment
Programmes. After over a decade of experimentation with the lives
of people, the poor are worse off than ever. School enrolment has
dropped, real wages have fallen, deaths from preventable illnesses

have risen. The number of poor in Sub-Saharan Africa increased from 184 million in 1985 to 216 million in 1990.[3]

World Bank and UN statistics are quoted not because they are necessarily more reliable than any other, but because they are likely to be conservative. The Bank is anxious to prove that its strategies are working, and yet its own figures belie this optimism. The real situation on the ground for the poor is far worse. Development has failed in Africa.

The reasons for this failure are many, and contested in the theoretical literature. Some writers put it to civil strife and ethnic wars. Others put it to lack of democracy and transparency in matters of governance. All these are important factors. But in our view the fundamental cause is that Africans are not in control of their own resources.

In many parts of Africa they do not own their own land. Products of the land – cotton, coffee, cocoa, timber, biogenetic materials, minerals – are either directly controlled by transnationals or traded in the world market at prices far below their real (labour and biochemical) value. Given this massive outflow of value, Africa has no hope in hell ever to realise sufficient incomes to sustain its populations. That is the fundamental cause of Africa's poverty. All else – unemployment, lack of provision for diseases, civil strife, general ungovernability – are the children of that system.

So when we say that development has failed in Africa, we mean specifically that the market-driven development strategy has failed. It has more than failed. It is, in fact, the root cause of Africa's present misery.

So much of Africa's immediate past. What of the future?

The Rise of Global Apartheid

Africa's future must be assessed in the context of the post-Cold War New World Order. Our argument is that this is not likely to bring any relief to Africa. If anything, the New World Order is likely to be even more predatory than the previous one.

The collapse of Soviet-style Communism obscures a deep crisis facing Western powers. Other forces are emerging to challenge them. One is fundamentalism. The West had a clear answer to Soviet communism, but has no answer to Islamic fundamentalism where the issues go beyond the development paradigm. Against Islamic fundamentalism, the West offers its own forms of Christian fundamentalism, but that only worsens the contradictions. Fundamentalism of all kinds is thus one new emerging force.

Another force is China, and other Asian powers. By the year 2020, China's economy is projected to be 140 per cent larger than that of the United States, and the economies of Japan, India and Indonesia will be among the world's five largest.[4] Clearly, the balance of economic power is shifting from the Atlantic to the Pacific.

A third force is the increasing awareness in the West of its own shortcomings and vulnerabilities. This gives rise to a sense of insularity and insecurity. The Cold War eclipsed these for a time. Now they are fully exposed. Among the vulnerabilities are the increasing lack of public control over speculative financial flows, the phenomenon of 'jobless growth', the rise of permanent unemployment and mounting burdens on welfare services. Compounding crises at economic and social levels are crises at ideological and cultural levels. The very values of 'modernisation' are under question. Challenges from, among others, the feminist and ecological movements are not just reformist challenges, but 'systemic' ones, going to the very core of Western self-assurance.

And the reaction is perverse. Western agents want to retain their powers (over nuclear weapons, markets and resources) and sell ideas of democracy and human rights. But the West sees enemies everywhere, particularly the poor. Thus it wants to ghettoise itself in the citadels of its cities. It erects immigration barriers against hordes of people of colour knocking at its gates. The result is increasing polarisation between the white Christian, Judaic Western nations and the rest of the world. A kind of 'global apartheid' has emerged.

Recolonising Africa

At present Africa is *as yet* too weak to challenge the West. It is beset by internal turmoil. It is divided and in debt. Its political leaders are in ideological crisis, not knowing in what direction to lead their people. They are captives to the dictates of the World Bank and IMF.

Given this weakness, Western interests have a free hand to recolonise Africa.[5] During the Cold War, Western powers found it necessary sometimes to compromise with the petty 'sovereign' sensibilities of African peoples so as not to push them into the Soviet camp. That factor is no longer of any consequence. The West is now openly advocating direct intervention in Africa's internal affairs. It is being argued that Africans have misused the autonomy they were allowed over the preceding 30 years: they abused their power, indulged in corruption, committed large-scale violations of human rights, ruined their economies by creating bloated armies, inefficient state enterprises and elaborate social welfare (especially health and education) systems. Moreover, they wasted all the 'aid' that the West poured in.

Ironically, this is all more or less true. A further irony is that these practices were tolerated, even encouraged, by the West. But that era has passed, and Western powers are chiselling their weapons to intervene in Africa on deep economic and political levels. They are laying down new ground rules to justify either sanctions or direct intervention. Withdrawal (or threat of withdrawal) of 'development aid' may now be used to sanction countries which

- do not conform to structural adjustment programmes;
- have a poor human rights record;
- spend too much on arms;
- refuse to privatise public utilities;
- reject multi-party or other arrangements not deemed democratic;
- refuse to enact environmental laws;
- refuse to limit population growth.

This is the scenario of Africa's future. The new discourse is of 'management' of Africa's politics as well as its economics. The West is laying down the instrumentalities and modalities of a new technocratic order in Africa.

The Role of the Private Agencies[6]

The foregoing provides the context for assessing the role Western private aid agencies will play in Africa. There are exceptions, of course, but in general the private aid agencies are the advanced guard of the new era of Africa's recolonisation. They are the missionaries of the new era. Just as in the colonial era the missionaries neutralised the ideological defences of colonised peoples and thus prepared the ground for colonial occupation, so now the Western agencies play this role in the new era.

During the slave period there were in the West voices opposed to slavery. During the colonial period there were those who opposed colonialism. And today there are voices in the West who condemn the free-market system of development. But these are minority voices. The *main* thrust of Western civil society is to preserve their own lifestyle and civilisation against the danger of encroachments from the South.

Some of the truths in the critique of 'aid' are worth recalling here. Against the massive flow of resources leaving Africa, aid is only a trickle. Aid is directed primarily to serve Western, not African interests, as illustrated by the political aims behind US policy to put Israel and Egypt at the top of the list of its aid recipients. European aid has gone to the Lomé Convention countries mainly to sustain a neo-colonial linkage.

In this context what role have private aid agencies planed? Essentially there have been four kinds of roles: diversionary, ideological, pacification and destructive of African institutions.

At a guess, between a quarter and a third of private aid agency money has gone into programmes such as population control and micro-enterprise support. These are *diversionary* in effect, and probably in intent. They draw attention away from the real causes of Africa's poverty. Neither population growth nor lack of enterprise are basic causes of Africa's poverty.

The *ideological* roles involve professing claims of universality for Western values of democracy, human rights, feminism and environmentalism. Private aid agencies promoting imported versions of these concepts have so thoroughly brainwashed a section of the middle class (living as they do, on lavish donor funds and international conferencing) that there are now signs of reaction against them. Slowly emerging is a return to African culture and traditions. These are seen as the place to begin. A return to the roots is also the place from which to challenge iniquitous and dangerous shortcomings of some of those traditions, as well as to avoid wholesale import of the West's ideological ragbag.

Pacification of people suffering from the effects of structural adjustment programmes is another role. This absorbs between a quarter and a third of private agency funds. Besides being diversionary, they tend to legitimise structural adjustment measures and World Bank/IMF strategies. Of course, these fail. The problem is much larger than their petty donations can solve.

The fourth role is that of *destroying African institutions* – of education, traditional agriculture, traditional healing and health practices and governance. In his book *Mozambique: Who Calls the Shots?*, Joe Hanlon has documented how private aid agencies systematically undermine the ability of the government to play its legitimate role of governing the country. Similar examples litter the African continent.

It is important to reiterate that there are exceptions to the general picture just painted. Nevertheless, the African grassroots and radical critique of the imperial project has been subverted by most private aid agencies. Faced by crises at home and the emerging new forces – notably Islam and China – the agencies' roles would be to help their governments and civil societies contain these new forces.

Now within the Western neoliberal tradition it is acceptable for a non-governmental organisation to take a position ostensibly opposed to its government. Thus, a number of activist NGOs and private aid agencies helped the struggle against apartheid even as their governments supported it. But this is all part of a larger scheme of containing change within controllable parameters. In South Africa, it was the combined efforts of private aid and its governmental backers that managed to neutralise the more radical and revolutionary actors in that country's liberation.

The language of 'empowerment', 'participatory development' and 'decentralised cooperation' are all part of the ideological baggage of private aid agencies to *manage change* in Africa. African poverty will remain big on the agency agenda in the years to come. Poverty will become a commodity to nurture the missionary and humanist pretext for intervention in Africa. With it will come all the Western ideological ragbag of democracy, human rights, feminism, secularism, efficiency, empowerment, participatory development, green development, accountability and so on.

The funny thing is that they are all praiseworthy values. You cannot object to them. But watch out for their real content. You will see that they are aimed, essentially, at the four functions identified above.

The Challenge Before African NGOs

This essay was commissioned to concentrate on the role of Northern private aid agencies. But it cannot end without a word on the role that African NGOs might play. Of course the bulk of them are appendages of Northern agencies. They are comprador NGOs or COMPRANGOs. Whilst there are minor contradictions between them and their donors, they act essentially as agents of Western programmes to control change in Africa within manageable parameters, to divert attention from the root causes of African poverty, to pacify and to peddle Western values and civilization.

However, there are those amongst them who offer a genuine critique of the neoliberal development model, who are conscious of the great traditions of African civilisation, who are sensitive to African culture with all its limitations and shortcomings, and who are not part of the neo-colonial governance of their societies. In the years to come they will provide a right focus for analysing the new forces emerging in the world. Possibly, they will help build grassroots structures for political action.

Those NGOs will strengthen African civil society and move it in a progressive direction if they can field a programme rooted in African culture and civilisation and independent of the development paradigm dictated by donors, including the private aid agencies.

Private Aid Agencies in Brazil

John Schlanger

For many years, the dominating vision in Latin America was that the state should be responsible for the welfare of its citizens. Globalising trends, and an increasing disbelief in state, government and politicans are making us question that vision. We would now say that the state has become too small for the big things, as it has become too big for the small things.

Ironically, Latin American governments are more democratic than before. The military regimes that dominated the continent from the 1960s to the mid-1980s are no more. And the NGO community, supported by private aid agencies, helped bring that about.

Welfare problems, however, remain. Economic and social inequality has grown in the last decade. In Brazil, 32 million people (about 20 per cent of the population) live in absolute poverty. Elsewhere in Latin America it is not much different. Inequality not only undermines the social basis for effective citizenship, it also distorts the democratic process by creating and consolidating differences in political power, leaving millions of people out of any process whatsoever. These are the 'excluded'.

But despite the pessimism this situation can produce, people are acting together to solve problems. And they have, sometimes successfully, demonstrated the importance of civic engagement.

The Case of Brazil and the Role of the Aid Agencies

For more than 20 years, most foreign development agencies have been supporting projects and programmes in Brazil oriented towards what is today called 'strengthening civil society'.

With the support of some Northern agencies, several hundred NGOs all over the country gained capacities to mobilise and empower people. These NGOs came to advise popular organisations such as trade unions, slums groups, peasant workers, etc. to question the military government and fight for their rights as citizens.

The support from Northern agencies came basically in the form of funding. Brazilian social leadership made the sending of foreign volunteers unnecessary. At the beginning of the 1970s, during the worst period of the military regime, funding started to change from 'assistencialism', promoted mainly by the Catholic Church, towards more politicised activities.

Later, in the beginning of the 1980s, support moved towards institutional development. Brazilian NGOs started to relate to social movements, locally and nationally. They relied on funding for programmes, not merely projects. In 1979, the Workers Central Union was one of the first to receive funding for training union leaders; in several states this work was done by NGOs, with the blessing of that trade union.

Though there is still a long way to go in the struggle for social justice, it may be stated that citizens' movements in Brazil have created an entirely new environment for participation at different levels. Brazilian NGOs played an important role in this process. It would have been impossible to get to this point without the support of a number of foreign agencies.

As NGO activity at the time was considered subversive, there was no possibility of survival without the support of the agencies. Many people working in (semi)clandestine conditions had their projects supported confidentially. At the end of the 1970s, many political exiles returned. Their arrival was followed by an important growth in the number of NGOs. Today, the largest NGOs of Brazil are directed by former exiles.

Today there is more to be done. We would like to suggest four fields of action that private aid agencies could stimulate in the coming years.

Breaking Down Old Shibboleths

The Brazilian government's attitude toward NGOs is changing. Until recently they were feared and repressed. Today, the government has come to acknowledge citizen organisations as partners in development. In his inauguration speech, President Fernando Henrique Cardoso, himself for many years director of an important research NGO, invited NGOs to take part in the development of a better society.

But how to structure this, if the organisations created by citizens in the last 20 years are so diverse? Some groups are local, others work on a national level. Some have existed for many years already, while others have sprung up just to reach an immediate goal. Other actors, such as private enterprises and traditional philanthropic organisations have come into the arena of development projects.

The sources of finance are also diverse. Funds coming yearly to Brazil from aid agencies, could be somewhere between US$130–150 million a year. The combined annual grants of three Dutch private aid agencies (Cebemo, ICCO and Novib) alone add up to US$25 million.

Among the new actors, philanthropic arms of business play a very important role. Large to middle-size corporations increasingly are promoting social projects – thereby gaining tax advantages, of course.

The InterAmerican Foundation commissioned research showing that 58 corporations sponsored projects up to US$115 million in 1993.

Some 30 corporations have founded the GIF (Group of Institutes and Foundations) comprising corporations with social programmes, most of them beginning their support only in the middle of the 1980s.

No figures are available for what municipalities are doing in partnership with civil society organisations. With the decentralisation of state revenues after 1989, municipalities have had more monies available. Several of them are looking for partnerships with civil society organisations.

State companies in Brazil are giants. They hold huge amounts of idle lands. One of the successes of the Hunger Programme (see Box 6.1) was to get state companies to put land at the disposal of rural populations to produce food, with technical support of the state companies themselves.

Brazilian NGOs have, with few exceptions, tended to remain at the margin of these initiatives. But in the long run, these corporate and local government-based initiatives may form important 'competition' for NGOs. Strengthening society alone does not fill stomachs, and the activities carried out by these new actors do.

Promoting Dialogue

This forces NGOs – and their supporting agencies – to reflect on existing stereotypical images: government is bad by definition, business's only interest is profit-oriented, and therefore there is no reason to dialogue with them. In a recent meeting with aid agencies, Brazilian NGOs defended the idea that efficiency and efficacy were 'capitalistic concepts, unsuitable for social work'.

The difficulty NGOs have in dialogue with other actors has to a certain extent blocked their vision. Things have changed a bit. Government may not be good, but not all governments are bad, as local government experience has shown. Business is profit-oriented, but if part of the profit comes back to society in the form of projects for the poor, this is not *per se* a bad thing. To overcome this polarisation will demand a big effort, and the only way out is dialogue.

Thus the first thing private aid agencies should consider in the case of Brazil is how to promote dialogue not only between NGOs, but between NGOs and social actors beyond their target-groups.

Donor organisations in Brazil (mainly from the US and Europe) held meetings in Brazil in 1993 and in April 1995. The purpose was to discuss their policies in the country and to consult Brazilian partners about educational activities the agencies carry out in their home countries. Curiously, Brazilian foundations, that is, organisations belonging to private entrepreneurial groups, were not invited to these meetings, even when they increasingly support similar projects. On the other hand, the business philanthropies are more and more inviting NGOs to participate in their meetings.

The same argument is valid for local governments. Brazil has almost 5,000 municipalities. In many of them, more socially involved mayors were elected and started social programmes with participation of local organisations. Why not dialogue with them – if not to support them directly, which might not be possible for many agencies – but to listen to what they have to say and look for opportunities?

By promoting this dialogue with other actors not yet acknowledged in the 'development scene', agencies could help spread and multiply activities, thus avoiding the isolation so common in the NGO community. Besides, the amount of funds business corporations, municipalities and state companies have at their disposal is immense.

Mobilisation of Popular Movements

Several NGOs in Brazil are now key role players, even at national levels. In the city of Rio de Janeiro at least three NGOs have the ability to mobilise nationally. They are consulted by national and local governments, and by public and private enterprises on issues concerning social, political and economical development.

These organisations (Citizen's Action against Misery, Hunger and for Life, the Viva Rio movement, and Roda Viva) are, like most NGOs, animated organisations. They are challenged to look for and even demonstrate new approaches, not just to criticise existing policies.

These organisations started important new social movements. Citizen's Action is nationwide. Viva Rio is oriented to the city of Rio de Janeiro. Roda Viva focuses on street-children. All three work within existing NGOs whose funding stems from development agencies of Europe and North America. However, with few exceptions, the agencies would not support the mobilisation work these movements are doing.

Local and foreign funds can be raised for basic needs development projects, but these organisations lack the professional skills to carry out these type of activities. People who can run small-scale business projects with social goals (employment generation, market knowledge to link offer to demand, etc.) are necessary but not available.

There are thousands of possibilities for projects emerging from citizen's organisations. The idea is not for private aid agencies to fund a few of them, but to find ways of helping NGOs respond to this demand. Not with their own knowledge, because most agencies do not have it. But they can promote partnerships with other organisations in their countries who have this know-how, but lack funds to support capacity-building abroad.

Self-Reliance
The third point derives from the first two: there is a growing impression that private aid agencies will substantially cut back their support to Brazilian NGOs in the coming years. Some agencies have already begun doing so. This is, in a certain sense, non-negotiable, for he who has not, cannot give. Financial limitations for agencies means also limitations in the expansion-potentials of NGOs. Some important NGOs have already begun laying off experienced personnel because of budget cuts.

On the other hand, Brazil is not a poor country, it is an unjust country. Too few have too much, too many have nothing. But especially among those who have too much, there is a growing consciousness that if they do not return something to society, sooner or later some kind of an outburst will be difficult to avoid.

This means growing possibilities for raising local funds. These funds cannot be raised in the more traditional European ways, as there is no culture in Brazil yet for charity and philanthropy, except in situations of natural disasters.

What is appearing in Brazil is the willingness of certain sectors within private enterprises to support social projects. The Citizen's Action and the Viva Rio movement are good examples of how to involve enterprises in social projects. Private agencies should not only encourage this, but also develop efforts to press enterprises in their countries who have activities in Brazil to support their partners. The German airline Lufthansa, for instance, has collected over US$12,000 dollars from its personnel for a project in Brazil. The huge Dutch-German clothing concern C&A has supported NGO-activities since 1990.

Yet as they reduce their grant making, private aid agencies have done little to stimulate NGOs to look for ways of fundraising locally. The third field of agency attention is thus an obvious one.

Overcoming Publicity Shyness
The fourth and last point for agency attention concerns publicity and mass media. Brazilian NGOs never tire of saying how they had to work in a semi-clandestine way during the military regime. And many continue acting that way. To come out in the open means not being afraid of the press, radio and television. The press is free, even if dominated by interest groups. To show what you do, to inform a broad public, creates an image different from operating clandestinely.

Box 6.1: The Citizen's Action against Hunger, Misery and for Life

The Citizen's Action against Hunger, Misery and for Life grew from the Ethics in Politics movement that had mobilised millions of people against the corruption of former President Fernando Collor, impeached by Parliament in 1992. After the impeachment, the leadership of the movement decided to launch a national campaign against hunger.

Led by Herbert de Souza (better known as Betinho), Director of the NGO IBASE (Brazilian Institute for Social and Economical Analysis), the campaign had, two years after its official launch in June 1993, mobilised more than three million citizens.

The campaign was set up along three lines:

- Partnership with the government, involving a joint governmental-civil society Food Security Council.
- Mobilisation of Civil Society, based on decentralised action by local citizens working in 20,000 local committees. There were no formulas on how to do it. The message was: if you want to do something, do it. And many people did. Not only citizens, but also public and private enterprises and several municipal governments joined in. And they were not excluded, as would have been the case in past years. They are the new partners in the struggle against social exclusion. The prognosis that the committees would have a short life proved wrong. Two years after the campaign was launched, they were still active.
- Use of the mass media: IBASE undertook to inform the broad public about the results. This is important because there is no tradition of accountability in Brazil. The newspaper *Jornal da Cidadania* (Citizen's Newspaper) is published every two weeks; 200,000 copies are distributed all over the country. All costs are financed by the publicity of public and private enterprises that support the campaign. A series of three-minute videos have been made, showing the experiences of those who took part. To the surprise of even the leaders of the campaign, the videos were shown weekly on national TV-Networks, without costs.

Results were impressive. Millions of tons of food were collected and distributed to needy people. The Christmas without Hunger campaign was set up in November 1994. It resulted in more than four million tons of food being collected in six main cities. In the second year of the campaign, the main theme was generation of income. Thousands of initiatives were taken that generated some kind of income for the poor, with surprising results.

Analysts of the campaign state that it helped bring solidarity, lost during the military regime, back into Brazilian life.

However, many NGOs criticized the Citizen's Action for being 'assistencialist', aimed at charity not change. For Brazilians, however, it is a success story. It changed the vision of many people. Like it or not, society has been strengthened. And it was set up by a local NGO.

NGOs have taken actions that have attracted the media and gotten space in newspapers and TV. This is part of democracy. But to do this better, professional support is needed. Private aid agencies could provide this, either by disseminating their own experiences in Brazil or by supporting contacts between NGOs and press or publicity agencies.

In this limited space we have tried to suggest some new fields of attention for private aid agencies. Up to now, only a few of them have responded, mainly by intuition. But this needs to happen on a larger scale.

Conclusion

Aid agencies, who certainly do not work in isolation in their countries, can contribute not only to support projects, but to help NGOs in Brazil overcome their isolation. Some NGOs are doing this on their own, most are not. The suggestions given above may stimulate agencies to find new ways of supporting their partners in Brazil. And it should happen soon, because if they don't, the progressive NGOs are in danger of turning conservative.

The Challenge of Intercultural Partnership

Edith Sizoo

Strange Enough

The historian Joseph Ki-Zerbo of Burkina Faso once said: 'The Northern development agents think they are having a dialogue with their African counterparts. In reality they only hear the tropicalised echo of their own voice ... In this way they too often *sacrifice the important to the urgent.*'

The South–North relationship badly needs rethinking. One way to begin is to stop, to pause beside the urgencies of the moment, and to try to grasp what we and others are really talking about when using the ample vocabulary of 'development cooperation'. This means breaking codes and exposing cultural assumptions.

It also means seeing international cooperation as a quintessential intercultural act. Strange enough, neither Northern nor Southern 'partners' took this obvious fact as a starting point for reflection. Yet time and again, cooperation programmes have led nowhere because no one paused to speak about unspoken assumptions guiding two important currencies of power: money and language. Any attempt to call these two into question creates deep feelings of insecurity, with attendant negative responses.

Can private aid agencies respond positively? Their futures will in no small way depend on how well they address this insecurity, overcome distorted assumptions and convert cultural liabilties into assets for meaningful relationships beween people from different parts of the world.

Security at Stake

During the first three decades of development cooperation, donor agencies in the North were at ease. Their power position gave them two-fold security. They enjoyed financial security, that is, they had the money to intervene; and they enjoyed 'sense security', the notion that Western-style development was universally valid and an unmitigated good.

Those who defined themselves as 'developed' (NB: past tense, a state of completion!), justified their aid interventions by taking themselves as the reference. This allowed them to define people in other parts of the world in negative terms. They were *non*-Western, *under*-developed, *on the way to* development, *non*-industrialised. Their economies were *in*formal, their knowledge *traditional* (that is, *un*-scientific), their political systems *un*-democratic, and their people *poor*. *'Grassroots'* suggest an image of people of 'low' level. A more accurate and positive term might be *community-based actors*. A great many terms could be jettisoned and replaced.

None of these labels were devised by the people concerned. Moreover, words like 'development', 'planning', 'progress', 'economic growth', 'democracy' often do not exist in many local languages. Yet the international cooperation business insisted on the use of such terms, thus imposing a 'common' language. This was, in short, an exercise in power, and a way of reinforcing a sense of security.

Money-power in development aid usually determines whose instructions are written on the road signs. But this does not necessarily obliterate other ways of making sense of reality. 'Common' terminology was not *communis causa* at all. Rather, the 'tropicalised echo' was practised and perfected. And monies thereby obtained. But these were often skilfully rerouted and used in ways more closely matching local notions of reality.

There is a lot of fashionable talk about the failure of development projects and the lost decade for development take-off. But projects do not fail by themselves. Rather, they fail where people resist an alien and alienating development model that does not fit into their relationship with the Earth, their vision on the role of community, family and the individual.

Decline of the West's Development Model

Today, the powers of money and language still in the hands of donor agencies, both governmental and private. But their sense-security has begun eroding in at least two ways:

- First, environmental destruction and social decay are putting the development model of the industrialised societies into question on home ground.

- Second, the dubious results of development interventions in countries of the South calls into question not only the applicability of the Western development model, but also its universal value.

In short, unease with the concept of 'development' is growing apace. There is a sense of crisis and calls for a new paradigm. At least among the *thinkers*. However, at the level of *decision makers* and *practitioners*, the remedies for development failures add up to ... more of the same: a continuous provision of West-remains-best recipes for structural adjustment, democracy, good governance and management. Is there a problem? Get the latest tool, such as the Logical Framework or the Objective Oriented Project Planning, or 'ZOPP' method designed by USAID and refined by the German Ministry for Development Cooperation.

Shifting the conceptual approach from 'top-down' to 'bottom-up', as many private aid agencies have proclaimed, does not solve the problem if the thinking moves along the same Rostowian evolutionary line from underdevelopment to development. The real alternative is not one but rather a diverse set of alternatives in accordance with diverse local contexts. There 'development' in its original sense (unfolding of the inner potential) takes place from within.

Such challenges to mainstream notions are emerging from the relatively new debate on cultures and development. It pleads for a pluralistic approach, and takes culture as a starting point, especially the strength and diversity of coping systems, that is: the ways in which people through the centuries continue to find their own solutions to the challenges of their natural and social environment.

Aid agencies have begun paying lip-service to such arguments. But few have taken them on board. The idea of a culture-conscious approach undermines the sense security of those who have to decide on funds and those who have to act in concrete situations.

A Common Agenda? The Credibility of Private Aid Agencies as Civic Actors on Home Ground

In a way it may be fortunate that the damage caused by economic concepts of productivity, accumulation, never-to-be-satisfied needs and maximum output with minimum (labour) input, is not only felt in the South but in the North as well. The ecological and social consequences of the dominant paradigm pose a common agenda, North and South, of those who do not accept these consequences as inevitable.

Non-governmental development agencies in the North and the South may be of different types – operational, co-financing, servicing, solidarity, etc. – but all claim some kind of commitment to shaping society. Now to shape one's society is a profoundly cultural act, with deep ramifications for the people concerned.

It seems only logical that the more an agency is involved in shaping its *own* society, the greater the credibility of its claim to speak about societies anywhere. And, conversely, the less it is involved in shaping its own society, the less right it has to make its voice heard.

Strangely enough, few private aid agencies have any civic involvement on home ground. Yet their countless policy documents, guidelines, criteria, priorities and evaluations underpin an implicit claim that they know what is best for other societies. For those at the receiving end in Southern countries, this pretention (once discovered) is naturally irritating.

Responsibility = Ability to Respond

Private aid agencies and NGOs in the South usually find themselves somewhere at the middle, or 'meso' level of society. They occupy a space between 'macro' economic and political decision makers and the micro-realities of community-based groups. Although their existence is linked to the channelling of resources from providers to receivers, they also play a role as civic actors. Credibility cannot be acquired without taking responsibility, which literally means ability to respond.

The credibility of agencies and NGOs as civic actors should therefore be tied to their ability to respond to at least the following prerequisites:

- Their knowledge of the history of their *own* people and their understanding of the cultural presuppositions which guide the shaping of their *own* society;
- Their willingness to use that historical knowledge and to put on record what happened to their *own* people 'in the name of devel-

opment' from the peoples' point of view, how these people reacted and why they react the way they do; and

• Their active involvement in concrete issues which are crucial for civic control over political decisions which direct the shaping of their *own* society.

Giving New Meaning to 'Partnership'

In the 'global village' of today, decisions taken at national and international levels have ever-wider repercussions. The need for world-wide horizontal contacts, exchange of experiences and views, as well as alliances, is more obvious than ever. At macro-levels (UN agencies, GATT, G-7, European Union, multinationals, the international banking system, etc.) this need is amply satisfied. And this fact helps explain increasingly monochromatic policies and practices.

However, for those operating at micro- and meso-levels, the needs for clear channels and active interchange are largely unmet. Yet if it is recognised that ill-development is everywhere, and that solutions have to be found everywhere, then

> the common agenda for NGDOs in all parts of the world would be to oppose uniform solutions imposed by the economic and political powers that be. A first point on that agenda is to gain political space for shaping the immense variety of societies in ways that make sense to the people concerned according to their own history and cultural context.

In this perspective 'partnership' between private aid agencies, NGOs and other organised groups will acquire its real meaning, a meaning which is closely related to the concept of 'mutuality'.

Mutuality ... or Equality in Diversity

Is 'mutuality'[7] at all possible in the context of a relationship which (a) contains dissimilar interests on both sides, (b) is not equal with regard to political and financial means, and (c) is intercultural? Such factors imply diversity at all levels. If we assume the ethical norm that diversity, that is, cultural difference, is no reason for inequality in the relationship, we might have to revalue what is contributed by the respective partners in the relationship.

Everyone who is familiar with development cooperation knows that money introduces some of the most damaging viruses to the relationship. It would be naive and unrealistic, however, to put a moratorium on providing funds. Money is needed for building up civil society. In spite of interesting attempts by a few private aid agencies to share some of their powers, such as through programme financing, partner consultations and local advisory bodies, the conditions for transferring money have remained the most important element in the relationship.

It is taken for granted that the NGO partner in the South has an interest in receiving money. The fact that the private aid agency in the North has just as much interest in providing money is hardly ever openly acknowledged or used in negotiations around the transfer of funds. In reality, aid agency work does involve the pursuit of interests, both at the organisational and the personal levels: it justifies the agency's existence, provides job satisfaction, unusual friendships, fieldtrips and so on. Recognising these interests on the donor side would make for much more honesty in the relationship between partners from the North and South.

> *The challenge is not to allow the balance of power to be determined by the possession or lack of financial means, but to find an equilibrium in the value accorded to the material and (more important): non-material contributions from both sides. Pooling of each of these resources and then deciding together on the use of them would be an important step forwards.*

Bridge-Building

Real partnership, however, will come about only when the common objective would shift from a one-way money transfer to a two-way dialogue around action for a responsible international civic society.

> *The challenge of intercultural partnership implies a shift from intervention in other peoples' societies towards interaction between credible civic partners.*

NGDOs – that is, groups beyond the private aid agencies – are perfectly well placed to act as intermediaries for bridge-building between 'peer groups' within their respective societies as well as between them. Groups of people with similar interests and activities such as farmers, women, artists, teachers, human rights activists, environment movements and those working with people with AIDS, learn more from each other than from (very expensive) so-called 'development experts'.

Intercultural and interreligious dialogue around conference tables is non-committal and hardly challenges people's own views.

> *Real intercultural dialogue takes place around action, when it becomes apparent that choices have been made and are to be made, when people discover that each choice is rooted in a specific socio-cultural context, and that sense giving is a way of interpretation of reality.*

Intercultural decoding is a prerequisite for partnership in an international context. A dialogue between those who would like to act in 'partnership' in the real sense, would automatically lead to creating together a *real-life vocabulary and a pattern for cooperation which would put people and their activities in their own rightful place*. It might finally bring about a relationship of equality in diversity. And it might give priority to the important over the urgent. Perhaps the first important question to ask each other is: would it be time to take time?

Notes

1. Tomaz Mastnak, in J. Benderley and E. Kraft (eds), 1994, *Independent Slovenia: Origins, Movements, Prospects*, St Martin's Press, New York. This quotation is drawn from Paul Stubbs, 1996, 'Humanitarian Organisations and the Myth of Civil Society', *ArkZin*, No. 55, based on an earlier paper presented at the European Conference of Sociology in Budapest, September 1995, 'Nationalisms, Globalisation and Civil Society in Croatia and Slovenia'.
2. World Bank, 1989, *Sub-Saharan Africa: From Crisis to Sustainable Growth*, Washington DC, p. 1.
3. World Bank, 1991, *Implementing the World Bank's Strategy to Reduce Poverty: Progress and Challenges*, Washington DC.
4. World Bank, 1994, *World Economic Prospects*, as reported in *The Economist*, 1 October 1994.
5. See Y. Tandon, 1994, 'Recolonization of Subject Peoples', *Alternatives*, 19, pp. 173–83.
6. See Y. Tandon, 1991, 'Foreign NGOs, Uses and Abuses: An African Perspective', *IFDA Dossier*, No. 81.
7. The booklet *Beyond Development Cooperation* published in 1993 by The Netherlands Association for Culture and Development (Amersfoortssetraat 20, 3769 AS Soesterberg, The Netherlands) provides some useful observations with regard to the notion of 'mutuality'. It says that the basic meanings of 'mutuality' and 'reciprocity' are not exactly the same. The English word 'reciprocal' literally means 'going back and forth' and in the figurative sense 'to make a return for something done, given or said' (Webster). In other words: action–reaction. The English word 'mutual' literally means 'coming from both sides'. It does not primarily mean action–reaction, but rather denotes an independent action from both sides. It implies equilibrium in the relationship and equality in diversity.

7

Calculation, Compassion ... and Choices

David Sogge and Kees Biekart

Must today's private aid agencies, like the poor who justify their existence, always be with us? And must they go on getting and spending in the ways described, and questioned, in the preceding pages? If the findings and views presented here are right, the answer to both questions is: Not necessarily. The agencies have no Manifest Destiny. Their righteous calling confers no special immunities and privileges, such as a 'right' to intervene. They are not captive to some immutable economic laws of motion, however much commerce grips them in its hammerlock. Rather, their futures are matters of *choice*. Staffs, Boards and members can make them, as can those outside the agencies, notably funding authorities (including legislators and individual donors) and even grantees and 'partners'. All have a stake and all have powers to choose.

Paying attention to institutions tasked with fighting poverty and exclusion, including the modest roles of private aid agencies, is no trivial pursuit. Public discourse of contentment in the 1990s commands and celebrates an active indifference towards the poor, North and South. As collective sector efforts are slashed or abandoned, what the agencies and domestically-focused non-profits do, or neglect to do, will affect the lives of millions. Here the contented classes respond, 'Let the charities fill the gap.' In the face of such cynical solicitude, our counsel for the private aid agencies would be: 'Choose to refuse to be used.'

Ownership and Control

Writers in this book signal several areas of choice. One concerns where power is ultimately located. Hence the questions, who owns the private agencies? To whom are they accountable?

Down through the decades, active citizens have pressed for, and sometimes achieved, new rules by which philanthropic trusts, public welfare bodies, charities and bureaucracies of official aid are supposed to act with greater transparency and accountability. Also politely tapping or impertinently hammering on the doors have been investigative journalists, researchers, parliamentary inquirers, public prosecutors and tiny bands of activist groups pushing for responsive philanthropy, and for a radically different course in foreign aid. A few progressive aid agencies have even joined them.

Criticised or pressed to account for what they do, agencies tend to respond defensively, their rejoinders often boiling down to restatements of their good intentions (which may indeed be blameless). Some in recent years have grudgingly agreed to independent evaluations of their less embarrassing aid projects. As of 1996, however, no private aid agency has agreed to undergo a Social Audit of itself and its works overall, although a number of firms and NGOs have done so.

Agencies' uneasiness in the face of public inquiry stems in part from a sense that their ownership structure is weak. Their roots among members, defenders and allies are shallow, and not getting any deeper. Some agencies could easily topple over in the first strong wind. The fact is that staff oligarchies tend to dominate; the 'voluntary' quotient made up of members and other putative owners is dwindling. Grantees and allies from poor regions, although occasionally providing *couleur locale* in advisory councils, are usually nowhere to be seen in the grey corridors of power among senior managers and their asset managers, donation brokers, or those other funding authorities outside the agency.

Meanwhile, Cold War imperatives have slackened and official aid turnover is shrinking in aggregate terms. But compulsions to get the agencies 'into the tent' have intensified. Funding authorities in the official aid system of governments, multilateral banks and UN agencies bestride centre ring with freer and more practiced whip hands. They choose the acts, select and drill the performing beasts, and orchestrate the perilous stunts of structural adjustment that put the lives of millions on the high wire. To the agencies and other NGO performers fall the tasks of holding tattered safety nets.

Now visible is a trend, already established in domestic welfare programmes, toward private agencies as official aid contractors, and a diminished quotient of 'privateness' in their ownership. Now if those official aid system authorities were to adhere in fuller measure to norms of transparency and democratic control, then private agencies, as contractees, might be better held to public account. But that would represent the triumph of hope over experience. Much of the official aid system remains opaque and unaccountable, and the advent of quangos affords even dimmer prospects for public oversight.

Trends like these underscore the urgency of the need for private aid agencies to make choices about who calls the shots. A valid choice, posed in the second chapter of this book, is to re-centre themselves as organisations rooted in civil society around a critical trinity of their publics:

- supporters (including public funding authorities or asset managers) who provide money out of commitment to an agency's values;
- members, an agency's constitutional owners; and
- those an agency serves through its activities, the intended beneficiaries of its mission.

A corollary here is that agencies reground themselves at home; that is, to become national organisations with an inter-nationalist perspective rather than rootless international bodies which happen to have offices or postboxes in a given country. By so doing they can also choose to address poverty and exclusion on home ground, in alliances with other actors North and South who are working for social justice.

Impact

Aid-of-suffering does not aim to suppress suffering. Philanthropy is at the same time necessary and useless ... In one sense, humanitarian action is not to be judged by its results ... Solidarity is no longer under discussion, but its value is measured by the number of persons it manages to mobilize rather than the results it obtains ... aid is fundamentally for the donor.[1]

Choices about who owns, and what drives, the agencies become more urgent as publics begin to ask what permanent differences they make. As Chapter 4 explains, many agency claims about their impact are grossly exaggerated, if not often completely hollow. Many claims are vulnerable because of real difficulties in attributing impact to an agency's acts and omissions. But where research hurdles have been overcome and valid evidence assembled, the weight of that evidence fails to support most claims. That so many agencies continue to gain revenues and standing independently of their programmes' long-term results, seems all the more astonishing – and less tenable – with every passing year.

After examining Swedish, Finnish and British agency efforts, one set of independent researchers also conclude that most agency claims of impact do not withstand scrutiny. And yet:

This does not mean that nothing can be done. The case studies suggest [agency] work that is most likely to have an impact when it directly addresses the social relationships that underlie poverty – such as land holding relationships, territorial conflicts, or having greater power to influence the distribution of profits – and which increases the ... capacities of the poor to tackle these relationships for themselves.[2]

Only a small minority of agencies support work along these – highly political – lines. They do so commonly as one element of an activity portfolio otherwise full of service-delivery projects. Only a few agencies have come to gear efforts systematically toward the 'deep structure' issues of power and poverty. One agency in Sweden has recently decided to make that shift, in part as a result of the just-cited impact study: it is winding down its support to conventional modernisation projects in order to concentrate on long-term efforts by which the poor achieve power. Moral judgements no doubt influenced that agency's choice, as it is religiously-based; but weighing heavily was sheer pragmatism: it chose to support things with the best chance of making a real difference.

Today, the universe of private aid agencies able to defend claims to permanent impact on poverty may come down to a mere handful. Tomorrow there may be more, but given trends in agency choices, not many more.

Agencies need to make choices on several fronts. The choice to start levelling with the public is self-evident: to say that there is no quick fix, no magic bullet to kill poverty; to admit that many projects fail, even on their own terms, and to state that aid is far less important than other factors. Such demystification may be traumatic for some, but secularised publics of the late twentieth century have withstood the collapse of far more profound illusions with no ill effects.

Just as urgent for most agencies, and potentially easier because it entails less immediate risk of public humiliation, is the choice to stop fooling themselves. Out of the glare of the public media, agencies can take long, sober looks at their activities and draw conclusions about the norms and paradigms that have guided them up to now. A problem, as signalled in Chapter 4, is that most agencies simply do not have a set of conceptual handholds explaining the problems they say they are addressing.[3] Most are groping, as in a darkened stairwell without a handrail.

No one can be summoned to install ready-made handholds. But there are usually a few people inside with a flashlight, and some outside willing to throw open a window or two, especially toward the South, but not only in that direction. Choices can be made to promote internal debate, external exposure and a rethinking of identity, ownership and rootedness in an agency's own society, which *itself* faces problems arising from 'social relationships that underlie poverty'. Choosing to reflect and debate on such issues, rather than adopting some off-the-shelf toolkit proffered by an imposing 'expert' institution, could allow agencies to find the conceptual handholds they need.

Commerce

Similarly, agencies can make choices to deal with, and indeed set limits to the invasive influence of the market. Chapter 3 looked at the matter. Without denying the force of spontaneous public compassion, and subliminal yearnings to see heroic myths of rescue replayed in sequel after televised sequel, agencies can choose to contest the 'laws of the market'. Choices largely pivot on a willingness to relinquish growth – the achievement of transnational status, for example – as a main criterion of agency success. Much also depends on a resolve to realign public aims and profile with an agency's professed principles of solidarity and sustainability. The alternative, already established in child sponsorship and right-to-intervene relief agencies but reasserting itself in anti-poverty agencies, is self-absorption in a fast-cycle, closed-loop, perpetual motion machine driven along a ratcheted sequence of (a) relief-in-aid (b) crisis-defined-as-mainly-humanitarian and prolonged as such (c) appeal for funds (d) relief-in-aid. But even many agencies in the 'structural anti-poverty' branch are hooked on a system of incentives and internal supervision little different from those of a common business enterprise, where gain through exchange generates the bottom line.

Informed Persuasion

When it comes to agency communication we can begin to talk about rather profound and sustained impact – both in respect to what agencies now are and what they could become. Today, many can beam out images and marketing messages with considerable sophistication. However, the logic of this kind of communication pivots on expanded reproduction of aid – relief intervention, the modernisation project in a faraway land – of the kind alluded to in the preceeding paragraph. Not many are willing to break with this logic and turn this communicative power to other, much more strategic purposes.

While most agencies cling to what one of the most seasoned and thoughtful of them now terms 'a mistaken belief in their own operational importance',[4] they tend at the same time to underestimate their powers to shape attitudes and policies. Together with such mass-media institutions as *National Geographic* and adventure comic strips, the agencies are already among the foremost influences on Western public perceptions of people and issues in the South. At a different level, the old endowed foundations have framed the thinking of anti-poverty policy elites both North and South for generations. Theirs were among the most important invisible hands in the 'marketplace of ideas'. They paid, in a sense, for the best mainstream policy paradigms that money could buy.

Today, knowledge-based NGOs – organisations with no real resource-transfer roles – offer stiff competition to mainstream sources of paradigms and policy. They do so on far smaller budgets than the university and thinktank projects financed by big foundations. Agencies can choose to make common cause with these pushy, analytical NGOs North and South; where such choices have been made, the results in agenda-setting can be far-reaching, as shown, for example, in the UNCED process culminating in 1992 in Rio. Agency project staff and Southern collaborators are witness to trends in human events of potential importance. They are often the *only* outside witnesses to those things. Here too, new conceptual lenses are needed. These would allow agencies to focus and to 'see' what they are witnessing, and to transform that into images and facts to illustrate points of wider significance. A few agencies have chosen to do just that by helping monitor the social effects of structural adjustment programmes or of environmentally destructive megaprojects. Here too the results, such as in shifts of World Bank lending practices, are not altogether discouraging. A choice for an agency may be simply to become a *conscious witness*.

Scenarios and Premonitions

The dogs may bark, but the caravan of mainstream institutions moves on down the shining path of neoliberalism. A banner over the narrow gateway reads, 'There is No Alternative'. Many go along in the irresistible flow, but some private aid agencies hang back, unsure if they should join the procession. The 1990s are a time of painful self-doubt for them and for kindred institutions bearing the stamps of Keynesian, Social Democratic or even Christian Democratic principles of social protection and citizen activism. Within the agencies, adherents to those principles skirmish with the born-again believers in the thrusting norms of 'market managerialism'. They reject the 'No Alternative', shining-path orthodoxies, and point to other paths more consistent with agency origins and professed ideals.

To imagine what lies ahead is tricky, but the attempt could yield insights, as shown in this book's interlude between Chapters 1 and 2, 'Looking Back from 2010'. We would conclude by offering the following scenarios, none of them exclusive of the others:

- Head Chefs in a Global Soup Kitchen – Humanitarians-without-borders extend their global reach as mega-agencies, capturing official aid contracts and surging flows of monies from televised appeals. Their sentinels in non-Western lands assure the media and official aid bodies of a steady parade of crisis spots requiring air-lifted action and live television coverage. Enormous cash surpluses from the most successful of these campaigns become start capital for global health and relief businesses; these funds stimulate joint ventures (also involving insurance companies worried about the spread of crime and AIDS) for social service and 'youth offender' programmes in poor countries, where the budgets and even staffing of health and other social Ministries are set only after negotiations with agency headquarters in Paris or New York.

- Agencies for Sale or Rent – Official aid bodies sign more and larger contracts with Southern NGOs, banks and specially-created Southern agencies to manage social 'safety nets', small-business promotion schemes, and basic social services. Many agencies get bypassed. This, combined with deteriorating returns in scandal-plagued charity markets and alienation of constituencies in the North, force bankruptcy or merger on increasing numbers of small and medium-sized private agencies. Investigative journalists, and a spate of new 'consumers guidebooks to charitable giving', add to the pressures. Outstanding among the survivors – who come to resemble, and to compete with, firms of consulting engineers – are those contracted by official aid bodies to manage packaged 'turnkey' projects on a 'no cure, no pay' basis. But engineering approaches aren't everything, especially where *savoir-faire* is needed as in Central Asia, the Middle East and Africa to challenge militant Islamic groups on the terrain of social welfare and community organising.

- Newcomers in the Running – Domestic organisations in the North normally outside the circuits of foreign aid, many grounded in specific communities, professions or sectors (city councils, public health nurses' associations, ghetto activist groups), extend and deepen ties to kindred organisations in non-Western regions. They add North–South, rich-poor dimensions to the work and discourse of their domestic interest groups. They dig into their own pockets, and tap a variety of emerging public funds, some of them not managed by the official aid power brokers. By so doing, these 'amateurs' rub shoulders with, and sometimes shoulder aside, some of the generalist private aid agencies. Politicians and big business, even if hostile, begin to pay respectful attention.

Meanwhile, knowledge-based Northern and Southern NGOs (on policy terrains like genetic resources, transport, or reproductive rights) begin gaining hearings in global communities of policy-influencing specialists, hitherto inaccessible to generalist NGOs like the private aid agencies.

Mainstream aid agencies awaken too late as the 'upstarts' move ahead, capturing the volunteered time and money of specific publics. After decades of unchallenged primacy, those agencies with vague intentions to get into 'policy dialogue' find themselves just one more competitor – for government subsidies, for political standing and public attention.

- The Common Agenda, and Reinvention – Pressed by allies and confronted with mounting social and environmental decay in the North, some agencies begin to rethink and recast themselves along lines of a common agenda (the world environmental movement having pioneered the approach in many respects). They drop their exclusive focus on problems 'out there' in the South. Structural adjustment, and widening social fissures, are now also realities of the North as well as the South. Agencies seek areas of joint interest with bodies hitherto focused on home ground, including local authorities, and with knowledge-based NGOs in the North. They develop pragmatic divisions of labour with activist and knowledge-based Southern NGOs. Tasks revolve around capturing and channelling information, exploring and comparing notes on policy innovations. In staff size, these agencies stay small; in volunteers and donating memberships they grow. The latter are drawn into *ad hoc* and perennial campaigns (about making choices in consumption, mobility, safe streets) that touch everyday life North and South. In short, a scenario in which generosity and solidarity dethrone calculation and cold charity.

Of these four scenarios, the first and second reflect today's prevailing trends, as agencies seek survival in caravans along the shining path of market dogmas. Yet other paths to survival and renewal beckon. The third and fourth scenarios are now emerging. They reflect natural evolution, but also difficult, conscious departures from past practice. They become more plausible as pioneering agencies and their allies make choices, demonstrate alternatives and thus gain new powers – even the power to render 'aid' as we know it obsolescent.

Notes

1. M.D. Perrot *et al.*, 1992, *La mythologie programmée. L'économie des croyances dans la société moderne*, PUF, Paris, p. 172. Cited in B. Hours, 1992, 'Les ONG: mercenaires du village planétaire ou gardiennes des ghettos', *L'Homme et la Société*, No. 105–6, juillet–décembre, p. 38.
2. R.C. Riddell *et al.*, 1995, *Promoting Development by Proxy. An Evaluation of the Development Impact of Government Support to Swedish NGOs*, SIDA Evaluation Report 1995/2, SIDA Stockholm, p. 79.
3. In a damning recent article on Save The Children USA, the most telling observations were not about high overheads, the article's main theme, but about the agency's lack of '"a commonly accepted and understood theoretical perspective" on which to carry on and evaluate its own work ... "Then the programs must be focused. Few of Save's projects fit these criteria. It's because of a lack of commitment. Save has no detailed objectives, no strategy. If you know what you do, you don't waste time and money."' Shelby Miller, quoted in Michael Maren, 1995, 'A Different Kind of Child Abuse', *Penthouse*, December, p. 51. It is a bit unfair to single out Save The Children USA, as many private aid agencies suffer the same shortcomings.
4. *The Oxfam Poverty Report*, 1995, Oxfam, Oxford, p. 207.

Index

Index by Auriol Griffith-Jones